FRANCE IN AMERICA

1497-1763

WILLIAM PITT

FRANCE IN AMERICA

1497-1763

BY

REUBEN GOLD THWAITES, LL.D.

SECRETARY OF THE STATE HISTORICAL SOCIETY OF WISCONSIN

WITH MAPS

HASKELL HOUSE PUBLISHERS Ltd.

Publishers of Scarce Scholarly Books

NEW YORK, N. Y. 10012

1969

First Published 1905

HASKELL HOUSE PUBLISHERS LTD.
Publishers of Scarce Scholarly Books
280 LAFAYETTE STREET
NEW YORK, N. Y. 10012

Library of Congress Catalog Card Number: 68-25272

Standard Book Number 8383-0288-2

Printed in the United States of America

CONTENTS

xiv CONTENTS

MAPS

EDITOR'S INTRODUCTION

IN laying out a series like *The American Nation*, one of the fundamental difficulties is to bring into its proper relations the French colonies and their influence on the British settlements. Beginning simultaneously with the earliest English colonization, the French colonies, except in Maine and Acadia, were during their whole history separated from the English by immense expanses of trackless forest. Hence it is not until well into the eighteenth century that the two parallel threads of neighborhood colonization are really intertwisted.

It has seemed wise, therefore, to treat French colonization as a continuous episode, especially because so far in this series there has been no account of the French colonies, except the chapter on commercial companies in Cheyney's *European Background* (vol. I. of *The American Nation*), the chapter on the Florida settlements in Bourne's *Spain in America* (vol. III.), a brief chapter on Colonial Neighbors in Tyler's *England in America* (vol. IV.), and the chapters on the English and colonial side of the border wars from 1689 to 1713 in Greene's *Provincial America* (vol. VI.).

Dr. Thwaites has therefore a free field to carry the whole subject through, from the beginning of Gallic settlement to the expulsion of the French from North America in 1763.

After a brief account of the planting of New France (chap. i.), the author devotes three chapters to the three fields of French adventure and settlement—Acadia, the St. Lawrence, and the Mississippi; besides a separate chapter (iv.) on the fascinating subject of the discovery of the Mississippi.

Having thus shown how the colonies came to be, he devotes chapters vi. and vii. to the wars by land and sea in America between 1713 and 1748; then, after an interesting chapter (viii.) on the people of New France, about half the book (chaps. ix. to xvii.) is devoted to the French and Indian War and its territorial results; then follows a review, which will be found novel and serviceable, of the conditions of Spanish Louisiana from 1762 down to the cession to the United States in 1803.

The literature of this subject is widely scattered and in several languages, and the student will find convenient the summary in the Critical Essay on Authorities: it deals rather with the fundamental works and collections than with special material on small points.

Although the first part of the book is chronologically parallel with several others of the series, and especially with Greene's *Provincial America*, it does not repeat, but gives between two covers a

succinct account of the origin, progress, and over-
throw of the French empire in America. The
western explorations, posts, and settlements of the
French have especially interested the author, and
are illustrated by original maps which almost for
the first time reveal the immense possibilities which
the French had before them.

AUTHOR'S PREFACE

THE story of the rise and fall of New France is the most dramatic chapter in American history. It has been so admirably related by Francis Parkman that to follow in his footsteps may seem a daring venture. But the work of Parkman runs through twelve octavo volumes, and in this busy world comparatively few are willing to undertake the task of reading them all, despite the fact that *France and England in North America* is quite as entertaining as the best of fiction, and possesses the additional charm of verity. There would seem to be needed a one-volume history of New France, from the stand-point of relationship with her English neighbors to the south. Indeed, so intimate were these relations, and so far-reaching their consequences, that no history of the American nation can be considered complete that does not, as fully as space will permit, outline the remarkable career of Canada under the French régime.

One cannot treat of this subject without constantly acknowledging indebtedness to Parkman, and rising from the task with a keen appreciation of the many-sidedness of that great master.

Yet it must be remembered that the word of no
historian is final.   Much has been learned since
the *Pioneers of France in the New World* went to
press in 1865, and not a little since the series was
completed in 1892 with *A Half-Century of Conflict*.
On both sides of the international boundary, more
particularly among the French writers of Canada,
there has for over a quarter of a century past been
an unceasing search into the "deeper deeps" of
the history of New France.   New stores of material
have been brought to light and published, scores
of trained historical students have each had a turn
at these fresh sources, old theories have been criti-
cally re-- examined; and not unnaturally many
scholars have come to entertain opinions differing
in some respects from those held by the older
writers.

So far as space and the aim of the series allow,
an attempt has been made in the present volume
to give the story of New France as it appears to
modern investigators.   Had this book been intended to stand alone, more attention would of course
have been paid to English colonial institutions and
events, as contrasted with and influencing those of
the French; but as these matters are sufficiently
treated in other volumes of the series, repetition of
facts was undesirable.   Some of the characteristics
of New France and its people, and certain features
of its history, are susceptible of much more liberal treatment than is herein given; but it is neces-

sary to fashion the garment to the wearer's need, and the faithful reader of the series will doubtless find contained in other volumes most if not all of that which he may miss in this. It has been customary to close the history of New France with the treaty of Paris, or in any event the conspiracy of Pontiac; the present writer has, however, in the interest of dramatic continuity, thought it desirable in the concluding chapter briefly to follow the subsequent fortunes of the French in Louisiana, until their absorption into the American nation.

REUBEN GOLD THWAITES.

FRANCE IN AMERICA

FRANCE IN AMERICA

CHAPTER I

THE PLANTING OF NEW FRANCE
(1497–1632)

"THIS year [1497] on St. John the Baptist's Day,"
did "our well-beloved John Cabot, citizen of
Venice," bravely set forth from Bristol in *The Mat-
thew*, a little lug-sailed vessel of fifty tons manned
by less than twenty West-of-England sailors. The
veteran mariner and his associates had been commissioned by Henry VII. to "set up our banner on
any new-found land . . . upon their own costs and
charges, to seek out and discover whatsoever isles
. . . of the heathen and infidels, which before the
time have been unknown to all Christians . . . [and]
to pay to us the fifth part of the capital gain so
gotten for every then voyage." Fifty-three days
out, Cabot sighted land somewhere within or
bordering the Gulf of St. Lawrence. The location
cannot be stated with definiteness; an animated
controversy has been waged over the question for

3

several years, Cape Breton Island, Newfoundland,
Prince Edward's Island, and Labrador having each
had its champions.   The opinion of Dawson, that
the landfall is in the neighborhood of North Cape,
on Cape Breton, is, however, growing in favor.[1]   Of
more immediate consequence to American history
was the fact that Cabot carried back to England
news of the rich possibilities of the cod - fishery
thereabout, especially off the cliff - girt bays of
Newfoundland.[2]

Ever since the middle of the fourteenth century,
and perhaps before, Englishmen, chiefly from the
port of Bristol, had been catching cod off the shores
of Iceland, if, indeed, the Labrador coast were not
included in the range of their activities.[3]   But
Cabot's report turned the attention of Bristol men
to Newfoundland, and thenceforth the Icelandic
catch held but second place.   When, the following
year, the discoverer departed upon his second

[1] Harrisse, "Outcome of the Cabot Quarter-Centenary," in
Am. Hist. Review, IV., 38–61, would place it in Labrador.
Dawson, in Can. Royal Soc., *Transactions*, XII., § 2, pp. 51–112;
2d series, II., § 2, pp. 3–30; and 2d series, III., § 2, pp. 139–268,
prefers North Cape, as above.   See summing up in Winship,
Cabot Bibliography, Introd., who thinks Dawson's theory probable but not proven; and that on the return Cabot's vessel
skirted Newfoundland as far as Cape Race.

[2] Cabot's charter, dated March 5, 1496, cited in Weare,
Cabot's Discovery, 96; Prowse, *Newfoundland*, 8.   For a more
detailed discussion of Cabot, see Bourne, *Spain in America*
(*Am. Nation*, III.), chap. v.

[3] Prowse, *Newfoundland*, 24–29, summarizes the data concerning early Icelandic fisheries.

voyage, Devonshire fishermen and traders—moved by the lusty ambitions of a decade wherein the habitable portion of the globe had suddenly been doubled by the discoveries of maritime adventurers —joined forces and sent "out of Bristow [Bristol] three or four small ships fraught with sleight and grosse wares, as coarse cloth, caps, laces, points, and such other," their purpose being to make hauls of fish and to barter with the savages of the "new isle" and the neighboring American littoral.[1]

It is not unlikely that Norsemen were at Newfoundland early in the eleventh century; but they do not appear to have made any settlement upon this new coast, which with its dense forests of conifers and almost countless fiords and island fringes so closely resembles Norway itself. Claims are made, also, that Spanish Basques, who were among the most venturesome of deep-sea fishers, had in their large, hulky craft preceded Cabot by a hundred years; but it is doubtful whether they went in force much before 1545. Portuguese fishermen appear to have arrived in 1501, and Normans and Bretons three years later.[2] Thereafter, for a century and a half, hundreds of fishing-vessels annually resorted to the rugged fiords of Newfoundland, their "winter crews" of boat-builders and scaffold-men settling themselves in small longshore colonies according to

---

[1] Stowe, *Annales*, 482.
[2] Prowse, *Newfoundland*, 43-49; Harrisse, *Découverte et Évolution Cartographique de Terre-Neuve*, xxxvii.-lxv.

nations—English, French, Portuguese, and Spanish.
Enormous hauls of cod were made, the fish being
flayed and dried upon great stagings which lined the
shores, in much the same manner as to-day;[1] while
many vessels searched in northern waters for seals
and whales. Throughout this long period, although
the French fisheries were for several generations
greater than their own, the fierce and hardy men of
Devon remained in chief control at the stormy isl-
and outpost — but only as the result of frequent
bloody struggles with still ruder Basques and
Bretons—fit training for the destruction of the
Spanish Armada and the ousting of France from
the American main-land nearly two centuries later.
After the dispersal of the Armada in 1588, against
which many a Newfoundland fishing-craft was
pitted, England was recognized as mistress of the
seas, and Spanish ships became almost unknown on
the Grand Banks, where for forty years they had
mustered fully two hundred sail and six thousand
seamen.[2]

Upon this enormous traffic in dried fish, much of
which was, and still is, marketed in Mediterranean
ports, and upon the accompanying trade for furs
with neighboring savages, several towns in northern
France and western England greatly prospered.
The numerous landlocked harbors of Newfoundland were, in those early days, also centres of a

[1] Prowse, *Newfoundland*, 21, 59, 61, etc.
[2] *Ibid.*, 51, 60, 81.

very considerable international barter—the cloths,
hats, hosiery, and cordage of west England being
carried thither in square-bowed fishing-craft, and
exchanged for oils, wines, and prints brought by the
larger vessels of Spain and Portugal.

St. John's was, as well, a port of call for most
maritime adventurers to North America, of which
Newfoundland was early recognized as the portal.
Verrazzano (1524), Cartier (1534, 1535, 1541), Roberval (1541), Hawkins (1565), Parkhurst (1578),
and Gilbert (1578, 1583) were but a few of the earliest in the long procession which sought water, provisions, and recruits in a harbor which by this time
was almost as familiar to the seamen of western
Europe as any of their own.   Later, the first settlers of both Virginia and New England found it
necessary occasionally to resort for succor to their
Newfoundland compatriots, whose island colony—
oldest of England's plantations beyond seas—had
preceded their own by a well-rounded century.

What acquaintance European seamen who fre-
quented Newfoundland had made with the river
St. Lawrence before the arrival of Jacques Cartier
is now unknown;[1] but it is not unreasonable to suppose that in their wide range for fish and furs—
during which Labrador was commonly visited—
they must not infrequently have entered the great
estuary and found its coasts narrowing to the banks
of a tidal stream.   Hakluyt makes such a claim for

---

[1] Discussion in Winsor, *Cartier to Frontenac*, 10-15.

English sea-rovers early in the sixteenth century. But voyages of this character were seldom recorded, and tradition is an uncertain guide.

In 1534, Cartier, a master-pilot of St. Malo—a port which for thirty years had annually despatched many vessels to the American fisheries—set out under the commands of his royal master, Francis I., with the definite purpose of formally extending the bounds of France. After touching at Newfoundland, he explored the St. Lawrence "until land could be seen on either side." The next year he repeated his voyage, and, ascending to Lachine Rapids, the head of navigation from the sea, named the island mountain at their foot Mont-Royal. His report[1] of a winter's experience (1535–1536) in this inhospitable climate, near the gray cliff of Quebec, gave pause to Frenchmen in their western colonizing schemes; further, the king was now engaged at home in serious difficulties with Spain, and had neither thought, time, nor money for continuing the exploration of North America.

When at last a truce had been declared between France and Spain, Cartier was made captain-general and pilot of a new fleet of five vessels which was to bear to America the king's viceroy, Jean François de la Roche, better known as Roberval, from his estates in Picardy. A month later than the time set, Roberval having failed to arrive, Cartier set sail

---

[1] *Brief Récit*, printed at Paris in 1545 and since included in Pinkerton, *Voyages*, and other collections.

with three ships (May, 1541), and in August was again at Quebec, where he built a post which he abandoned in the spring, thence returning to France. It is said that in the Gulf of St. Lawrence he met the belated Roberval coming with supplies, and with colonists who had for this purpose been liberated from French jails. The Picard remained for a year at Quebec, whose crude fortifications he restored and bettered, and he attempted some interior exploration; but his community was one requiring a liberal use of the lash and the gibbet, and gave him little peace. There are reports that Cartier was sent to bring him home in 1543. After the king's settlement of the accounts of the joint expedition (April 3, 1544), both Cartier and Roberval pass from our view.[1]

France was now in the throes of civil war; the Huguenots, struggling bitterly against the domination of a hierarchy which rigidly controlled the state, engaged all of the king's means of repression. Seeking a refuge for his persecuted countrymen, the great Huguenot leader, Admiral Coligny, attempted to establish a colony of French Protestants in America. His Port Royal, planted in 1562 on the river Broad, proved a failure; and a settlement of two years later, on St. John's River, was razed by jealous Spaniards sallying from St. Augustine.[2]

[1] Winsor, *Cartier to Frontenac*, 23–47; Tyler, *England in America* (*Am. Nation*, IV.), 284–286.
[2] Bourne, *Spain in America* (*Am. Nation*, III.), chap. xii.

It was not until 1598[1] that another attempt was
made by France, this time to found a colony on the
St. Lawrence.   In that year Troilus du Mesgoñez,
Marquis de la Roche, headed two ships laden with
the usual crowd of degenerates—for in that day
the sweepings of jails and gutters were commonly
thought to furnish proper material for colonization
over-seas.   Landing his unmanageable vagabonds
on lonely Sable Island, he essayed to search for a
site on the main-land, far beyond; but storms drove
his ships back to France, where he at once fell into
political difficulties which resulted in his imprison-
ment.   It was not until five years later that a
chance rescue came to the abandoned colonists, who
had had a pitiful experience, dallying with death
upon this sandy reef which lies in a region of almost perpetual mists and chilling blasts.

In 1600 a commercial partnership was formed between François Gravé, the Sieur du Pont (commonly called Pontgravé), a St. Malo trading mariner
who had been upon the St. Lawrence as far up as
Three Rivers; a wealthy Honfleur merchant, Pierre
Chauvin, who was a Calvinist friend of Henry IV.;
and another rich Calvinist named Pierre du Guast,
Sieur de Monts.   Despite the vigorous protests of
St. Malo merchants, who asserted that their long
protection of French rights in that quarter gave
them a claim to the American trade, to these three
men was granted a royal monopoly of the fur-trade

[1] Possibly 1578; Winsor, *Cartier to Frontenac*, 76, gives 1590.

in the New World.[1] They made two successful
voyages to Tadoussac, but the majority of the men
left behind to build a fort met death from cold and
starvation.

Chauvin dying, he was succeeded by Amyar de
Chastes, a prominent friend of the king, who contracted a partnership with Pontgravé and several
Rouen and St. Malo traders. In 1603, Pontgravé
took out with him Samuel de Champlain, commissioned by the king as pilot and chronicler of
the expedition, which proceeded as far as Lachine
Rapids, and returned with large cargoes of furs.
Champlain was an experienced seaman who had
commanded a vessel in West Indian waters, and
now entered upon a career which has made him
perhaps the most famous figure, as he certainly is
one of the most picturesque, in the romantic history of New France.[2]

Upon reaching Honfleur they learned that De
Chastes had died, thus leaving without a head the
colonization scheme on which Pontgravé and Champlain were to report. By permission of the king,
however, his place was taken by that equally distinguished nobleman the Sieur de Monts—"a gentleman of great respectability, zeal, and honesty,"
declares Champlain—whose voyage to Tadoussac

[1] Biggar, *Early Trading Companies of New France*, "traces the
birth and growth of commerce down to the year 1632."
[2] Slafter, memoir in Prince Soc. ed of *Champlain's Voyages;*
Gravier, *Champlain.*

we have already chronicled. De Monts was given the viceroyalty and trade monopoly of all of North America between the fortieth and forty-sixth degrees of latitude, with directions to found a settlement. It was specified in his commission that Huguenot colonists were to be granted religious freedom; but the savages must be instructed in the faith of Rome.

De Monts, Champlain, Pontgravé, and a friend of De Monts, the Baron de Poutrincourt, set forth in three ships, accompanied by some six score of artisans, both Catholics and Protestants, who were respectively served by "a priest and a minister." Touching in the neighborhood of what is now Annapolis Royal, Nova Scotia—at Lower Granville, on the northwest shore of Annapolis Basin—Poutrincourt concluded to settle there, and, styling the place Port Royal, returned home for his family. The others proceeded to St. Croix Island (June, 1605), at the head of Passamaquoddy Bay, near the present boundary between Maine and New Brunswick; but the following spring, after a winter of rare suffering and death-dealing scurvy, moved to Port Royal, which thus was the first enduring French settlement planted on the main-land of North America. An entertaining and spirited account of life at this lonely outpost has come down to us from the pen of Lescarbot,[1] a lawyer-poet who was of the gay company whom De Monts and his colleagues had gathered

[1] Lescarbot, *Histoire de la Nouvelle France.*

about them. But an alleged wholesale conversion of natives by the priest of the party, widely heralded at the time, appears to have been a clever pretence to win the favor of the Catholic court.[1]

The superior defensiveness of Quebec was early appreciated; nevertheless, the Bay of Fundy, and particularly the isolated eastern peninsula, early called Acadia, was strategically of immense importance to the coast of New France. Hence, Acadia was firmly held against English claims and suffered the usual hard fate of a buffer colony.

England claimed North America by virtue of the discoveries of the two Cabots (1497–1498), France by that of Verrazzano (1524), and the Spanish by Columbus's voyages, quickly followed by internal exploration. The sixteenth century witnessed abortive colonizing efforts north of the Gulf of Mexico by all three nations; but it was not until the opening of the seventeenth that the contest seriously commenced. Eight years after Henry IV. of France had given to De Monts the country between the fortieth and forty-sixth parallels, Louis XIII., disregarding this grant, conveyed (1612) the region between Florida and the St. Lawrence to Madame de Guercheville and the Jesuits. Early in the century James I. of England began also to parcel out the continent, his first beneficiaries being (1606) the combined London and Plymouth companies.

[1] See Thwaites, *Jesuit Relations*, I., for details and for Lescarbot's memoir on the event.

In 1613, Samuel Argall, "a Virginia sea-captain of piratical tastes," who was later to be governor of that province, without warning swooped down upon the French colonies at Port Royal and on Mount Desert Island—the latter a Jesuit outpost on the firing-line—burned the buildings, and expelled the inhabitants.[1] Nine years after this outrage (1622), and while the former residents were gradually repeopling the shores of Annapolis Basin, James I. conveyed to Sir William Alexander, Earl of Stirling, the Acadian peninsula which the French held by right of occupation, but which the English king now claimed and rechristened Nova Scotia. In addition to Nova Scotia, Sir William was granted a generous strip three hundred miles wide, up the gulf and river of St. Lawrence. The new owner of Acadia brought over a few Scotch and English, who settled at and refortified old Port Royal, the French *habitants* having several years previously removed to the site of the present Annapolis Royal, some twelve miles farther up the basin. But it was impossible to make headway against their French neighbors. The latter soon absorbed the fresh arrivals, whose descendants, Gallicized both in name and blood, in the following century took sides against Great Britain.

Although stronger than Sir William's handful of immigrants, the French colony in Acadia was still feeble. Few of the settlers were adept at agricult-

[1] Tyler, *England in America (Am. Nation,* IV.), 72, 289.

ure; the native population was small, and the
hunting-ground was limited, with consequent re-
striction of the fur-trade. The original seigneur,
Poutrincourt, had lacked sufficient resources, and
owing to the fickleness of the Versailles court was
able to give slight assistance. His son and successor,
Biencourt, became a *coureur de bois*, and long lived
on much the same scale as his aboriginal companions; while his successors, the La Tours and d'Aulnay, rival fur-trade chiefs and corsairs, fought a
bloody feud that lasted until the death of the latter in 1650.[1] This internecine war, abounding in
piratical raids of the most furious character, kept
the shores of the Bay of Fundy in a constant and
unprofitable turmoil throughout nearly half a century; the unfortunate *habitants*—fishers, trappers,
hunters, and roving adventurers, many of them
half-breeds, but none of them paying much more
attention to their fields than did the Indians—
being ranged like feudal retainers in the service of
their respective lords. "They belonged to an
epoch that is lost in the mists of antiquity. Biencourt, d'Aulnay, the two de la Tours, Saint-Castin,
Denys, Subercasse, Marpain, are so many legendary
heroes whose names are still re-echoed by forest

---

[1] See detailed narrative by Parkman, "The Feudal Chiefs of
Acadia," in *Atlantic Monthly*, LXXI., 25, 201; Mass. Hist.
Soc., *Collections*, 3d series, VII., 90–121; Quebec Hist. Soc.,
Transactions, III., 236–241; Hazard, *Hist. Collections*, I., 307–
309, 541–544; Charlevoix, *New France* (Shea's ed.), III., 124–
138.

and rock from New Hampshire to the inmost recesses of the Bay of Fundy." [1]

Sir William Alexander was able to maintain a
nominal hold upon the country only by spasmodically coming to terms with whichever fur-trade
faction chanced at the moment to be uppermost—
a feat of opportunist diplomacy imitated by the
French court, whose authority the prevailing chief-
tain also privately acknowledged. Throughout all
the nominal changes in political mastery, this little
theatre of discord witnessed the same play of miserable international intrigue, reprehensible to all concerned, which was to end in the ruin of the unhappy
Acadians.

Convinced that the rock of Quebec was far better
suited than Port Royal for the needs of a stronghold of French power, Champlain induced De Monts
to authorize a colony there. The latter thereupon
secured for his friend the governorship of New
France, and sent him out with Pontgravé in two
well-equipped ships to found (July, 1608) the
capital of the king's western possessions. It was
a fortunate site, not only far removed from the
meddlesome English, who were now established at
Jamestown (1607), and were freely examining the
Atlantic coast with a disposition to regard the
French as intruders, but advantageously situated
for commanding the Indian traffic of an immense

[1] Richard, *Acadia*, I, 28; Tyler, *England in America* (*Am.
Nation*, IV.), 289, 306–310.

drainage basin, and for despatching exploring expeditions to the interior. The cliff overtowering the little settlement on the strand of Quebec was under ordinary conditions practically impregnable, and seemed an ideal situation for a fortress guarding the door of a vast continent.

Various motives contributed to the establishment and maintenance of New France. The king very naturally was moved by a passion for territorial expansion; the church was eager to convert the heathen savages of the New World; the fur-trade, although abounding in great risks, was at times so profitable as to stimulate the cupidity of merchants; the hope of finding deposits of precious metals was predominant in the minds of speculators; the army and the navy were ambitious for gallant exploits; and the French people in general were in that eventful period imbued with a generous yearning for adventure in strange lands. Conquest, exploration, missionary zeal, and the fur-trade were, therefore, for a hundred and fifty years the controlling and often warring interests of New France.

Champlain, who loved to roam, in person conducted several exploring parties, chiefly up the Saguenay and the Ottawa, and into the country around Lake Champlain. In 1615 he was upon the shores of Lake Huron, vainly searching for a westering waterway through the heart of the continent. In 1634 one of his agents, Jean Nicolet, penetrated as far as Wisconsin and made trading compacts

with the tribesmen of that distant land.[1] The
year following (December 25, 1635), the adventurous, pious, and tactful governor departed from
this life. With its back to the wall, the hamlet of
Quebec had under his guidance defied savage enemies, the forbidding climate, the meagre soil, and
all the numerous train of obstacles which at first
beset European colonization in the North American
wilderness. From a political point of view, Champlain had laid deep the foundations of New France;
he had spread the sphere of French influence northward to the barren lands of Labrador and Lake St.
John, westward as far as the interlocking streams
which in Wisconsin form the principal canoe route
to the Mississippi, and southward to the banks of the
Mohawk and the Hudson; while through the active
vehicle of intertribal barter Paris-made weapons
and utensils had penetrated into the most distant
tribes of the continental interior.[2]

In another important particular, however, Champlain's dreams had not been realized. He earnestly
sought to make of New France an agricultural
colony; but we have seen that the enterprise originated with a commercial monopoly which, while

[1] Butterfield, *Discovery of the Northwest; Wis. Hist. Collections*,
XI., 1–25.

[2] Specifically, Sagard, *Histoire du Canada* (ed. of 1866), 193,
194; Marquette, in *Jesuit Relations* (Thwaites's ed.), LIX., 127;
La Chesnaye (1697), in Margry, *Découvertes et Établissements
des Français*, VI., 3.   On the whole subject, Parkman, *Pioneers
of New France*, 230; Turner, *Indian Trade in Wisconsin* (*Johns
Hopkins University Studies*, IX., Nos. 11, 12).

pleasing the court with a pretence of concern for Christianizing the heathen, doubtless had no further desire than to extract from the country its full measure of profit in trading with the natives for furs. Until 1663 the colony on the St. Lawrence maintained a precarious existence under the baneful management of a succession of self-seeking corporations. The winning of a sustenance from the reluctant soil of eastern Canada required greater toil and thrift than mercantile adventurers were willing to bestow; the far-stretching rivers were a continual invitation to explore and exploit the wilderness and its strange inhabitants; the fur trade was the only apparent source of wealth—just as cod-fisheries were accounted the one valuable asset of Newfoundland and of the maritime colonies on the shores of Acadia, where Poutrincourt and his successors and rivals were leading factious but picturesque careers.

The trading and colonizing charter granted to De Monts had been cancelled in 1609. For two years Champlain kept the plantation alive mainly by the aid of merchant adventurers in Rouen; when they withdrew (1611) he secured the formation of a new company, composed of merchants in Rouen, Havre, St. Malo, and La Rochelle. This concern finally went to pieces through jealousy, and amid a storm of complaints that certain members were selling arms and ammunition to the savages and thus endangering the Quebec settlement. The Company

of Associates was thereupon organized, with Champlain and De Monts as the most prominent members; but religious and commercial differences arose, and in the midst of the quarrels Champlain for a time stood in danger of losing his command. In 1620 the corporation was dissolved, its successor being what is known as the Company of De Caen. Seven years later Richelieu secured the dissolution of the latter and the substitution of his own monopoly, commonly called the Company of the Hundred Associates. This powerful organization was granted almost sovereign jurisdiction throughout the vast transatlantic claims of the French, extending from Florida to the arctic circle, and from Newfoundland to the "great fresh lake" of Huron.[1]

Previous monopolies had included Protestants in their membership, and much of the trouble originated from religious dissension, for it was a time when men could not peacefully agree to disagree in such matters. The Hundred Associates,[2] however, admitted none but Catholics. Huguenots and foreigners were not permitted to enter New France, and for fifteen years the company was to maintain and equip priests at each settlement or station. While internal harmony was thus secured, the result was most unfortunate; for among the Hugue-

[1] See analysis and references upon this charter in Cheyney, *European Background* (*Am. Nation*, I.), 156-160.
[2] Actually one hundred and seven. See list in Du Creux, *Historia Canadensis*, sig. b; the charter and other interesting particulars in Sulte, *Histoire des Canadiens-Français*, II., 27-33.

nots now being harried from France were some of
the best material in the nation; and, forbidden to
enter Canada, these vigorous people were soon employed in developing rival English colonies to the
south.

From the first, the court, largely influenced by
the church, was much concerned with the conversion of the Indians. The Calvinist De Monts had
been allowed to take out Huguenot ministers for
those of his companions who wished them; but
missions to the natives must be conducted solely
by Catholic clergy. Jesuits had been ordered to New
France by King Henry IV. as early as 1610; but
their experiences were not happy, for at Port Royal
Poutrincourt's son opposed them, and we have seen
that at Mount Desert English sea - rovers from
Virginia demolished their settlement (1613). In
1615 Champlain introduced to Quebec four members of the fraternity of Recollects, the most au-
stere of the three Franciscan orders. For ten
years these gray friars practised the rites of the
church in the Canadian woods, all the way from
the fishing and trading-post of Tadoussac, at the
mouth of the Saguenay, to the western lake of
the Nipissings, on the road to Lake Huron. But
when Richelieu began to assume control, the argument was advanced that ministrations of a sterner
order were needed for this work. The Recollects
were therefore induced to invite the aid of the powerful Jesuits, who just then were conducting suc-

cessful missions in Asia, Africa, and South America. In 1625 three of the "black gowns" appeared at Quebec, and immediately the field of operations broadened, although it was soon seen that the successful promulgation of the peaceful doctrines of Christianity was to be no holiday task among the warlike tribes of the great Algonquian family.[1]

In July, 1628, a predatory English fleet under Admiral Sir David Kirk took possession of Tadoussac, and a year later secured the unresisting surrender of Quebec from the hands of Champlain, who had with him only sixteen combatants. The governor, together with the missionaries, were transported to England, but eventually they were allowed to proceed to France. Three years later (1632) Canada was retroceded to France,[2] the Hundred Associates now began their work in earnest, and the Jesuits were allowed a monopoly of the interior missions, which they rapidly developed; the Recollects being thereafter confined to the maritime districts—the ill-defined region to which was now applied the general term Acadia, heretofore chiefly confined to the Nova Scotia peninsula.

[1] Details in Thwaites, *Jesuit Relations*, passim.
[2] Cf. Tyler, *England in America* (*Am. Nation*, IV.), 290.

CHAPTER II

THE ACADIAN FRONTIER
(1632–1728)

ANOTHER wave of foreign war reached the shores of Acadia in 1654, when Port Royal, Fort St. Jean (the St. John of our day), and other little strongholds on the Bay of Fundy, fell victims to a New England force under Major Robert Sedgwick, a sturdy Cromwellian soldier who held a commission from the Protector. Thirteen years later (1667) the peninsula was restored to France by the treaty of Breda, the white population at that time being only about four hundred souls, of whom less than a fourth lived beyond cannon-shot of Port Royal.[1]

Isolated, neglected by France, having but slight communication with Canada, and constantly exposed to naval assaults from the English colonies to the south, the little band of Acadians had by this time acquired characteristics all their own. They had become toughened by the harsh condi-

[1] In estimates of Acadian population, we follow Richard, *Acadia.*

tions of a protracted civil war, the frequent struggles now imposed upon them by English invaders,
and the roving character of their life, to an independence of thought and action seldom met with
elsewhere in New France. Affairs were discussed
and decided in public meetings, much after the
fashion of New England, and the *habitants* were accustomed to the necessity of thinking for themselves. The frugal habits and simple tastes and
manners of their forebears were tenaciously retained;
bookishly ignorant, they were easily satisfied as to
material things; they held devotedly to the Catholic
faith, being content to allow the priests, men quite
of their own type, to influence their action in temporal as well as in spiritual affairs. Hating the
English as they had good right to—for heretic
raiders from New England, bent on burning and
harrying these coastwise settlements, had become
an annual possibility—nevertheless, they were apt
to find themselves happier under English rule,
which, when the carnage ceased, at least left them
free to manage their own domestic affairs; whereas
fussy French officialism, seeking to fasten upon
them the feudal conditions elsewhere prevalent
in New France, greatly annoyed these honest
folk who had become accustomed to town-meeting
methods.

There were, and could be, no definite bounds between New England and New France, each growing
and aggressive. The Bay of Fundy region was in

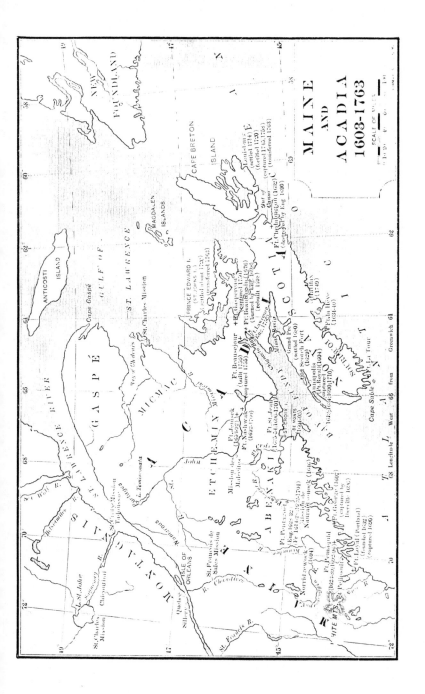

MAINE
AND
ACADIA
1603-1763

SCALE OF MILES

constant dispute.   To France it was necessary as
protection to her portal, the Gulf of St. Lawrence;
to the English this argument was in itself sufficient
reason for covetousness.

Thus far there had been no serious attempt on
the part of English colonists to venture westward
of the Alleghany barrier; but they were now eagerly
spreading all over the Atlantic slope, and the adventurous spirits of New England and New York
found their outlet to the north.   Their stockaded
trading-posts, soon surrounded by hamlets of backwoodsmen, were being established all along the
eastern frontier of Indian tribes who in the west
and north were the neighbors of New France.   The
French, on the other hand, were reaching down into
Maine and New Hampshire with their fur-trade and
mission stations.

A clash was inevitable.   Frenchmen upon the
Bay of Fundy had had long and severe military
training; among them were competent Indian leaders, and Algonquian blood coursed the veins of some
of the most prominent of the men of European race,
while the spirit of conquest was abroad.   The English borderers, in their block - house farmsteads,
were not long in discovering that Acadia had become a hotbed for French and Indian marauding
parties that fought with torch and tomahawk.
Acadian fishermen also sought to capture English
fishing-vessels that entered upon their waters.   It
is small wonder that between the treaty of Breda

and 1710 Port Royal alone suffered five assaults from New England expeditions.[1]

King William's War (1689–1697) occurred when the entire population of New France was not greater than twelve thousand, whereas New England and New York alone held a hundred thousand inhabitants. New France would have suffered severely in a struggle with the English coast colonies, had it not been for the help of her Indian allies, the strategical strength of her important posts, the fighting capacity of her well-trained militia, and the dissensions which existed in the councils of the English colonists.

French operations in this war, under Governor Frontenac, were vigorous, consisting of three winter expeditions (1689–1691), in which Indians were chiefly engaged, savagely attacking the long line of English frontier at widely separated points—New York, New Hampshire, and Maine. Great alarm was thereby occasioned in the English colonies, and small wonder; for, despite the relative strength of her children over-sea, at this time the population and resources of the mother-land were less than half those of France, which was the strongest country in Europe; and Louis XIV. was actuated by a lust for land which in the end was to prove fatal, but to

[1] In 1680, 1690, 1704, 1707, 1710. Calnek and Savary, *County of Annapolis*, 34–62; Charlevoix, *New France*, III., 211, V., 170, 191–201; *Nova Scotia Hist. Collections*, I., 59–64; Hutchinson, *Hist. of Mass. Bay*, II., 143–171, 182–184, 196–204.

the Englishmen of his time appeared seriously to threaten English colonization in America.

The Iroquois and several of the western tribes, notably the Ottawa, were egged on by them to attack the French, which they did with a barbarity quite equalling the Algonquian forays on English backwoodsmen. For a time these irregular counter raids seemed insufficient, and the first colonial congress was held at New York (May 1, 1690) to devise joint expeditions against Canada. The result proved feeble, but the convention was historically important as furnishing a precedent for future colonial co-operation.[1] A New England fleet with eighteen hundred militia commanded by Sir William Phipps, captured Port Royal that summer, and consequently Acadia; but in the following season, Phipps having left too small a garrison, the French *habitants* retook the district, and their king retained it under the treaty of Ryswick (1697).[2]

Other incidents of the war were the yielding of Newfoundland to the French (1696), who held the great island until obliged under the treaty to surrender it the following year; and five years of irregular bushranging along the New York and New England border, both sides freely using Indian allies, a practice in which the French were by training, temperament, and association the more expert.

----

[1] Frothingham, *Rise of the Republic*, 90–93, gives material from Massachusetts archives not readily accessible elsewhere.

[2] Cf. Greene, *Provincial America* (*Am. Nation*, VI.), chap. viii.

The treaty did not, however, bring peace to the harassed borderers.   Intercolonial hostilities of a merciless character continued spasmodically along the frontier throughout the period of five years between the treaty of Ryswick and the breaking-out, in 1702, of Queen Anne's War, known in Europe as the War of the Spanish Succession. The military operations of the latter were of a character similar to those of the preceding war. Of three attempts made by New England troops to recapture the peninsula (1704, 1707, and 1710), the last was successful, Port Royal surrendering to Colonel Francis Nicholson after an heroic defence of nineteen days.

By the terms of the treaty of Utrecht (1713),[1] "All of Nova Scotia or Acadia, comprised in its ancient limits, as also the city of Port Royal," was definitively ceded to Great Britain, in whose hands it thereafter remained, the first solid step in the conquest of New France. The indefinite, indeed curiously clumsy, phrasing of this description, of course settled nothing as to the boundaries between New France and the English colonies. These were to be determined by a joint commission, which was, however, never appointed, possibly because the questions involved were of too delicate a nature for arbitration; a half-century later they were referred to the arbitrament of war.

[1] Text in Chalmers, *Treaties;* Gerard, *Peace of Utrecht;* Houston, *Docs. Illus. Canadian Constitution.*

In the absence of definitive boundaries, the French now stoutly asserted that by the term Acadia was meant only the peninsula of Nova Scotia, a plausible contention in view of the treaty phrase; and the English were caustically notified not to meddle with the rest of the country, especially to the west and southwest of the Bay of Fundy, involving most of the hotly disputed border-line between New France and New England. The French claim extended to the Kennebec River, and up to that stream they proceeded to strengthen their defences.

On the other hand, the English contended for what they claimed to be the common understanding: that Acadia (which in 1691 was included in the new charter of Massachusetts) comprised also Cape Breton, New Brunswick, and so much of Maine as lay beyond the Kennebec. This position found abundant warrant in old French documents, it being proved that therein, so long as the French were in control, the term Acadia was accepted among them as embracing the entire stretch of country between the Kennebec and the St. Lawrence. As Lahontan said in 1703: "The Coast of Acadia extends from Kenebeki, one of the frontiers of New England, to l'Isle Percée, near the Mouth of the River of St. Lawrence. This Sea-Coast runs almost three hundred Leagues in length."[1] Already Eng-

---

[1] Thwaites, *Lahontan's Voyages*, I., 323; see also documents in Parkman, *Half-Century of Conflict*, App., 273–287.

lish fishing and trading stations had crept up along
the coast as far as the Kennebec, and preparations
for a still farther advance were evident.[1]

The Kennebec forms with the Chaudière, which
empties into the St. Lawrence opposite Quebec, a
possible although difficult portage route for war
and trading parties, and was frequently used by
French and Indians upon their marauding raids.
Indeed, the long and undulating water-shed between
the St. Lawrence and the Atlantic drainage abounds
in chains of lakes and opposite-flowing rivers which
can be used in short-cut journeys between the lower
St. Lawrence and the sea.   Throughout all this interesting region of forest and stream, English and
French traders and adventurers frequently met and
fought; but the Kennebec, as the chief trade-route
and war-path, with memories of both King William's
and Queen Anne's wars, was adopted by the French
as their boundary, and became the bone of a heated
contention.

The Massachusetts policy of maintaining among
the tribesmen official trading-posts, with fair prices
for furs, had, south of the Kennebec, secured to the
Puritans the friendship of the natives and a long
peace.   But the Abenaki, in the Kennebec valley
and to the north, remained firm in their adherence
to New France.   Jesuit missionaries had converted
them, and taught their wards to hate the overbearing and land-grabbing English, who would ruin the

[1] See Tyler, *England in America* (*Am. Nation*, IV.), chap. xvi.

hunting - grounds by converting them into farms.
After the treaty of Utrecht the French strengthened
this alliance, and stockaded the native villages, thereby seeking to create a dense line of Indian opposition along the Kennebec that could not be
penetrated by importunate borderers from the
south.[1]

The most important Abenaki town was Norridgewock, seventy - five miles above the river - mouth.
Its spiritual director was Father Sebastien Rale,
concerning whose ability and energy as a missionary,
and skill in savage leadership, there can be no
doubt; but politically he was a bigot, and hated
Englishmen as though the children of the evil one.
Agricultural settlements from Massachusetts steadily increased in this quarter. It maddened the
nervous and excitable Rale to find the English
frontiersmen stolidly indifferent to arguments and
threats. The new-comers obtained lands by purchase from certain Indian chiefs; but the authority
of these chiefs to dispose of the common hunting-
ground was denied by Rale and the rank and file
of the tribesmen—properly enough, for the Indian
polity is intensely democratic, and the chief can only
act when his followers consent; moreover, Indians
could not in those early days comprehend the

---

[1] Documents and discussions in Baxter, *New France in New
England;* N. Y. Docs. Rel. to Col. Hist., IX., 909–912, 933–935;
Thwaites, *Jesuit Relations*, LXVII., 55–65, 97–119; Franklin,
Writings (Sparks's ed.), IV., 7, 8.

meaning of a permanent land transfer, their notion being that the courtesy of a temporary occupancy was alone sought, and that in due time they would be permitted to regain their hunting-grounds.

While Rale, in the intensity of his Anglophobia, may not have personally incited his people to actual warfare, he nevertheless maintained close touch with the officials at Quebec and Louisburg, who neglected no means of fostering bad blood; and he connived at the introduction of war-parties of Ottawa, who stirred his flock to frenzy. In 1721 the New England border was cruelly swept by savage raids, the inception of which was easily traceable to Norridgewock. The usual quarrels and jealousies between the Massachusetts governor and assembly led to a two years' delay in retribution; but in 1723 an initial raid was made by Massachusetts men upon the Penobscot, and a French missionary village was destroyed; this being followed the next season by a further punitive expedition of two hundred volunteers, who proceeded up the Kennebec, successfully stormed Norridgewock, and in the ensuing massacre killed Rale himself.[1] All along the Kennebec, Abenaki were now slaughtered without mercy by bands of Massachusetts rangers, whose zest for killing was, when jaded, stimulated by an

[1] Baxter, *New France in New England*, 237–273; Parkman, *Half-Century of Conflict*, I., 229–239; Charlevoix, *New France*, V., 268–281; Thwaites, *Jesuit Relations*, LXVII., 231–247; *N. Y. Docs. Rel. to Col. Hist.*, IX., 936–939; Mass. Hist. Soc., *Collections*, 2d series, VIII., 245–267.

official reward, for each savage scalp, of a hundred pounds in depreciated provincial currency.

This irregular border strife, which lasted throughout four dark and bloody years, while the mother-countries were still at peace, early extended as far west as the Hudson. As usual in such cases, in the end the blow fell heaviest upon the savages themselves. Left alone, the tribesmen might soon have pleaded for mercy from English wrath; but French officials on the St. Lawrence, and French partisans in the Acadian settlements, would hear of no yielding on the part of their dusky dogs of war, and so the weary strife went on. It meant the sapping of the strength of New France. To New England, the bitter experience proved a fit training-school for the independent yeomen who were in mighty struggles first to oust their French rivals, and then cast off the leading-strings of mother England herself.

CHAPTER III

THE ST. LAWRENCE VALLEY
(1632–1713)

FROM the time of the restoration of New France (1632) till the final catastrophe of 1759, Canada remained uninterruptedly French; and from the tide-water of the St. Lawrence as a base, French traders, soldiers, and settlers (*habitants*) spread westward, northward, and eventually southward. In the year of the restoration probably not over a hundred and eighty of its inhabitants might properly be called settlers, with perhaps a few score military men, seafarers, and visiting commercial adventurers. The majority of residents of course centred at Quebec, with a few at the outlying trading-posts of Tadoussac on the east, Three Rivers on the west, and the intervening hamlets of Beaupré, Beauport, and Isle d'Orleans. At the same time the English and Dutch settlements in Virginia, the Middle Colonies, and Massachusetts had probably amassed an aggregate population of twenty-five thousand — for between the years 1627 and 1637 upward of twenty thousand settlers emigrated thither from Europe. While the English government

34

was engaged in efforts to repress the migration towards its own colonies, the utmost endeavors of the powerful French companies, their arguments reinforced by bounties, could not induce more than a few home-loving Frenchmen to try their fortunes amid the rigors of the New World.

With all his tact, Champlain had committed one act of indiscretion, the effects of which were left as an ill-fated legacy to the little colony which he otherwise nursed so well. Seeking to please his Algonquian neighbors upon the St. Lawrence, and at the time eager to explore the country, the commandant, with two of his men-at-arms, accompanied (1609) one of their frequent war-parties against the confederated Iroquois, who lived, for the most part, in New York state and northeastern Pennsylvania. Meeting a hostile band of two hundred and fifty warriors near where Fort Ticonderoga was afterwards constructed, Champlain and his white attendants easily routed the enemy by means of fire-arms, with which the interior savages were as yet unacquainted.[1] His success in this direction was, through the unfortunate importunity of his allies, repeated in 1610; but five years later, when he invaded the Iroquois cantonments in the company of a large body of Huron, whose country to the east of Lake Huron he had been visiting that summer, the tribesmen to the southeast of Lake Ontario were found to have lost much of their

[1] Cf. Tyler, *England in America* (*Am. Nation*, IV.), 288.

fear for white men's weapons, and the invaders retreated in some disorder.

The results were highly disastrous both to the Huron and the French. The former were year by year mercilessly harried by the bloodthirsty Iroquois, until in 1649 they were driven from their homes and in the frenzy of fear fled first to the islands of Lake Huron, then to Mackinac and Sault Ste. Marie, finally to the southern shores of Lake Superior, and deep within the dark pine forests of northern Wisconsin. In the destruction of Huronia, several Jesuit missionaries suffered torture and death.

As for the squalid little French settlements at Three Rivers, Quebec, and Tadoussac, they soon felt the wrath of the Iroquois, who were the fiercest and best-trained fighters among the savages of North America. Almost annually the war-parties of this dread foe raided the lands of the king, not infrequently appearing in force before the sharp-pointed palisades of New France, over which were often waged bloody battles for supremacy. Fortunately logs could turn back a primitive enemy unarmed with cannon; but not infrequently outlying parties of Frenchmen had sorry experiences with the stealthy foe, of whose approach through the tangled forest they had had no warning. Champlain's closing years were much saddened by these merciless assaults which he had unwittingly invited; in the decade after his death the operations of his suc-

PROGRESS OF
FRENCH DISCOVERY
IN THE INTERIOR
1600 - 1702

Portages
British Possessions in 1713
French Possessions and Claims

SCALE OF MILES
0   50   100   150   200

cessors were largely hampered thereby. Montreal, founded by religious enthusiasts in 1642, during its earliest years served as a buffer colony, in the direction of the avenging tribesmen, and supped to the dregs the cup of border turmoil.

Not only were Frenchmen obliged to huddle within their defences, but far and near their Indian allies were swept from the earth. The Iroquois practically destroyed the Algonquian tribes between Quebec and the Saguenay, as well as the Algonkins of the Ottawa, the Huron, and the Petun and Neutrals of the Niagara district. The fur-trade of New France was for a long period almost wholly destroyed; English and Dutch rivals to the south were friendly to the Iroquois, furnished them cheap goods and abundant fire-arms and ammunition, and egged them on in their northern forays; while towards the Mississippi, and south of the Great Lakes, Iroquois raiders terrorized those tribes which dared to entertain trade relations with the French.[1]

In 1646, however, the blood-stained confederates, after nearly a half-century of opposition, consented to a peace which lasted spasmodically for almost twenty years; until in 1665 the French government found itself strong enough to threaten the chastisement of the New York tribesmen, and thereafter the Iroquois opposition, while not altogether quelled, was of a far less threatening character.

About the same time the government of Canada

[1] Cf. Greene, *Provincial America* (*Am. Nation*, VI.), chap. vii.

underwent a fundamental change, which gave new vigor to the attempt to penetrate into the unknown west. The Hundred Associates had agreed, in their charter, to send four thousand colonists to Canada before 1643, to lodge and support them during three years, and then to give them cleared lands for their maintenance; but the vast expense attendant upon an enterprise of this character was beyond the ability of the company, who had found no profit in any feature of their undertaking; therefore, after feeble attempts at immigration, they transferred to the inhabitants of Quebec their monopoly of the fur-trade, with all debts and other obligations, but retained their seigniorial rights as lords of the soil. Finally, in 1663, the associates willingly surrendered their charter, New France became the property of the crown, and thereby was ended the era of feudal tenure under the mastery of a grasping although unsuccessful commercial corporation. Thus, freedom from the control of corporate greed and measurable relief from the Iroquois horror came almost contemporaneously. New France, now over a half-century old, had at last been given the shadow of a chance.

So far the rivalry of England had, after the return of Quebec, been felt only in Acadia,[1] for the Iroquois acted as a barrier between the contending powers all along the northern frontier, both before and after the English acquisition of New York in 1664.

[1] See chap. ii., above.

England, Holland, and Sweden had all planted their North American settlements upon a relatively narrow seaboard, with the Appalachian range lying for the most part not to exceed a hundred miles inland. The coast abounds in indentations — safe harbors and generous landlocked bays, into which flow numerous rivers of considerable breadth and depth. By means of these the interior can readily be explored as far as the waterfalls which are formed by the lower benches of the mountain wall; beyond this the sailing craft of the early European settlers could not go—the traveller who would ascend farther by canoe must alight at each recurring rapids or falls, his progress retarded and his person exposed to possible assaults of the often hostile savages who lurked upon the bush-strewn banks. The forested peaks which fretted the western sky-line, while pygmies compared with the Cordilleras rimming the Mississippi basin on the farther west, at first seemed insurmountable to the men of the coast. In these altitudes the soil is thinner than upon the alluvial coast plain; moreover, beyond the mountains dwelt fierce tribes of aborigines with whom the colonists were as yet unwilling to cope. Thus hemmed in by a wide belt of rugged country, wherein nature was unkind, and bands of warlike barbarians held the streams and forests, it was natural that an agricultural, manufacturing, and seafaring people should as a whole spread inland only when pressed for room.

Among the English colonists, however, were many restless adventurers who sought new lands, fresh hunting-grounds, and the uncertain profits of the roving Indian trade. As early as 1650, Governor Berkeley, of Virginia, made a vain attempt to cross the Alleghany barrier in search of the Mississippi, of which he had vaguely heard from Indians. A few years later a Virginian, Colonel Abraham Wood, discovered (1654–1664) streams which poured into the Ohio and the Mississippi,[1] thus penetrating the Mississippi basin several years before the French discovery by Jolliet and Marquette.[2] Later explorers — Lederer[3] (1669, 1670), Batts[4] (1671), Howard and Salling[5] (1742), Walker[6] (1748, 1750), Gist[7] (1751), Finley[8] (1752, 1753), Boone[9] (1769), George Washington[10] (1770, to the mouth of the

[1] Coxe, *Carolana*, 120; Adair, *Am. Indians*, 308; *State of British Colonies* (1755), 107, 118.

[2] See chap. iii., below.

[3] Talbot (trans.), *Discoveries of John Lederer*.

[4] Beverley, *Virginia; N. Y. Docs. Rel. to Col. Hist.*, III., 193–197.

[5] Du Pratz, *Louisiana*, 62; Wynne, *British Empire in America*, II., 405; *Expediency of Securing Our American Colonies*. 25, 47.

[6] Walker, *Journal*, in Johnston, *First Explorations of Kentucky*.

[7] Gist, *Journal* (Johnston's and Darlington's ed.).

[8] *Maryland Gazette*, May 17, 1753; Filson, *Kentucky* (erroneous date); *Pa. Col. Records*, V., 570; "Boone Papers," in Draper MSS.

[9] Boone, "Narrative," in Filson, *Kentucky*, 47–54; Draper MSS.

[10] Washington, *Journal of a Tour to the Ohio*, in *Writings* (Ford's ed.), II., 285–316; Collins, *Kentucky*, II., 460, notes doubtful evidence, nowhere else confirmed, of Washington's presence earlier than 1770.

Kanawha)—pushing far in advance of the limits of continuous settlement, moved westward the conflicting claims of Pennsylvania, Virginia, and the Carolinas. But up to the middle of the eighteenth century these enterprises were sporadic and with slight result; New France had in her feeble way long held the vast basin of the Mississippi before the men of the English colonies seriously attempted any occupation of trans-Alleghany waters.

The stately flood of the St. Lawrence, sweeping past the cliff of Quebec on its journey to the sea, annually brought down to the little trading hamlets of New France fleets of birch-bark canoes, laden with peltries and propelled by lusty, swarthy savages from the mysterious forests and plains of the "upper country." Bedizened with paint and feathers, speaking many harsh, guttural dialects, as cruel and crafty as they were keen at a bargain, boastfully garrulous of their deeds on the war-path and the hunt, yet as fond of amusement as children, these strange people greatly excited the curiosity of the mercurial men of France. Adventurers were eager to join in the wild life of the far-away camps of the tribesmen; fur-traders scented untold profits in following these dusky hunters into the unknown wilderness; ecclesiastics foresaw in this heathen world a rich harvest of souls.

Explorers, fur-traders, missionaries, soldiers, rovers of every sort, and of such the population of New France was chiefly composed—for soil and character were unfavorable for agriculture, there was no manufacturing, and thus far from the sea the fisheries were unimportant—found themselves easily lured by the far - stretching and ramified waterways which led from and to the great northwest. The colony was no sooner planted than Champlain, a typical adventurer of his time, set the fashion of exploration. We have seen that the founder of New France personally reached the shores of Lake Huron, and that in 1634—the year before his death—his agent, Jean Nicolet, was treating with Wisconsin tribes upon the chief northwestern gateway to the Mississippi, which stream, however, he does not appear to have visited.[1]

The handful of colonists soon became widely diffused by means of these enticing wilderness paths. By the time New France was fifty years old, its population of three thousand souls was scattered all the way from far-eastern Acadia to the lonely trading-camps of the explorers Radisson and Groseilliers, in the wilds of central Wisconsin (1654–1655) —a stretch of over fifteen hundred miles along the great glacial groove of the St. Lawrence drainage system. Governor d'Avaugour wrote from Quebec in 1661: "As regards ... the settlements, they are scattered in a still more unsocial fashion than are the savages themselves ... less than three thousand souls residing over an extent of eighty leagues ... for a distance of a league and a half around Quebec

' See chap. i., above.

there is sufficient to support a hundred thousand souls." [1]

That the French at first made much larger claims to the interior of North America than did the English, was due less to their undoubted avarice for territory than to their early enterprise as explorers. They held tenaciously to the far-reaching theory, in that day by no means singular to France, that if one of their compatriots was the first white to reach strange waters, the king of France was thereby entitled to the lands drained by all streams which might directly or indirectly flow into or from the waters thus discovered. This assumption ignored the presence of the aboriginal inhabitants, who had not sought to be discovered; but as they were ignorant of European civilization and its accompanying theology, it was taken for granted that they possessed no rights which a Christian need consider.

By means of formal proclamations of "taking possession," accompanied by the burial of engraved leaden plates upon the banks of rivers and lakes, and the rearing of posts bearing metallic insignia of France, amid religious and civil ceremonial, her adventurers rapidly pushed her claims through the heart of the continent. They stoutly and honestly held, according to the tenets of their time, that such discovery and rites, backed as they soon were by a line of water-side posts, gave them unquestionable jurisdiction over the vast drainage systems of the

[1] Thwaites, *Jesuit Relations*, XLVI., 151.

St. Lawrence, the Mississippi, the Winnipeg, and the Saskatchewan.

Holding such claims to be the logical result of exploration, partially occupying the country with their fur-trade and military stations, and enjoying therein a widely diffused commerce with the natives, with the majority of whom they were on kindly terms, Frenchmen long felt confident that the English colonists, thus far giving small evidence of land hunger, might permanently be restricted to the narrow eastern slope of the Appalachians; and perhaps to such fur-bearing littoral in the extensive north as might be controlled by the powerful but unadventurous "Governor and Company of Adventurers of England trading into Hudson Bay."

The establishment in London (1667) of the Hudson's Bay Company, as the fruit of the defection from French interests of two of their most noted explorers in the region of the upper Great Lakes—the sieurs Radisson and Groseilliers[1]—proved the opening wedge of that English commercial rivalry which was ultimately to shatter New France. The charter granted (1670) by King Charles II. to this notable company, upon whose rolls were Prince Rupert, the Duke of York, and other court favorites, quite after the fashion of the most exorbitant French claims, bestowed the entire region drained by waters flowing directly or indirectly into and from Hud-

[1] See Scull (ed.), *Radisson's Voyages; Wis. Hist. Collections*, XI., 64–69; Campbell, *Radisson and Groseilliers*.

son Bay; to this enormous drainage basin being later added large grants upon the Arctic and Pacific slopes. Over a wilderness as vast as Europe, the company were to enjoy the "whole, entire, and only liberty, use and privilege of Trading and Trafficking," with absolute powers both as to civil and military affairs, including even the making of war or peace with other peoples.[1]

While the Hudson's Bay Company was deliberately settling itself upon the lonely shores of the bay, and from the first enjoying large profits, the French were making brave strides in the interior to the far south. La Salle, with his ambitious fur-trading schemes, was reaching out towards Louisiana; with much official display, Saint Lusson was taking possession at Sault Ste. Marie of the upper Great Lakes (1671); Jesuit missions for the Christianizing of the savages were being opened along the shores of these inland seas; Jolliet and Marquette were rediscovering the Mississippi by way of the Fox-Wisconsin route; Perrot, Duluth, and their fellows were exploiting the forest trade, and by turns wheedling and bullying the tribesmen as occasion demanded; the lilies of France were surmounting many a log stockade—half fort, half trading-station; and on every hand it appeared likely that French overlordship had come to stay.

The French were not long in discovering that

---

[1] Full text of charter in Mills, *Statutes, Documents, and Papers ... respecting ... Boundaries of the Province of Ontario*, 29–37.

the great English company of the north was a
dangerous rival in the fur - trade. "These smug
ancient gentlemen," as Lord Bolingbroke once con-
temptuously called them, were not keen after exploration of their sub-Arctic domain. Their shop-
keeping servants at first showed a curious reluctance
to venture farther inland than could be seen from
the walls of their stockaded "factories"—although
in later years there were not lacking among them
adventurers whose names stand high on the roll of
American explorers. But having the freedom of the
seas, they could cheaply import to the gates of their
bayside forts a high grade of goods. Although
merciless in bargaining with the natives, they were
able to offer the latter better prices and merchandise
than could be found at the posts of the monopoly-
ridden French. The result was that the Quebec and
Montreal merchants, who were operating through
Mackinac, Sault Ste. Marie, and Lake Superior
stations, found the Indians, who cared little for the
time element, often willing to travel long distances
to reach the better customer. Moreover, such were
the difficulties of transportation met by the French
of the interior, with their long and arduous portages,
that they purchased from the natives only the
lighter and more expensive furs, such as beaver,
marten, and fox; while the English, able to load
pelts upon sea-going vessels at the wharves of their
Hudson Bay posts, were customers for every variety
of skins. Some idea of the profits of the trade, as

reaped in these earlier years of the Hudson's Bay Company, may be obtained when we read that in 1676 the value of the merchandise which they exported to their agents at the bay, for purposes of barter, was but £650 sterling, while that of the furs imported into England from the same source was nearly £19,000.[1]

Serious rivalry began in 1671, when the Jesuit Albanel was sent overland from Canada to report upon the English trade and make commercial overtures to their customers. Thereafter much uneasiness was displayed by the company, for it was found that the French were actively at work along the southeastern fringes of their territory, drawing off customers from the bay factories and prejudicing the minds of the natives.

In the summer of 1685 a party of eighty bushrangers under Chevalier de Troyes and the Sieurs d'Iberville, de Sainte Hélène, and de Marincourt—sons of the Charles le Moyne of whom we shall presently hear [2]—approaching James's Bay by way of the Ottawa River, captured Moose factory and Fort Albany.[3] Until the treaty of Utrecht (1713), nearly every season witnessed picturesque armed contests between French and English upon the dreary shores of Hudson Bay. Intermittently, the French were during several seasons in almost complete

---

[1] Willson, *The Great Company*, 173.
[2] See chap. v., below.
[3] Bryce, *Hudson's Bay Company*, 51.

mastery of the situation. But their trade in this district proved to be far from profitable. France was weak in sea-power; the vessels of her bay traders were subject to pillage and destruction by the all-conquering navy of Britain.[1] Even had communication with France been uninterrupted, the traders were victims of the commercial monopoly which fettered New France; they could not meet the prices for furs which had been established among the seaboard savages by the British. At Utrecht, in 1713, it was agreed that the bay should remain the property of its first exploiters. The "Old Lady of Fenchurch Street," as the great company was derisively termed by hostile critics, once more assumed control — greatly weakened, however, through long years of adversity.

[1] Bryce, *Hudson's Bay Company*, 52-60.

CHAPTER IV

DISCOVERY OF THE MISSISSIPPI

(1634–1687)

AT the head of the east and west trough of the
St. Lawrence Valley the French discovered another low area, extending transversely north and
south, practically between the Arctic Ocean and the
Gulf of Mexico, with the Mississippi flowing through
the greater part of its enormous length. The basin
of the Mississippi is separated from that of the St.
Lawrence by a low and narrow water-shed running
closely parallel to the Great Lakes, approached from
the latter by short rivers easily ascended, and
readily crossed by portage paths varying in length
from one mile to ten; at the end of the carries were
streams, for the most part flowing leisurely into
larger rivers emptying either directly or indirectly
into the Mississippi. From Lake Erie, the west-
going travellers would first reach a route to the
waters of the Ohio by way of Lake Chautauqua;
next, from the site of the present Erie (the Presq'isle
of the French), could be reached French Creek,
which flows into the Alleghany, one of the two
forks of the upper Ohio; other portages led over to

49

the Beaver, the Muskingum, the Scioto, and the
Wabash. From Lake Michigan, the river St. Joseph might be ascended to its source, and a carrying trail found, by which the Maumee could be
reached and descended to Lake Erie, thus cutting
across the base of the great Michigan peninsula; or,
at the great bend of St. Joseph (South Bend, Indiana), a marshy trail led over to the Kankakee,
which pours into the Illinois, itself an affluent of
the Mississippi. At Chicago River was another
trade - route over a narrow, swampy divide, by
which could be reached the Des Plaines, a tributary
of the Illinois. The favorite path of all, however,
was that by which Lake Michigan was connected
with the Mississippi by ascending Green Bay and
the Fox River, crossing a boggy plain of a mile and a
half in central Wisconsin (at the modern city of
Portage), and descending the broad, island-strewn
Wisconsin River, which is edged by picturesque
bluffs alternating with rich alluvial bottoms.

The portage routes between Lake Superior and
the Mississippi were of great importance in the control of that inland sea, but were seldom used in
ordinary travel between the extremities of New
France. The Bois Brulé is a narrow stream in
which rapids and pools succeed each other through
the heart of the overhanging forest; a carrying path
of a mile and a half leads to the often turbulent St.
Croix, wherein cataracts and billowy rapids neces-
sitate several bank-side portages. At the southwest

extremity of Lake Superior the foaming St. Louis
was ascended to a trail by which was reached the
lake-strewn region of the Mille Lacs, whence the
initial waters of the Mississippi peacefully emerge.
Ascending Pigeon River, on the present boundary-
line between Minnesota and Manitoba, it was possible by means of a score or two of portages and
short-cuts, through a vast net-work of lakes and
divergent streams, to reach Lake Winnipeg; and,
beyond that, the inlets to Hudson Bay and the far-
stretching systems of the Saskatchewan and the
Assiniboin, which touch the feet of the Canadian
Rockies and lead to other portages connecting with
waters flowing into the Arctic and Pacific oceans.

So low is the height of land between the divergent
drainage systems that empty respectively into the
Gulf of St. Lawrence and the Gulf of Mexico, that
at some points—notably the Chicago and the Fox-
Wisconsin routes—spring floods occasionally enabled
traders and explorers to propel their canoes and
bateaux from one system to the other without a
carry, the waters of the upper Wisconsin flowing
over into the Fox, across the portage plain, and
those of Lake Michigan setting southward towards
the Mississippi, through the Chicago River, which
was, in an earlier geological period, an outlet of
Lake Michigan instead of an inlet.

It did not take French explorers long to realize
that these drainage troughs furnished means for the
trade and military control of the vast interior of

the continent, between the Alleghanies and the Rockies, from the frozen lands of the far north to the sub-tropical region bordering the Gulf of Mexico. French progress up the St. Lawrence system was throughout much of the eighteenth century interrupted by the hostility of the Iroquois, who held the lands to the south of Lake Ontario and along the Niagara portage. Champlain's early assault upon these,[1] the most warlike of American savages, had engendered a hatred which would not down, and the manifestation of which was only ultimately abated by growing powers of reprisal on the part of New France.

Champlain and several succeeding generations of explorers found Lake Huron by laboriously stemming the numerous rapids of Ottawa River—the original outlet of that inland sea, but a slight geological upheaval had created a rim, which thereafter separated the waters of river and lake. Thus Huron was, by this direct but difficult route, the first great lake to be discovered (1615); Ontario (1615), Superior (1616), and Michigan (1634), with their respective portage routes to the Mississippi, being next unveiled in the order named. Erie, known to the French as early as 1640, was not navigated by them until 1669, save by occasional unlicensed traders, who were surreptitiously bringing furs to the markets of the English and the Dutch allies of the Iroquois; and there is a possibility that

[1] See chap. iii., above.

in this early period Englishmen and Dutchmen
themselves may have threaded its waters on a like
errand, although the establishment of a French fort
at Niagara (1678) did much to hamper this traffic.[1]
It was not until the establishment of Detroit (1701)
that the northwest could safely and regularly be
reached by means of the Great Lakes; and even
later the Ottawa River route was occasionally used
by French traders and explorers during uprisings
of the New York Indians, when the passage of the
Niagara portage was attended with danger.

From the time of the first European landfall in
North America, the discovery of a transcontinental
waterway that should shorten the route to China and
India had been keenly desired by Spain, France,
and England in turn.   That such existed was for
over two centuries an article of faith with European
geographers, and American annals abound in records of attempts to find it.   Navigators of different
nations carefully examined every inlet along both
coasts, from the south upward, and explorers of
the interior were led hither and yon by Indian
traditions of such waterways—for the wily American savage, seeking either to please his unwelcome
guest or to induce him to move on, was wont stoutly to assert that somewhere beyond the horizon lay
the very thing the stranger sought, be it precious
metals or a transcontinental passage.   Gradually,
after centuries of endeavor, the wished-for water-

[1] *N. Y. Docs. Rel. to Col. Hist.*, IX., 289.

way was moved northward upon the maps, until at last the fabled "Northwest Passage" came to be relegated to the impenetrable Arctic.

Very early in the history of New France, knowledge of the Mississippi reached Quebec. Indian reports obscurely spoke of it as "a great water," emptying into some greater sea, thus leading the French at first to suppose that it was either the Pacific (or South Sea) itself, or in direct communication with that ocean. It is quite improbable that any one tribe possessed complete information regarding the entire river, in advance of white men's discovery and exploration. Certain stretches were, of course, well known to the bands dwelling along those portions of its banks; and to some extent the lower reaches of its affluents were known to them—but no doubt superstitious fear, jealousy of neighboring tribes, and absence of that curiosity which impels civilized man to exploration, combined to keep them within their own bailiwicks. Traditions and theories were passed on from one tribe to another; but the result was only vague, purblind knowledge based upon no definite conception of the geography of the continent. Thus the first white explorers—fur-traders and missionaries—often found such aboriginal information sadly perplexing.[1]

The lower reaches of the Mississippi were early visited by roving Spanish adventurers from Mexico

[1] Elaborated in Thwaites, "The Great River," in *The World To-day*, VI., 184–192, 383–391.

and Florida.   Alonzo de Pineda is credited with the
honor of first exploring the great river (1519) and
calling it Rio del Espiritu-Santo; Pamfilo de Nar-
vaez met his death in the delta nine years later;
Hernando de Soto was buried in its waters in 1542.
But from these adventures nothing resulted beyond
a shadowy claim on behalf of Spain.[1]

Certain distorted information had come to Champlain concerning the characteristics and name of
the Indians at the mouth of Fox River, in Wisconsin — which, we have seen, was one of the chief
gateways to the Mississippi—leading him to suppose that these people might be Chinamen, and
Green Bay the entrance of the much-sought route
to Cathay.[2] His agent, the daring Nicolet, was
much disappointed to find there only breech-
clouted Winnebagoes, an expelled offshoot of the
Dakota of the west.   His long and difficult journey (1634)—the most important exploration thus
far undertaken for New France—brought him little nearer to a solution of the great geographical
problem.

It is possible that twenty years later (1655),
Radisson and Groseilliers—"anxious to be knowne
with the remotest people" and "to discover the
great lakes that they had heard the wild men speak

---

[1] Bourne, *Spain in America* (*Am. Nation*, III.), chap. x.
[2] Parkman, *La Salle*, xxii., xxiv.; Butterfield, *Discovery of the
Northwest*, 37–39, 58, 59; Hebberd, *Wisconsin under Dominion
of France*, 14–16.

of"—were upon the "great river" which flowed southward to the Spaniards; but Radisson's journal, written years after their visit to Wisconsin, has no map and is couched in vague terms. Only the year before (1654), a writer in the *Jesuit Relations* averred that the sea which separates America from Asia was but nine days' journey from Green Bay— about the time necessary for a canoe trip from Green Bay to the Mississippi by the route of the Fox and Wisconsin rivers.[1]

At the Jesuit mission on Chequamegon Bay of Lake Superior, Father Claude Allouez obtained from the Indians (1665) some disjointed data concerning the great south-flowing waterway.[2] His successor, Father Jacques Marquette (1669), became especially interested in the Mississippi, the hazy reports which he received from his naked parishioners but increasing his curiosity and whetting his desire to Christianize the savages along its banks. Four years later (1673), in the company of an official explorer, Louis Jolliet, he ascended the Fox and made an easy portage to the Wisconsin, at whose mouth they found the Mississippi (June 17).[3] When they started from the Jesuit mission at Mackinac Straits, the travellers were confident that the river either emptied into the South Sea (Pacific) or coursed southeastward to the Atlantic; but by the time the mouth of the Arkansas was reached, whence they

---

[1] Thwaites, *Jesuit Relations*, XLI., 185.   [2] *Ibid.*, LI., 53.
[3] *Ibid.*, LIX., 86–163.

returned northward, it was definitely learned from tribesmen of the lower reaches that the broad flood poured into the Gulf of Mexico and not into either ocean.

The long-sought transcontinental waterway, east and west, could not, therefore, be in this direction. It was, however, now evident that New France possessed, for the light and shallow river craft of that day, a practically continuous waterway from the Gulf of St. Lawrence to the Gulf of Mexico, through the heart of the continent. Bark canoes could readily penetrate into the most far-reaching waters, sailing-vessels could plough the lakes, while a chain of little bank-side forts of logs might over-awe the Indians, monopolize the fur-trade of the vast interior, and probably confine the English to the Atlantic coast.

Marquette remaining among the western savages, Jolliet had hurried back to Quebec with the news of their discovery. Maps and other papers were lost in the wreck of his canoe in Lachine Rapids, near Montreal,[1] but his verbal report greatly excited the colony. Among those who recognized the possibilities of this vast extension of the bounds of New France, with an ice-free port upon the Gulf of Mexico, were the bold and sturdy Governor Frontenac and his afterwards famous protégé, Robert Cavelier, known to history as the Sieur de la Salle.

[1] Thwaites, *Jesuit Relations*, L., 322; LVIII., 93, 109; LIX., 89.

Born of a wealthy Rouen family, in 1643, La Salle became in his youth a Jesuit novice, and thus was legally debarred from inheriting his father's fortune. Of an imaginative, daring, and ambitious mind, he appears to have fretted under monastic restraint, and in his twenty-third or twenty-fourth year to have left the order, wherein it appears that he had taken the three requisite vows, served as a teacher, and been known as Frère Robert Ignace.[1] Although parting on good terms with his brethren, in later years he became a fierce opponent of the Jesuit missionaries in Canada, chiefly because his vast fur-trade projects, with the inevitable traffic in brandy, were regarded by them as tending to demoralize the Indians, and his proud spirit could brook no opposition.

Arriving in Canada in 1666, La Salle found here an ample field for his adventurous nature. He at once started upon a careful study of Indian methods and languages, and soon became a recognized expert therein, freely confided in by Frontenac, a man of kindlier character but of a like lofty ambition. It is known that during these early years of his Canadian experiences La Salle was a wide traveller. He was much with the Iroquois, both in their own country and upon hunting trips on the Ottawa; and the claim is made that, probably in 1671, he was first of white men at the Falls of the Ohio (Louisville) — indeed, that about that

[1] Thwaites, *Jesuit Relations*, LX., 319, 320.

time, prior to Jolliet's tour, he actually discovered
the Mississippi; but these early exploits are not
proven, and there is strong ground for doubting
them.[1]

When, in 1672, Frontenac conceived the idea of
erecting a fort on Lake Ontario, to intercept Indian
trade which might otherwise be deflected to the
English at Albany, and with a view also of carrying
the trade nearer to its forest customers, he selected
La Salle as its commandant.   Fort Frontenac was
accordingly erected (1673) on the site of the present
Canadian town of Kingston, at the outlet of Lake
Ontario.

The following year (1674) La Salle, burning with
plans for trade and discovery towards the Mississippi,
whence Jolliet had just returned, went to France,
endorsed to the king by the governor, and secured
from his sovereign the seigniory of Frontenac, on
condition that the fort should be reconstructed of
masonry and thereafter be maintained at his charge.
In the summer of 1675, now a member of the Canadian *noblesse*, he returned to New France, two of
his fellow-passengers being men with whom his
name was thenceforth to be indissolubly connected
—François-Xavier de Laval-Montmorency, the first
bishop of Quebec, and Father Louis Hennepin, a
Recollect friar, in cowl and sandals, whose insatiable
desire to achieve adventures had caused his superi-

---

[1] See arguments in Parkman, *La Salle*, 22–27; and documents
in Margry, *Découvertes*, I., 87, 330, 436.

ors to despatch this frocked worldling as a missionary to the wilds of America.[1]

In 1676 we find La Salle developing Fort Frontenac as a trading station, founding a settlement around its stout walls, introducing cattle to the district, building vessels for trading upon the lake, and spending thirty-five thousand livres on his costly although as yet somewhat unprofitable enterprise. The next year he was again in France— one marvels at the frequency with which the great traders of New France crossed the ocean, despite the weary slowness of their storm-buffeted tubs of vessels; also at their tedious and almost annual visits in laboriously propelled canoes from far-distant points in the interior to the commercial centres on the lower St. Lawrence. This time he presented to the court a memorial setting forth the advantage of Fort Frontenac as a base for far-western trade, and the undoubted profits of a traffic in buffalo wool and skins towards the Mississippi Valley. A patent was granted him to build forts in that wonderful land, "through which would seem that a passage to Mexico can be found"; but he must not involve the crown in any expense— French explorers were then expected to pay their way out of a monopoly of the fur-trade in new regions—nor should he trade with tribes already regularly trafficking direct with Montreal.

[1] For life and characterization of Hennepin, see Thwaites, *Hennepin's New Discovery*, Introd.

Even better than a patent was his acquisition of
a lieutenant, in Henri de Tonty, a young Italian
soldier of fortune who had served as an officer in
the French army, but lost his right hand at the
battle of Libisso.   La Salle found in Tonty a nature
as bold and adventurous as his own, and possessing
that tact and kindliness in which he himself was
conspicuously lacking.   La Salle had a cold, hard,
domineering manner, and made few friends; it is,
however, highly creditable to him that among these
were such men as Frontenac and Tonty.[1]   The
seignior and his lieutenant arrived at Quebec in
September, 1678, equipped with anchors, cordage,
sails, and other supplies for a vessel to be built above
Niagara for fur-trading on the upper lakes.   In
the following January they arrived at the falls, of
their company being the Recollect Fathers Hennepin, Ribourde, and Membré—for missionaries to
the Indians must needs accompany most exploring
expeditions in New France, and La Salle would
have no Jesuit in his train.

While a block-house was being erected at the outlet of Niagara River, and their vessel, the *Griffon*—
in allusion to the two griffins on La Salle's coat of
arms—was being constructed at the mouth of
Cayuga Creek, above the cataract, the leader and
a small party returned to Fort Frontenac, mostly
overland through the Iroquois country.   The *Grif-*

[1] Legler, "Henri de Tonty," in Parkman Club *Papers*, I.,
37–57.

fon, a vessel of fifty tons burden and bearing five guns, set sail on August 7, 1679, carrying the reunited party, and twenty days later cast anchor off Point Ignace, on the Straits of Mackinac, where was the Jesuit mission from which Jolliet and Marquette had departed on their voyage six years before.

For nearly a quarter of a century past, since the days of Radisson and Groseilliers, independent French traders (*coureurs de bois*) and black-robed Jesuit missionaries, particularly the former, had roamed quite freely through the region of the upper lakes, and very likely the upper reaches of the Mississippi. Some of these traders were at Mackinac when the *Griffon* arrived; and with them several men whom La Salle had sent up with goods in advance to barter for a cargo of furs. The leader found that his agents had been corrupted by the western itinerants, who looked askance at these wholesale and organized methods of trade, thinking that they spelled ruin to their calling. La Salle arbitrarily arrested the malecontents, who were poisoning the minds of the tribesmen against him and plotting his disaster; he also sent a detail to quiet another group of critics quartered at the neighboring Sault Ste. Marie.

The *Griffon* thence proceeded to Green Bay, where a rich store of peltries awaited her, amassed by those of the seignior's buyers who had remained loyal. The Ottawa, hereabout, being a tribe that

annually carried furs direct to Montreal, dealings
with them were by the terms of his agreement illegal; but he appears to have suffered no qualms of
conscience over the transaction. The *Griffon* was,
however, soon thereafter lost in a gale on Lake
Michigan, so that the question was never raised.

At Green Bay, La Salle and Tonty had left the
vessel, which was to be taken to Mackinac by her
crew, and it was many months later before they
heard of the disaster. The former, with fourteen
men, proceeded in canoes up Lake Michigan along
the west shore, and the latter led a like contingent
by the east, the two parties reuniting at the mouth
of St. Joseph River. Descending to the Illinois by
way of the Kankakee portage, the party were at
Peoria Lake on New Year's Day, 1680, in the midst
of a considerable population of Illincis, to whom
Marquette and Allouez had ministered at this point.
Here the adventurers stopped, and built a palisade
which was named Fort Crèvecœur—apparently in
compliment to Louis XIV. in allusion to his capture (1672) of a Netherlands stronghold of that
name.

La Salle now found it essential to return to Fort
Frontenac for naval supplies, to fit out a vessel
with which he designed exploring the lower Mississippi. Four days before his departure he despatched an expedition to the upper waters of that river.
This was headed by Michel Accau (Ako), who was
accompanied by Antoine Augel (nicknamed "le

Picard") and Father Hennepin—the latter merely
the usual ecclesiastical supernumerary, but as the
chronicler of the voyage quite generally accepted by
historians as its leader.[1] Accau's party, leaving
Crèvecœur on the last day of February, eventually
reached the Falls of St. Anthony (the site of the
modern Minneapolis), about five hundred miles
above the mouth of the Illinois. Taken prisoners
by the Sioux, they were treated as kindly as possible by their captors, but sometimes necessarily
lived on short commons. After extended wander-
ings in northeastern Minnesota and northwestern
Wisconsin, during which they shared with the natives abundant hardships, they were rescued by
Tonty's cousin, Duluth, who, with four followers,
was visiting the Sioux in the interests of Frontenac's fur-trade. Duluth escorted the party down
the Mississippi, and over the Fox-Wisconsin trade-
route to Mackinac, where the Jesuits entertained
them handsomely until spring, when they could
proceed down the lakes to Niagara and Fort Frontenac.

On his return to France, not long after, Hennepin wrote an entertaining account of his remark-
ably varied American experiences, which was published in 1682 under the title of *Description de la
Louisiane*,[2] and had a large sale in several succeed-

---

[1] Up to this point Hennepin is the chief authority relative to
the first western voyage of La Salle.

[2] La Salle had used the term "Louisiane" as early as 1679.

ing editions in French, Italian, Dutch, and German.
But in 1697 he brough forth another work, *Nouvelle Découverte*, in which—La Salle now being dead
—he unblushingly claimed that his party not only
explored the upper Mississippi in 1680, but on their
return south descended the great river to its mouth.
His description of this feat, one quite impossible
in the time at their command, was but a clumsy
plagiarism from the report of his colleague, Membré, upon the voyage to be mentioned below, which
that friar made in La Salle's company in 1682.
This bold assumption was soon discredited, however, and the erratic Hennepin's last years were
spent in obscurity, his own order deeming him a
conceited braggart.   However, Hennepin's work on
America is, aside from this one fault, an invaluable
contribution to the history of New France and to
American ethnology.[1]

When La Salle had departed Tonty, now in
charge, occupied Starved Rock, a steep, high cliff
on the banks of the Illinois, and built thereon Fort
St. Louis.   During the spring and summer most
of his men deserted—for the employment was not
popular, and rival fur-traders were continually trying to seduce La Salle's following; so that when,
in September, the Illinois were attacked by an
Iroquois war-party, Tonty and his four remaining
companions—three men and Membré, Father Ri-

---

[1] See Thwaites, *Hennepin's New Discovery*, Introd., for argument and summary; text for details.

bourde having been killed by Kickapoo—retreated northward out of harm's way. Crossing over to Lake Michigan, they descended along the west shore, at a time when La Salle himself was hastening up the east coast to their relief. Delayed by bad weather and Tonty's illness, it was December before his party reached the Jesuit mission at Green Bay with their story of disaster.

Meanwhile, La Salle had had a severe trip; he discovered that the *Griffon* was lost, that his agents had robbed him at Fort Frontenac, and that his creditors were not only trying to foreclose his estate but were defaming him; while commercial and political enemies were multiplying on every hand. Nevertheless, he obtained fresh credit and supplies at Montreal, and, as related above, unwittingly passed Tonty on the return voyage. Finding nothing but traces of disaster on the Illinois, he retreated to St. Joseph River, where he built Fort Miami. The next spring (1681), having at last heard of the whereabouts of Tonty and Membré, he hurried on to join them at Mackinac, the party thence journeying to their base at Fort Frontenac.

In August, with credit once more extended, but leaving behind him an enormous debt, the undaunted adventurer again started for the west with Tonty and Membré, their party consisting of fifty-four men, of whom twenty-three were French, a contingent later increased to thirty French and a hundred Indians. Dividing into two sections, they reached the Illinois both by the Chicago and St. Joseph-Kankakee routes, and on February 6, 1682, entered the Mississippi River (then called Colbert). March 9, when among the wandering Arkansas, La Salle took formal possession, for his king, of the vast basin of the Mississippi; and April 9 repeated the ceremony, with elaborations, at one of the mouths of the Mississippi. But food was scarce, the country was unhealthy, the Indians were treacherous, and La Salle was for forty days ill with fever; the expedition, therefore, returned to Mackinac. This was the futile voyage which Membré described, and which Hennepin, so far as the discoveries were concerned, appropriated as his own experience.

During this summer Frontenac, La Salle's friend and fur-trade partner, had been replaced as governor by La Barre, who discredited the explorer and did what he could to ruin him. Moreover, the Indian trade of the lakes was, despite all efforts, fast being absorbed by the English. Nevertheless, La Salle and his faithful Tonty descended in the autumn to the Illinois, rebuilt Fort St. Louis on Starved Rock, and carried on a profitable trade in buffalo hides with the six thousand Illinois who had reassembled in the neighborhood. In the autumn of 1683 La Salle started for Quebec to propitiate La Barre, and on the east coast of Lake Michigan met the Chevalier de Baugis, who had been sent out by the governor to relieve La Salle of command in the Illinois. With more tact than customary, La

Salle sent back word to Tonty to yield gracefully,
and soon after this La Barre's traders were swarming into the region.

La Salle himself reached Quebec safely, and,
without waiting to concern himself with the govern-
or, at once sailed for France to lay his case before the
court.   Hennepin's first and reasonably veracious
book was now upon the market, and Canada was
much in the public eye.   The explorer of the far
interior of this land of mystery accordingly made a
good impression and found ready listeners.   La
Barre was ordered by the king to restore Fort Frontenac, Fort Miami, and Fort St. Louis of the Illinois
to La Salle; and the latter was authorized to found
colonies in Louisiana, also to govern the country
between Lake Michigan and the Gulf of Mexico.
He was further assisted in this imperial enterprise
with four ships and nearly four hundred men.

At last heading an expedition worthy of the
cause, La Salle set out from Rochelle (July 24, 1684)
in high spirits.   But the principal vessel was commanded by Captain Beaujeu, and soon there was
bad blood between him and the often haughty and
arrogant leader.   The Spanish captured one of
their ships, and the other three failed to find the
mouth of the Mississippi.   Rendezvousing in Matagorda Bay, in January, 1685, far west of their destination, another vessel was soon grounded and lost.
La Salle landed his pioneers in February, and built
another Fort St. Louis; but disease was rife, the

tools had largely gone down with the wreck, and
the Indians were hostile.   A month later Beaujeu
left the wretched and ill-equipped colony and sailed
to France, and the remaining ship was wrecked
later in the year.

Vain were all efforts to find the mouth of the
Mississippi.   The colony was being wasted in toilsome expeditions up and down the forests and
morasses edging the gulf, desertions frequently occurred, and a spirit of mutiny arose.   Early in
January, 1687, La Salle, his brother Abbé Jean
Cavelier, Father Douay, Joutel, the journalist of
the colony,[1] and a small party—in all, seventeen
weak, ragged, half-starved, and desperate men, including two or three Indians—started out, on horses
obtained from the natives, to reach Canada overland and secure aid and reinforcements by sea from
France.   Twenty were left behind as a garrison.   On
March 19, while upon the bank of Trinity River,
when conditions were at their worst, La Salle was
ambuscaded by some of his disaffected companions,
shot dead, stripped of clothing, and the naked corpse
left to the wolves.   The assassins soon quarrelled
among themselves and disappeared into the woods,
leaving La Salle's friends to go their way.

When Joutel and his handful of comrades arrived at the mouth of the Arkansas, they found there
two of Tonty's followers; for the faithful lieuten-

---

[1] For details, consult Joutel, "Relation," in Margry, *Découvertes*, III.; also the former's *Journal Historique*.

ant had long been searching for his master, at the
head of a party of twenty-five French and eleven
Indians, and had left these men here on special
detail.   Tonty's party had descended the river, explored for thirty leagues on either side of the mouth,
and returned disheartened.   Tonty left in the hands
of a native chief a letter for La Salle, and this was
the missive which fourteen years later was handed
to Iberville, as elsewhere related.[1] Joutel joined
Tonty at Starved Rock, and, being outfitted by him,
proceeded to Mackinac and eventually to Quebec.
Apparently impelled both by a desire to obtain
supplies en route, from friends of La Salle, and the
wish of his relatives among the survivors to be on
hand at the distribution of an estate which would
surely be quarrelled over by creditors, the survivors
concealed the fact of their leader's death, and the
truth was not known until after their arrival in
France, in October, 1688.

As for the score of miserable colonists left by
La Salle at Fort St. Louis, on Matagorda Bay, the
heartless king made no effort for their relief; but
the Spanish, jealous of French encroachments,
launched four expeditions to find them.   In May,
1689, an overland party from Mexico discovered
the battered palisade, and found it desolate, save
for three bodies.   Prowling Indians had attacked
the starving crew, and either killed or imprisoned

[1] See chap. v., below.   Letter dated Village des Quinipissas,
April 20, 1685, in Margry, *Découvertes*, IV., 181, 190, 191.

all. Later, Spanish officials humanely ransomed some of the survivors from their savage captors. Thus closed one of the most tragic chapters in American exploration.

Of all the characterizations of La Salle, who undoubtedly was, with all his shortcomings, one of the greatest pathfinders in history, none is more discriminating than these words of Joutel, coming from a loyal supporter who knew him intimately, in the period wherein great triumph was succeeded by the most abject adversity: "His firmness, his courage, his great knowledge of the arts and sciences, which made him equal to every undertaking, and his untiring energy, which enabled him to surmount every obstacle, would have won at last a glorious success for his grand enterprise, had not all his fine qualities been counterbalanced by a haughtiness of manner which often made him insupportable, and by a harshness towards those under his command, which drew upon him an implacable hatred, and was at last the cause of his death." [1]

[1] *Journal Historique*, 203.

CHAPTER V

LOUISIANA AND THE ILLINOIS

(1697–1731)

WHEN the treaty of Ryswick (1697), closing the Palatinate War — known in America as King William's or Frontenac's—brought to Europe a temporary cessation from armed strife, Louis XIV. was prevailed upon to make an official undertaking of what had originally been so largely supported by the slender purse of La Salle. The reports of that ill-fated explorer had fired the imagination of Frenchmen in both hemispheres, and the time now seemed ripe for another attempt to execute his ambitious project of a French establishment at the mouth of the Mississippi, to be connected with the St. Lawrence colonies of New France by a continuous line of forts along the two great interlocking continental drainage troughs.

Among the men whose ambitions had been stirred by the deeds of La Salle were two hardy and chivalrous sons of Charles le Moyne, of Quebec, colonial interpreter and captain of militia — Pierre, known to history as Iberville, and his younger brother Jean Baptiste, whom from his seigniory we

call Bienville. Iberville, a born buccaneer, whose
daring naval expeditions against the English on
Hudson Bay had made him a marked figure among
the adventurers of New France,[1] was selected to
lead the enterprise. He departed from Brest in
the last week of October, 1698, when in his thirty-
eighth year, with two frigates escorting two transports laden with a well-selected company of two
hundred soldiers and colonists, among the party
being Bienville, then a midshipman but eighteen
years of age, the young Sieur de Sauvole,[2] and
Father Anastase Douay, a Recollect friar, who, as a
survivor of La Salle's last expedition (1684), possessed much valuable local knowledge. The leader
was equipped with instructions ostensibly ordering
him to explore the Amazon, the intention being to
deceive the English in case they proved of a jealously inquisitive turn of mind, for they themselves were
covetous in the direction of the Mississippi delta.[3]

Iberville touched at Santo Domingo for rest and
supplies, but was refused permission to land by the
Spanish garrison at Pensacola, notwithstanding his
pretence that he was but going to arrest vagrant
coureurs de bois, supposed to be harbored along the
gulf. Pocketing the rebuff, the adventurers erected
huts on Ship Island, eighteen miles southeast of

[1] See above, chap. iv.
[2] Fortier, *Louisiana*, I., 33, thinks him a brother of Iberville
and Bienville; discredited by Hamilton, *Colonial Mobile*, 32.
[3] Margry, *Découvertes*, IV., 58–62.

the present Mississippi City; and in February (1699)
built Fort Maurepas on the Back Bay of Biloxi [1]
—a beautiful situation, backed by a forest of pines,
walnuts, chestnuts, and live-oaks, but with unsanitary conditions, unfit water, a sterile soil, and far
removed from a waterway by which the interior
might readily be penetrated.

Heading a party in row-boats and canoes, composed of Bienville, Sauvole, Douay, and forty-eight
men-at-arms, Iberville sailed in search of the Mississippi, rediscovered the river on March 2, "the water
all muddy and very white," and proceeded two
hundred miles up-stream, to the mouth of the Red.
Returning, Bienville descended by the way they
had come, while Iberville led half of the party
through the Bayou Iberville and lakes Maurepas
and Pontchartrain into Bay St. Louis, on the way
securing from the natives a letter which the Chevalier de Tonty, La Salle's lieutenant, had written
fourteen years before, when turning north from his
fruitless search for his chief's reputed colony at the
mouth of the great river. [2] Tonty had left word
that this document was to be handed to the first
Frenchman to appear in the region; and it was
welcomed by Iberville as indisputable evidence that
he had reached the country to which La Salle had
drawn the attention of France.

---

[1] Hamilton, *Colonial Mobile*, 31; Penicaut's "Journal," in
Margry, *Découvertes*, V., is the chief authority for the daily life
of the colony for several years.   [2] See above, chap. iv.

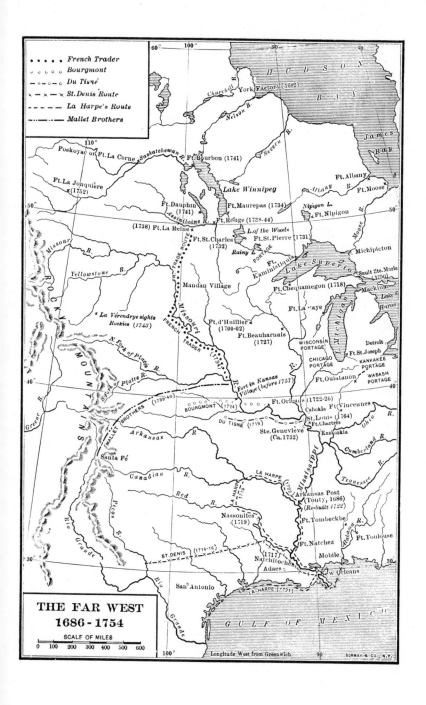

THE FAR WEST
1686-1754

Sauvole and Bienville had been favorably impressed with the present site of New Orleans—a relatively dry plain in the midst of the vast morasses of the delta—and reported it as a fit seat for the colony. But Iberville feared that an inland town would be subject to Indian raids, and remained at Biloxi Bay within sight of the gulf. In this extremely undesirable situation, the little colony of ninety persons, although nestled safely within the shadow of the substantially built palisade and bastions of Fort Maurepas, suffered severely from shortage of food, decimating fevers, and lack of Indian trade. Desertions, also, were not uncommon; for, bereft of soil suitable for agriculture, and lacking other occupation, the men wandered far into the interior upon independent quests for mines and for trade with the natives.

Tonty, who since La Salle's death had valiantly remained at Fort St. Louis of the Illinois, conducting a spasmodic trade in buffalo hides and vainly petitioning the court for aid in exploring Louisiana, was soon in correspondence with the gulf colony. We read of one of his men, Launay, who had several times journeyed down the Mississippi, being at Biloxi in 1699, drawing for Iberville a map of the river; and Tonty receiving a message from the latter, conveyed by returning missionaries.[1] It seems likely that some of the deserters may themselves have ventured to the Illinois, where Kas-

[1] Margry, *Découvertes*, IV., 453, 459.

kaskia and other prosperous colonies were now being established.

Early in May (1699) Iberville returned to France with the ships, leaving Sauvole in command at Biloxi, with Bienville as lieutenant. Thereafter the founder spent a large share of his time in France or upon cruises against Spanish treasure-ships, with but occasional visits to the colony. Early in 1702, just previous to his final departure—for death overtook him at Havana four years later—he directed its removal to Twenty-seven Mile Bluff, on Mobile River, where Fort Louis of Louisiana (named for the king, not the saint) was erected. This was a more favorable position, Iberville thought; for by the Tombigbee and Alabama rivers the Indians of a large district could be reached, and from here it was possible with their help to attack, if need be, the rear of the English colonies of Carolina and Virginia and intercept their forest trade.[1]   In 1710, under Bienville, another change of base was affected, because of floods — this time to higher ground, on the site of the modern Mobile.[2]

During the summer of 1700 Iberville ascended the Mississippi as far as the Natchez neighborhood, in company with a mining adventurer, Pierre Charles le Sueur, who at least seven years previous had been upon the upper reaches of the river, also upon the Minnesota, searching for copper, lead, and

[1] Margry, *Découvertes*, V., 587, 595-597.
[2] Hamilton, *Colonial Mobile*, 42-70.

colored earths. He had served as a commandant on Lake Superior as early as 1693, and two years later constructed a fort on Lake Pepin; but receiving no encouragement from Canadian officials to work his mines, he returned to France, where he met Iberville, and joined him at Biloxi. Accompanied by twenty experienced miners from France, Le Sueur renewed his northern quest, with the accustomed unsatisfactory result. Extensive explorations for mines were also made at this time by various prospecting parties in Louisiana, Mississippi, Alabama, Arkansas, and Tennessee.[1]

However, one important discovery was made by Le Sueur: an English trader at the mouth of the Arkansas—for even in this closing year of the seventeenth century English rivalry had commenced upon the lower Mississippi. The men of the middle colonies and Virginia were still impeded by the rugged barrier of the Alleghany range from other than feeble efforts towards reaching west-flowing waters; and the fierce tribes of the north were jealous of white men's intrusion on their domain—although Iroquois opposition to the French caused the New York tribesmen to permit English and Dutch fur-traders occasionally to pass the dividing ridge and barter for peltries with savage bands who would otherwise have sought the markets of New France.

[1] Penicaut's "Relation," in Margry, *Découvertes*, V., 416–420; Shea, *Early Mississippi Voyages*, 89–111; *Wis. Hist. Collections*, XVI., 173–200.

The southern end of the range breaks down into modest hills, which were easily traversed by the Carolina traders, who with pack - horses wended their way over a comparatively level trail leading westward through the country of the village-dwelling Cherokee, and even occasionally penetrated to the Red River tribes beyond the Mississippi. But the Indian population through this table-land was relatively sparse and the tribes of the Arkansas were far distant; then, again, horse - trail traders could carry but light loads, were more subject to attack than those who swept along the northern rivers in heavily laden and well-guarded canoes and bateaux; and in their cupidity the Cherokee were wont to rob and not seldom murder the English and Scotch-Irish forest merchants. Thus the French in Louisiana long enjoyed immunity from serious commercial competition from Carolina; nevertheless, Le Sueur's discovery was ominous, and in his report to the court that autumn (September 7, 1700)[1] Iberville alludes to the growing danger of English rivalry.

To add to their uneasiness, the Spanish governor at Pensacola had but recently visited Biloxi and filed with them a protest against this wedge of French settlement, now numbering some seven hundred persons, between the Spanish of Mexico and Florida. A few years later, during Crozat's régime, Spanish vessels freely preyed upon French

[1] Margry, *Découvertes*, IV., 370–378.

commerce passing through the Gulf of Mexico.
Taking advantage of the outbreak of war in Europe
between the Quadruple Alliance and Spain, Bienville, early in 1719, captured Pensacola; the Spanish
retook the fort, but Bienville won it a second time
in September; it was then restored to Spain by the
treaty of a few months later.

Another incident also gave the Biloxi colonists
pause. Bienville was descending the Mississippi
from one of his numerous exploring expeditions in
small boats, when (September 15, 1699), at a bend
in the river eighteen miles below the present New
Orleans, called English Turn, he met an English
frigate of sixteen guns. Its captain had been sent
out by Daniel Coxe, proprietor of Carolana and "all
the lands lying westward to the sea," to found a
settlement that should command the approach to
the interior of the continent. But he had left his
colonists at Charleston, and with a slender crew
was somewhat perfunctorily examining the lower
reaches of the Mississippi — a voyage afterwards
instanced by Great Britain as supporting her claim
to this region. The youthful commander of the
little fleet of small boats is said to have deceived the
formidable intruder with representations that the
French were already planted in force not far up-
stream, whereupon the Englishman politely withdrew.[1]

---

[1] Letter of Sauvole, in Margry, *Découvertes*, IV., 455, 456;
see also La Harpe, in *Journal Historique*, 19, 20. But the evidence as to the deception is inconclusive.

Iberville and Sauvole soon passing away, Bienville remained until 1743 the principal historical
figure in Louisiana. Others occasionally occupied
the post of governor; but Bienville, as devoted and
disinterested as Champlain, was throughout this
protracted period the chief actor, and powerfully
and beneficently influenced the colony. During his
long supremacy the wide-stretching region of Louisiana was the scene of many fruitful events.

Not unnaturally, Iberville's venture occasioned
great alarm among the fur merchants of Canada.
Just as their operations upon the upper Mississippi
were becoming important, this new danger arose, of
a probable diversion down that river of trade that
had heretofore sought an opening by way of the
St. Lawrence. Their concern was not lessened when
in 1701 Governor Callières received notice from the
court that the new province of Louisiana would be
governed direct from France, not from Quebec, Iberville being named as the king's representative in the
south.[1]

In 1712, Sieur Antoine Crozat was granted for
twelve years a monopoly of trade, mining, land
grants, and slavery in Louisiana, to which "the
laws, edicts, and ordinances of the realm, and the
custom of Paris" were extended; although the
grantee was given certain powers of nomination
that placed in his hands not a little political control. In this charter, which gave to Louisiana its

[1] Margry, *Découvertes*, V., 591, 606.

first civil government, the bounds of the province were officially mentioned; the imperfect state of geographical knowledge rendered it, however, impracticable to set definite limits.　In general terms, Louisiana was to extend from New Mexico to "the lands of the English of Carolana," to embrace the rivers Mississippi, Missouri, Ohio, and Wabash, and to run "from the edge of the sea as far as the Illinois"—while beyond the Illinois (which district probably extended to the mouth of the Wisconsin) the country was to be retained under the government of New France.　It is not certain from the phrasing of the grant that it was sought actually to include the Illinois in Louisiana; but as the patentee certainly exercised control over the northern district, no doubt it was understood at court to be a part of his domain.[1]　Crozat opened lead mines as far north as Missouri, but his great venture failed.　He resigned his monopoly to John Law's Company of the West (chartered 1717), which had contracted to settle six thousand whites and half that number of negro slaves within twenty-five years.

New Orleans, founded by Bienville in February, 1718, thenceforth was not only the seat of government but the metropolis of the far-spreading province.　Three years later Louisiana was divided into nine military districts, called Mobile, Biloxi, Alabama, New Orleans, Yazoo, Natchez, Arkansas,

[1] Text of grant in French, *La. Hist. Collections*, III., 38-42.

Illinois, and Natchitoches,[1] the last-named a buffer against the hostile attitude of the Spanish towards French encroachments to the southwest.

Prominent among the purposes of the founders of Louisiana was the development of an overland commerce with the Spanish colonies to the southwest. Texas was at this time claimed by the Spanish, and their trading caravans had visited the Indians of the district; but, thus far, there had been no attempt at settlement. The French also claimed the territory by virtue of La Salle's colony, which had been thwarted by Spanish machinations. In 1714, Bienville despatched an expedition under Louis Juchereau, the Sieur de St. Denis, who reached a Spanish mission on the Gila River. There he formed such pleasant relations with his hosts that he proceeded to the city of Mexico, and returned in 1716 with a favorable report to his superior. A second expedition under his charge, with which were associated six adventurous Canadians, followed the same route; the Canadians returned to Mobile after a profitable trade, but St. Denis was imprisoned by the Spanish, and two years elapsed before his release.[2] Meanwhile (1717), the French erected a fort at Natchitoches, near Red River, only seven leagues from a Spanish outpost in Texas.[3] This vantage was maintained throughout the

---

[1] French, *La. Hist. Collections*, III., 84.

[2] Margry, *Découvertes*, VI., 193–199; *Journal Historique*, 116, 129, 130.   [3] *Journal Historique*, 131; Margry, VI., 252–255.

French régime; but another, some eighty miles above, among the Caddo Indians, established (1719) by Bernard de la Harpe, was of a less permanent character.[1] La Harpe, a wide traveller, was engaged in several trading and exploring expeditions on the upper waters of the Red and Arkansas, and in 1722 built a post on the latter stream,[2] on a site which Tonty had garrisoned in 1686.

The Missouri River, also, was not neglected. Canadians were reported upon that waterway as early as 1704; while in the few succeeding years the traders Laurain, De Bourgmont, and Du Tisné undertook considerable journeys among the Pawnee, Osage, and Arapaho tribes. These overtures to their old-time customers were resented by the Spanish, who in 1720 undertook a retributive expedition among the Missouri allies of their neighbors, a movement which greatly alarmed the French of the Illinois. Two years later, De Bourgmont erected Fort Orleans on the Missouri—probably on the north bank, in the present Carroll County, Missouri—and there maintained himself with a strong garrison for four years; withdrawing gradually, the remnant of his force fell (1725 or 1726) victims to an Indian massacre.[3]

After the disaster at Fort Orleans, subsequent

[1] *Journal Historique*, 178–219; Margry, VI., 243–306.
[2] *Journal Historique*, 282–285; Margry, VI., 357–382.
[3] Du Pratz, *Louisiana*, 297; Villiers du Terrage, *Dernières Années de la Louisiana*, 17.

expeditions set forth from the Illinois rather than
from Louisiana.   Reports are extant concerning enterprises of this character in 1734 and 1739—the
caravan in the latter year being apparently headed
by two brothers, Pierre and Paul Mallet, who seem
successfully to have reached Santa Fé, the seat of
Spanish trade in those parts.   They returned by
way of New Orleans, where Bienville was delighted
at the result of so far - reaching an exploration.
Among the experiences of these adventurers, near
the head-waters of the Arkansas, was what was possibly the first sight by Frenchmen of the Rocky
Mountains, nearly four years before the celebrated
discovery by Chevalier Vérendrye of the Bighorn
Range, far to the north.[1]

French Jesuits had operated in the Illinois country as early as Marquette, but their ministrations
were in Indian villages along the Illinois River.   In
1699 the Sulpicians opened a mission at Cahokia,
on the Mississippi, and the year following the Jesuits removed their establishment to the neighboring
Kaskaskia.[2]   Fort Chartres (1720)—a stout fortress,
designed to check growing English encroachments
on the Ohio and the Mississippi—St. Philippe (1723),
and Prairie du Rocher (1733) followed in due course.[3]

---

[1] This record of French exploration in the southwest is based
chiefly on documents in Margry, *Découvertes*, VI.

[2] Thwaites, *Jesuit Relations*, LXV., 101–105, 263.

[3] So Moses, *Illinois;* Wallace, *Illinois and Louisiana under
French Rule;* Mason, *Chapters from Illinois History*.   But the
chronology is still in some confusion.

By the time of the founding of New Orleans, the little group of Illinois settlements had from their productive soil, facilities of transportation, and location at the centre of profitable Indian trade, already grown into a neighborhood of great importance in the agricultural and commercial development of New France. In 1719, Louisiana and the Illinois entered upon the brief period of "boom" which was inaugurated by Law's somewhat fantastic speculative scheme. Cahokia and Kaskaskia greatly increased in size and importance, eight hundred new settlers being imported, chiefly from Canada and New Orleans, and placed on large land grants; several stone-mills and storehouses were constructed, the *habitants* were encouraged to grow tobacco, and negro slaves were introduced.

Throughout the first half of the eighteenth century the Illinois became noted for agricultural products, which were shipped in large quantities to Detroit on the north, Ohio River ports on the east, and southward to New Orleans and Mobile, whence they found their way to the West Indies and Europe. At Kaskaskia the Jesuits maintained an academy; at Cahokia, the Sulpicians had a considerable school for Indian youth; and Fort Chartres was known as "the centre of life and fashion in the West." It is recorded that "about the year 1746 there was a scarcity of provisions at New Orleans," and the Illinois French "sent thither, in one winter, upward of eight hundred thousand weight of flour." In exchange for their products, the thrifty Illinois *habitants* received many luxuries and refinements directly from Europe and other French colonies— sugar, rice, indigo, cotton, manufactured tobacco, and goods of like character — and these interior settlements were long regarded as the garden of New France.[1]

At first the Illinois settlements were governed from Canada, although their trade relations were naturally more intimate with Louisiana than with the lower St. Lawrence. Indeed, despite the protests of the Quebec officials, who were alarmed over this diversion of the Mississippi trade, there was now but slight connection with Canada. The old portage routes connecting the divergent drainage systems of the St. Lawrence and the Mississippi had fallen into comparative disuse. Several causes contributed to this result: the reduction of trading-posts on the Great Lakes, under the economical policy of Governor Callières's administration; the continued hostility of the Fox Indians in Wisconsin;[2] the physical hardships of these routes; but in large measure the careful fostering of the more convenient southern trade and the growing bulk of exports. The people of the Illinois henceforth looked upon

---

[1] Contemporary descriptions in *N. Y. Docs. Rel. to Col. Hist.*, IX., 891; Du Pratz, *Louisiana*, 301 – 303; Pittman, *Present State of European Settlements on the Mississippi* (1770), 42, 43, 55; Charlevoix, in *Journal Historique* (1744), 394– 396.

[2] See documents in *Wis. Hist. Collections*, XVI., XVII.

the Mississippi as their natural highway to the markets of the world.

Law's financial project collapsed in 1720, but its
Louisiana branch had become merged in the Company of the Indies, which continued to operate
here for several years upon a dwindling career.
The enormous expense of a long but successful
war with the Natchez Indians was in the end the
determining factor, and at its close the corporation gladly surrendered its charter (January 23,
1731), Louisiana becoming once more a royal province.[1]

In the mean while both Louisiana and the Illinois
had materially prospered, chiefly as the result of
improved navigation facilities, and stimulation of
business and manufacturing enterprise, increased
immigration, and the efforts made to broaden not
only the area of tillage but the variety of crops.
From Louisiana rice, indigo, and tobacco were exported; fig-trees from Provence and orange-trees
from Santo Domingo had become acclimated; there
was also a small acreage of cotton; the population
along the lower Mississippi had increased from some
six hundred whites and a score of negroes to five
thousand whites and two thousand blacks. As a
province, Louisiana, in the leisurely fashion of the
subtropics, had continued to thrive. But in Illinois
the easy-going *habitants*—farmers, hunters, traders
by turn, with a strong admixture of unprogressive

[1] Margry, *Découvertes*, V., 590.

Indian blood — soon forgot the feverish and unwonted energy of artificial stimulus.   The villages
of the mid-country resumed their natural status of
sleepy little fur-trade and mission stations, and thus
remained until the downfall of New France.

CHAPTER VI

RIVALRY WITH ENGLAND

(1715-1745)

THE War of the Spanish Succession, in America called Queen Anne's War (1702-1713), had greatly impoverished France. Louis XIV. died in 1715, overwhelmed with disappointment, for the wide-spreading empire which he had reared was now shorn on every hand, and numerous domestic calamities faced the throne. Immediately following his death the country came under the practical control of the benign Cardinal Fleury, preceptor to the young king, and in 1726 he was made actual minister. Early in his career commercial restrictions were largely removed, to the immediate benefit of French commerce. We have already seen[1] that earnest, although economically unsound, measures had been taken for the development of Louisiana; Guadeloupe, Martinique, and the French half of Hayti also felt new life. In Canada, ice-bound half the year and with a roving population that lived largely on the fur-trade, feudalism seemed an ill-nurtured exotic;[2] but Louisiana and these West

[1] See chap. v., above.   [2] See chap. viii., below.

Indian possessions were, with their subtropical climate, particularly adapted to the profitable use of
slave labor and to the paternal form of government which France employed alike at home and in
the colonies. Coffee and sugar from the French
colonies began to drive from the European markets
the productions of the rival English islands of
Jamaica, Barbadoes, and their smaller neighbors;
England was also, for a time, losing ground along
the Mediterranean, in the Levant, and in far-off
India. French merchant shipping grew from three
hundred vessels, at the time of Louis's death, to
eighteen hundred in 1735.[1]

While Fleuri was dominating France, the English
prime - minister was Sir Robert Walpole. Both
statesmen strongly desired peace in western Europe,
and in the face of many difficulties long maintained
it. But there were irresistible forces at work, largely
originating in differences of temperament between
the two peoples, which tended to neutralize their
efforts at a good understanding. France and England were engaged in a long-standing rivalry for the
possession of lands over-seas, which might be col-
onized and thereby made to assist in the development of national commerce. Naval strength is the
predominant factor in colonizing and the pushing
of colonial trade. The mistress of the seas con-
trols the ocean lanes, can keep open against all
comers the necessary lines of communication be-

[1] Mahan, *Influence of Sea Power*, 243.

tween the colonies and the mother-land, and in
need can defend colonial coasts.[1]

England, more clearly than France, recognized
this principle, and in a measure acted upon it.
Her perception had not at the time of our narrative
attained to a thorough understanding; her efforts
were lacking in continuity and cohesion, and much
stupidity was sometimes displayed by her naval and
military boards; but, impelled in great measure by
the necessities of her insular position, she did much
better than France, whose statesmen were so steeped
in the back-door turmoil of continental dynastic
bickerings that they often quite lost sight of their
colonies and the sea.   The result was that soon her
neglected navy had shrunk to half the strength
of that of Great Britain, ill-manned and ill-equipped
as the latter generally was; and complications arose
for which France was unprepared and the reasons
for which were not always at once comprehended
by her leaders.

English trade rivalry among the tribes of both
the Ohio and the upper Great Lakes early became a
serious matter with the officials and merchants of
New France, and we find frequent references to it in
the French documents of the period.[2]   Not only did
wandering French and English traders visit and tam-

---

[1] On England's policy at this period, cf. Greene, *Provincial
America* (*Am. Nation*, VI.), chaps. vii., xvi.
[2] *N. Y. Docs. Rel. to Col. Hist.*, Index; also *Wis. Hist. Collections*, XVI., XVII.

per with each other's Indians; but, as pointed out in a
previous chapter,[1] there was much smuggling across
the lines—French merchants obtaining low-priced
goods from New York and Albany; Englishmen
purchasing peltries from French dealers, and even
directly from *coureurs de bois* who operated in the
region of Mackinac and Sault Ste. Marie and surreptitiously sought the English market. In 1724
it was affirmed by a careful observer[2] that, contrary to law, Albany merchants, instead of exclusively patronizing tribes allied to the English,
were obtaining four-fifths of their skins "from the
French of Mont Royall and Canada"; and several
English traders were prosecuted and punished for
this serious offence.

The issue relative to the proprietorship of the
trans-Alleghany region was soon raised by English
colonial officials. In 1686 Denonville reported to
Versailles that letters written to him by Governor
Dongan of New York "will notify you sufficiently
of his pretensions which extend no less than from
the lakes, inclusive, to the South Sea. Missilimak-
inac is theirs. They have taken its latitude; have
been to trade there with our Outawas and Huron
Indians, who received them cordially on account of
the bargains they gave." Denonville pleads for
definite information from the court, relative to the

---

[1] See chap. iv., above.
[2] Colden, "Memoir on the Fur Trade," in *N. Y. Docs. Rel. to
Col. Hist.*, V., 726–733.

French claims, based on "a great many discoveries that have been made in this country, with which our registers ought to be loaded." [1]   As usual, however, nothing was then done to check the fast-opening bud of English aspirations. Versailles waited until it had grown into a stout tree.

By the close of the first quarter of the eighteenth century Englishmen were conducting a profitable but adventurous fur-trade upon the upper lakes and upon the Wabash and elsewhere throughout the Ohio basin, even as far south as the Creek towns on the sources of the Tennessee. Virginia and Pennsylvania were also beginning to exhibit interest in their own overlapping transmontane claims. It had always been asserted that the charters of the coast colonies carried their bounds far into the hinterland; but in an earlier period the contention seemed idle, for the west was not then needed. Now that their citizens were creeping over the Alleghanies and meeting opposition on western waters, it seemed worth while formally to deny French ownership of the West. The king was, in 1721, requested by the Lords of Trade, on the recommendation of Governor Keith of Pennsylvania, to "fortify the passes on the back of Virginia"; also to build forts upon the Great Lakes, in order to "interrupt the French communication from Quebec to the River Mississippi." [2]   But England herself

[1] *N. Y. Docs. Rel. to Col. Hist.*, IX., 297.
[2] *Ibid.*, V., 624, 625.

was as yet in no hurry; she could afford to play a
waiting game.   Outside of the official class, the West
was to tide-water provincials but a misty region;
hence, for a generation longer, the rival forest traders
were allowed to fight it out among themselves.

In 1729, however, an official step towards strengthening the French position was taken by the chief
engineer of New France, Chaussegros de Léry, at
the head of a small military reconnaissance which,
during a lull in Iroquois opposition, proceeded to the
Ohio over the Chautauqua portage, and surveyed
the river down to the mouth of the Great Miami.
Up to this time the French, familiar with the
country eastward, had not penetrated much farther
to the northwest than the shores of lakes Superior
and Nepigon.   In common with the English, however, they were showing a renewed interest in seeking the supposititious waterway through the American continent that should more closely unite Europe with China and India.[1]   Between 1719 and
1747 the Hudson's Bay Company, reluctantly
spurred by popular demand, made several half-
hearted attempts to discover the Northwest Passage,
which many thought to emerge from the western
shore of Hudson Bay.

During the same period the explorers of New
France busied themselves with similar projects.
In 1720 the Jesuit traveller and historian, Father
Charlevoix, was despatched from France on a tour

[1] See chap. iv., above.

of observation with this end in view.   After visiting the Mississippi Valley and talking with traders and Indians, he did not think a continuous
waterway practicable, but recommended to the
court two trade-routes across the continent.   One
of these was to result from an exploration of the
Missouri to its source, thence reaching the Pacific
by means of some west-flowing river [1]—the identical
plan which Thomas Jefferson proposed to George
Rogers Clark in 1783, and which President Jefferson successfully inaugurated twenty years later
through the agency of Meriwether Lewis and Clark's
younger brother William.[2]   The other plan was to
establish a line of posts among the Sioux of the
plains, and thus creep into and across the interior.
This latter project was adopted; but nothing further
resulted than the erection (1727) of a post on Lake
Pepin, on the upper Mississippi, which was soon
abandoned owing to a fresh outbreak of the hostile
Foxes, who held the Fox-Wisconsin waterway.[3]

About the time of the abandonment of this
scheme, the commander at Lake Nepigon was
Pierre Gaultier de Varenne, Sieur de la Vérendrye.
His imagination fired by the optimistic reports of

[1] Charlevoix, *Journal Historique*, 300, 301, translated in
Wis. Hist. Collections, XVI., 417, 418; Margry, *Découvertes*,
VI., 531–535.

[2] Documentary material in Thwaites, *Original Journals of the
Lewis and Clark Expedition*, vii., 193.   See Channing, *Jeffersonian System* (*Am. Nation*, XII.).

[3] Margry, *Découvertes*, VI., 542 – 566; *Wis. Hist. Collections*,
XVII.

Indians, whose notions of geography were often
quite vague, he conceived a plan for seeking the
Pacific by means of the vast net-work of lakes and
rivers that stretches westward from Lake Superior
by way of Pigeon River, Lake of the Woods, Rainy
Lake and River, Lake Winnipeg, the Assiniboin,
and the Saskatchewan.   His report that the ocean
might thus be reached within five hundred leagues
from Lake Superior[1] won powerful official support;
he was accordingly granted a monopoly of the fur-
trade north and west of Lake Superior, upon the
supposed profits of which he was to undertake extensive exploring expeditions.

Vérendrye suffered from the customary fickleness
of court patronage, and through the machinations
of rivals soon found himself neglected and a bank-
rupt.   Nevertheless, with marvellous energy and
perseverance, he had by the year 1738 established
what was officially styled the "Post of the Western
Sea," a line of six "forts built of stockades . . . that
can give protection only against the Indians . . . and
trusted generally to the care of one or two officers,
seven or eight soldiers, and eighty *engagés*.   From
them the English movements can be watched "
and "the discovery of the Western Sea may be accomplished."   These outposts were St. Pierre on
Rainy Lake, St. Charles on Lake of the Woods,
Maurepas at the mouth of the Winnipeg, Bourbon

[1] Text in Sulte, *Histoire des Canadiens-Français*, VI., 145–
150.

on the east shore of Lake Winnipeg, La Reine on the Assiniboin, and Dauphin on Lake Manitoba; to them Vérendrye's successor, St. Pierre, added La Jonquière on the upper Saskatchewan, near the site of the modern Calgary. It was from La Reine that Vérendrye's son Pierre, known as the chevalier, made a famous expedition which resulted, on New Year's Day, 1743, in sighting the Bighorn Range, a hundred and twenty miles east of Yellowstone Park, long accounted the first view of the Rockies by white men.[1]

These explorations in the northwest, accompanied as they were by incidents which would make a thrilling volume of wilderness adventure, furnished a stirring object-lesson for the young men of France. They served a still stouter purpose in preserving the life of the colony. During much of the time from 1682 until the British conquest, and especially after 1712, the most important trade-route to the Mississippi, the Fox-Wisconsin waterway, was closed to the French, owing to the "bad heart" of the Fox Indians and their allies. At times the Foxes entered into compacts which, combined with the Iroquois barrier on the upper Ohio, practically closed the Mississippi from the north and east. Numerous and costly military expeditions against

[1] Parkman, "Discovery of Rocky Mountains," in *Atlantic Monthly*, LXI., 783–793. Margry's account, in *Statutes, Documents, and Papers . . . respecting . . . Boundaries of the Province of Ontario,* 68–80.

this formidable enemy were of small avail. The
fur-trade of the West, so essential to the life of New
France, was nearly paralyzed; the people of the
Illinois, on the farther side of the barrier, had become almost exclusively patrons of the southern
trade; profitable fur-bearing animals had retreated
from the hunters farther and farther inland; and
now little was left to the forest merchants of Quebec
and Montreal save the peltries snatched from the
barren lands of the far northwest.[1]

For a generation the " Post of the Western Sea "
caused grave concern among the "smug ancient
gentlemen" of the Hudson's Bay Company. The
southern half of the enormous territory which
Charles had so freely granted to them was dominated
by the adventurous French, who not only alienated
the confidence of the tribesmen, but won the native
trade. Rivalry such as this was farther - reaching than when the Canadians held the shore forts
upon the bay and attempted to operate them from
the sea, for the latter were now in their element as
wilderness rangers. Moreover, the men of France
now had at their back a chain of forts quite stout
enough for immediate needs, stretching across the
continental interior like a gigantic letter T, its
horizontal bar a transcontinental system extending
from the Gulf of St. Lawrence to the head-waters
of the Saskatchewan, and its stem commanding

[1] Documents in *Wis. Hist. Collections*, XVI., XVII., throw
new light on the Fox war.

the entire length of the Mississippi River and its approaches. The outlook for the English was not encouraging.

Spain's large colonial interests in Florida, Mexico, South America, Cuba, Porto Rico, and the eastern half of Hayti caused her to maintain a large navy. But her colonial policy was excessively narrow and arrogant; her colonists, forbidden to trade with others than herself, covertly encouraged English smuggling, which developed into acts of the most daring and often insolent character. Urged by her merchants, who saw their West Indian trade endangered by freebooting British rivals, Spain now adopted an overbearing and insulting attitude towards English ships, which often were stopped and searched on the high seas, with occasional maltreatment of officers and crews. This, and Spain's intrigues to regain Gibraltar, led to violent popular clamor in Great Britain, which, skilfully manipulated by the parliamentary opposition, of which William Pitt was one of the leaders, Walpole found himself unable to ignore, and against his counsel war was declared on October 19, 1739.[1]

Fleury's sincere desire for peace with England wrought good results to both nations, so long as Walpole could keep him apart from Spain. It developed, however, that six years previous there had been signed a secret family compact, by which

[1] *Gentleman's Magazine* (1739), 551; *S. C. Hist. Collections*, IV., 20.

the two Bourbon courts agreed to support each
other in case of the outbreak of war.   Under this
arrangement it now became necessary for France,
reluctant though she was, with all her forces to
assist Spain by land and sea.   While the former
was, therefore, not nominally a party to the struggle,
she became so to all intents and purposes.   Thus
the peaceful dreams of Walpole and Fleuri were
interrupted by a current of events which they had
vainly sought to stem.

Two years later the English peace minister was
driven from power by men who, like Pitt—his star
rising while Walpole's waned—felt that there should
be no further hesitation to compass that defeat of
the Bourbons which was essential to Great Britain's
growth as an imperial power; and who were beginning to perceive that such growth must largely
be based upon control of the sea.   A British ulti-
matum called on Spain to renounce the right of
searching vessels, and expressly to acknowledge the
English claims in North America — among these
latter being one relating to the undetermined southern boundary of the colony of Georgia, which had
been but recently established (1732) to the north of
Florida.[1]

Spain promptly despatched to the West Indies,
which both sides had selected as the logical battle-
ground, a considerable fleet convoyed by a French
squadron of twenty-two ships, for the presence of

[1] *S. C. Hist. Collections*, I., 203; Stevens, *Georgia*, I., 140-160.

which Fleuri made weak excuses. England's grim
reply was a general pillaging of the French merchant
marine upon the Atlantic, without, however, formally
declaring war against the Versailles government.
She had stolen a march on the enemy, by sending
to the scene of action a fleet under Admiral Edward
Vernon, in the last week of July, three months before
the declaration of war; its instructions being "to
destroy the Spanish settlements in the West Indies
and to distress their shipping by every method
whatever."

It had been the hope of Vernon, with his squadron of six ships, to find rich prizes in the Spanish-
American ports. But when (November 21) he
easily captured and destroyed Porto Bello, the
booty amounted to the trivial value of $10,000;
for the Spanish, also scenting trouble, had before
Vernon's arrival hurried off their treasure.

The reinforcements in ships and men, which
Vernon had asked for, were cheerfully sent. The
English colonies north of Carolina had been called
upon to assist, and owing to the current enthusiasm
they did so with surprising alacrity. The conjunction was effected at Port Royal, in Jamaica,
early in January, 1741. Thereafter the expedition—without doubt the largest armed force thus
far seen in the Gulf of Mexico, and much in excess
of the need—was unfortunately to have two leaders; Vernon remained as admiral of the fleet, now
numbering thirty fighting vessels, but Brigadier-

General Thomas Wentworth commanded the troops,
nine thousand in number.

The new-comers had suffered greatly on the voyage, from bad weather and sickness, and throughout the campaign there was a heavy mortality from
the wretched sanitary conditions.   March 3 the
forces again landed before Cartagena; but after a
long and weak siege, during which the troops suffered greatly from mismanagement and the leaders continually wrangled, the demoralized army
was (April 17) withdrawn in the fleet to England.
The grewsome horrors of the expedition, and the
unfortunate quarrel of the commanders, have been
preserved for us in literature by Smollett,[1] a supporter of Wentworth, and then a surgeon on one
of the ships of the line.   Later (1746), Vernon was
dismissed the service, his choleric temper having
led him into an open quarrel with the admiralty
board.

It had been the intention of the government to
aid Vernon with a co-operating expedition.   For
this purpose Commodore George Anson was ordered
from the west coast of Africa, where for three years
he had been protecting English trade against French
assaults, to round Cape Horn and join Vernon on
the Pacific side of the Panama isthmus.   Anson's
little squadron of six ships, with the usual poor

---

[1] *Roderick Random*, chaps. xxviii.–xxxiii.   For technical account of Vernon's expedition, see Clowes, *Royal Navy*, III.,
52–80.

equipment and meagre force of unseasoned and un-
drilled sailors, met with a severe storm at the cape.
His own ship, the *Centurion*, was the only one
neither destroyed nor driven back.

Arriving at Juan Fernandez on June 11, 1741, the
Centurion had but thirty men and officers fitted
for duty.   Later she was joined by the storm-
wracked *Gloucester* and *Trial*. The roll of the de-
pleted squadron now revealed the fact that out
of the 961 persons who had originally shipped on
these three vessels, 636 had died, leaving but 325
men and boys, an insufficient crew for the *Centurion*
itself.   Nevertheless, with this starveling company,
Anson ravaged the west coast of South America,
and would have joined Vernon at Panama but for
receipt of news of the latter's discomfiture.

The *Trial* and *Gloucester* had soon to be abandoned
as unseaworthy. The commodore was now left
with the *Centurion*, manned by but 200 men, at
last, however, efficient from long and careful training.   Imbued by the spirit of Drake and Hawkins,
he conceived the bold plan of striking out into
the Pacific, with a view of intercepting the Spanish
galleon yearly trading between Manila and Acapulco.
After a tempestuous voyage he came upon his
quarry near the Philippines, and challenged her.
The Spaniard was heavily laden with merchandise,
and her crew of 600 men were unskilled, so that she
readily succumbed (June 20, 1743) and yielded up
her cargo, worth $2,500,000.

The victorious Anson at once started for home by way of the Cape of Good Hope. Favored by a fog which hid him from the view of the French Channel fleet, he safely anchored at Spithead (June 15, 1744), having harried Spanish commerce around the globe.[1] England had at last good occasion for being in an ecstasy of joy. The gallant sea-dogs were paraded through city and country with bands and banners, and the government, which had contributed so slightly to the success of the brilliant expedition, made a rear-admiral of its commander, who in later wars was, as Lord Anson, to add still greater lustre to British arms.

[1] See Clowes, *Royal Navy*, III., 320–324, for details of Anson's expedition.

CHAPTER VII

KING GEORGE'S WAR
(1743–1748)

THE conflict between England and Spain was soon broken in upon by the much broader War of the Austrian Succession (1744–1748). England, Holland, and Hanover sided with Maria Theresa, queen of Hungary and Bohemia, and daughter of Emperor Charles VI., who claimed on his death (1740) the successorship to his domains. On the other side, Spain, France, Bavaria, Saxony, and Prussia contended for a division of the empire, and one of the aims of France was the acquisition of the Netherlands. At first France and England fought each other indirectly, as auxiliaries to rival claimants, the two governments being nominally at peace. But in 1743 French machinations so forwarded the Jacobite intrigues that Prince Charles Stuart was despatched in a French fleet to invade Scotland. At the battle of Dettingen (June 27), French and English came directly into deadly clash, and the French were so embittered at being expelled from Germany by English arms that at the close of the year's campaign it was seen that formal hostilities

must result.   March 21, 1744, the government at
Whitehall at last proclaimed war; had this decision
been made two years sooner, doubtless the struggle
might have correspondingly been shortened.   Our
present interest lies solely in events which now
transpired in America, where the encounter is known
as King George's War.

After the cession to England of Newfoundland and
Acadia, under the treaty of Utrecht, the French
troops withdrew to Cape Breton (l'Île Royale),
which they contended was not included in the
cession; although English claims classed that island
as a part of Nova Scotia, from which it is separated
by the narrow strait of Canso, a waterway about
the width of the Hudson River at New York.   At
the southern end of the strait was the important
English fishing station of Canseau, protected by a
stockaded block-house.

Selecting as their base a rugged harbor called
Port à l'Anglais, on the eastern coast of Cape
Breton, the French gradually erected there the
fortress of Louisburg, accounted the stoutest stronghold on the western coast of the Atlantic, being
planned by some of the most competent military
engineers of their day, and costing about thirty
million livres, equivalent to $10,000,000.   From
the first, Louisburg was a thorn in the side of
New England.   The sea - fisheries were quite as
necessary to the welfare of the English coast colonists as the fur-trade was to New France.   In sailing

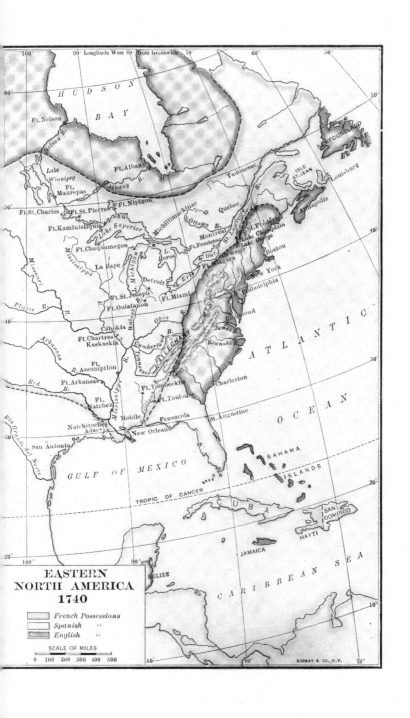

EASTERN
NORTH AMERICA
1740

French Possessions
Spanish   "
English   "

SCALE OF MILES
0   100 200 300 400 500

BORMAY & CO., N.Y.

to and from the Newfoundland banks, New England
fishers were subject to serious annoyance from the
French; officials from the fort were continually in-
flaming *habitants* and savages in Acadia, and encouraging assaults on English colonists in the
peninsula; at Louisburg, Indian war-parties returning from murderous and devastating raids on the
English borderers in Maine were cajoled and rewarded—indeed, they were often led by French
partisans; moreover, Cape Breton was held to be
English territory.   There was, however, some compensation in the fact that the Louisburg garrison
bought a large share of their provisions from Boston
merchants, and a considerable clandestine trade was
carried on between individuals of the rival colonies,
despite the regulations of both France and England,
by which it was sought to confine colonial trade to
vessels carrying their own flag.[1]

While Louisburg was being developed as protector of the entrance to Canada and as a serious
menace to New England, New France was, as we
have seen in previous chapters, strengthening herself in the interior of the continent.   Her line of
forts connecting Louisiana with Canada by way of
the drainage systems of the Mississippi, the Ohio,
the Great Lakes, and the St. Lawrence, was now well
established; and in the fur-bearing wilderness of the
far northwest the long "Post of the Western Sea"
was feeling its way towards the Pacific and barring

---

[1] Murdoch, *Nova Scotia*, I., 430; Bourinot, *Cape Breton*, 31.

to the south the operations of the Hudson's Bay
Company.[1]   A new fort at Niagara was designed to
overawe England's savage auxiliaries, "the devoring
Iroquois"; Fort Chambly was to protect Montreal
from further inroads by way of the now familiar
war route through the geological trough occupied
by the Hudson River and lakes George and Champlain; and Fort Frédéric, at Crown Point, on the
west shore of Lake Champlain, still further strengthened this line of defence.[2]

Meanwhile, in all North America, England's garrisons aggregated but nine hundred men.[3]   Her
colonists themselves were in each province torn by
dissensions, so that little was done save to rail at
the French.   Governor Burnet of New York, at his
own expense, built a fortified fur-trading post at
Oswego (1727) as a rival to Niagara; and it has been
told how Massachusetts advanced her firing - line
along the Kennebec frontier;[4] but further we find
slight progress on the part of the English bordermen,
between the treaty of Utrecht and the opening of
King George's War.   Indeed, it now seemed to
many observers quite possible for New France to
hem in her rival to the Atlantic slope; and there
were those among her master - spirits whose ambition stopped at nothing short of a policy of North
America for the French alone.

[1] See chap. vi., above.
[2] Parkman, *Half-Century of Conflict*, II., chap. xvii.
[3] Fortescue, *British Army*, II., 256.
[4] See chap. ii., above.

Yet there were certain tendencies that gave pause
to the wisest counsellors at Versailles.   The British
navy had shattered the American commerce of
Spain, and it seemed likely that the latter's colonies might follow.   The sea-power of England was
steadily on the increase.   To be sure, she had so
wide a field of sea to cover that her vessels were
often inadequately equipped and her crews insufficient; while the barbarous press-gang which was
employed to recruit the ranks generally developed
unsatisfactory material.   Nevertheless, France was
still weaker in this respect, and, relatively, her navy
persistently declined.   The possession of Louisburg
was of enormous strategic importance; but far-away
Quebec was of small value as a base—the integrity
of the outpost on Cape Breton depended largely on
keeping communication open with the mother-land,
and to this task it will be shown that the French
navy was unequal, in the face of England's domination of the Atlantic.

News of the declaration of war was received at
Louisburg by a French vessel two months before
information reached Boston.   Governor Duquesne
had thus an important advantage over the enemy,
and he immediately despatched an expedition of
several hundred soldiers and marines, under Captain
Duvivier, to reduce the neighboring British stockade
at Canseau, which was manned by about eighty ill-
equipped colonial militia.   Surrender promptly followed the appearance of the invaders, and the

prisoners being given their choice of retiring within a year either to England or one of the English colonies, many of them proceeded in the autumn to Boston.[1]

A like war-party, chiefly composed of Micmac and Malecite Indians, was sent against Annapolis (Port Royal), where Colonel Mascarene, governor of Nova Scotia, with a small body of men, stoutly stood his ground behind the old ramparts and a full equipment of cannon.   Duvivier joined the besiegers after the capture of Canseau, but could make no headway against the gallant Huguenot.   Reinforcements arriving from New England, Duvivier at the close of September retired to Louisburg, to be sneered at and censured for mismanagement.[2]

These attacks on their Acadian outposts had greatly exasperated the New-Englanders, and plans for the capture of Louisburg were formulated by several ingenious persons whose bitterness against the French was far greater than their knowledge of military science.[3] Parkman gives credit for the adopted scheme to William Vaughn, the intelligent, well-educated, but headstrong proprietor of large fishing interests at the mouth of Damariscotta River and on the island of Matinicus, off the Maine coast, and an officer in the attacking force.   Pepperrell claimed that Colonel John Bradstreet was the

[1] Bourinot, *Cape Breton*, 37.
[2] *Ibid.*, 37, 38; Richard, *Acadia*, I., 203–205.
[3] Parkman, *Half-Century of Conflict*, II., 83–85.

originator and planner of the campaign. Documents
of the period prove that other persons also offered
plans to Governor William Shirley, of Massachusetts,
to whom the chief credit is due for securing aid from
the provincial assemblies of Massachusetts, Rhode
Island, and Connecticut, and, in general, putting
the scheme on its feet.

Massachusetts, in particular, was the scene of
eager enthusiasm over the project. The enterprise
took on the nature of a crusade. Preachers uttered
prayers and sermons inveighing against the Catholicism of the French, which in the fervor of their
bigotry they styled "antichrist." In the opinion
of Massachusetts men, the Puritan army now being
raised "was Israel, and the French were Canaanitish
idolaters"; while the famous revivalist, George
Whitefield, furnished a motto for the flag which
savored of the religious character of the undertaking
—"Nil desperandum Christo duce." Colonies outside of New England scoffed at it as a crazy enterprise, save that New York gingerly contributed to
the extent of lending from her ordnance stores ten
eighteen-pounders.[1]

After seven weeks of feverish and unskilful prep-
aration, the crusaders were ready to sail (March
24, 1745). Shirley had selected as his lieutenant
William Pepperrell, a rich merchant with less military training than many of the 4270 men who were

[1] See *N. Y. Docs. Rel. to Col. Hist.*, VI., 284, for Governor
Clinton's letter.

placed under his command; but he was popularly
appreciated as a man of sense and tact, qualities
which soon were to stand him well in stead.   Of this
motley company of rustics and fishermen—some
of whom had been bushrangers on the Indian
frontier or had smelled powder on board New
England privateers but all equally guiltless of
regular military discipine — Massachusetts contributed 3300, Connecticut 516, and New Hampshire
454—150 of the New Hampshire men being in the
pay of Massachusetts; Rhode Island also raised 150,
but they arrived on the scene too late to participate.
The naval force, under Captain Edward Tyng, a
privateersman with some experience under fire,
consisted of thirteen armed vessels carrying an aggregate of 216 guns of all sorts and sizes, the
heaviest caliber being twenty-two pounders.   For
transports, there were taken into the service ninety
fishing-boats, in which the militiamen found slight
shelter from the "terrible northeast storm" which
now swept the Maine coast, and on the voyage they
suffered greatly from exposure and sea-sickness.[1]

Sadly buffeted by wind and waves, the fleet
gradually assembled in the port of Canseau.   While
a detachment of the land forces were rebuilding the
block-house, Tyng was cruising off Louisburg, and
captured several French prizes laden with supplies

---

[1] See MS. diaries of the period, chiefly preserved in the library
of the Mass. Hist. Society.   See Bourinot, *Cape Breton*, 41, for
lists of vessels and troops.

for the garrison. The expedition received on the
23d a fortunate and probably essential reinforcement. Commodore Peter Warren had been ordered
by the British government to co-operate with Shirley "for the annoyance of the enemy, and his
Majesty's service in North America." He now appeared with four ships—*Superbe, Mermaid, Launces-
ton,* and *Eltham*—and thenceforth assisted Pepperrell—effectively, although occasionally with some
not unnatural exhibitions of bad temper over being
obliged to acknowledge the precedence of a bungling
amateur militiaman.[1]

The arrival of Warren's fleet rendered it possible
to blockade the port of Louisburg against all comers.
While waiting for the ice to move in Gabarus Bay,
which is practically Louisburg's outer harbor, Pepperrell managed to instil into his command some
of the elements of drill; so that by April 29, the
day of the start, it was possible for them roughly to
manœuvre in battalions of four or five hundred men.

The fortress of Louisburg, whose walls embraced
about a hundred acres, occupied the greater part of
an undulating, rocky tongue of land projecting between the sea to the south and an inner harbor to
the north. The heaviest line of defence, protected
by four substantial bastions and ditch and glacis,
was along the southwest wall, which stretched for
twelve hundred yards across from the harbor well
towards the ocean. Fronting this wall, and ex-

[1] Parkman, *Half-Century of Conflict,* II., 155, 158.

tending to the sea-side, lay a wide expanse of morass, which was impassable for heavy bodies of troops. The narrow mouth of the harbor is strewn with reefs and islands, upon the largest of the latter being planted a strong battery; but this is dominated by Lighthouse Point, on the opposite side of the entrance. Westward of the bay, the country consists of low, rocky undulations, at the time of the attack clothed with a dense growth of cedar, stunted spruce, and other evergreens; this rough country, affording fine cover for an enemy, approached closely to the west gate. Upon the south shore of the harbor, a mile away, and abutting the hills, the Grand (or Royal) Battery, a small fortress in itself, also commanded the harbor entrance.

Pepperrell was without engineers; he had a few skilled artillerists, with experience on New England privateers worrying French and Spanish commerce, and Warren lent him several from the fleet; but neither the general nor his men understood the first principles of the arts of siege. Yet his landing, at the head of Gabarus Bay, on April 30 and May 1, was rather skilfully performed; the French outposts were easily driven in, batteries were soon established, and the English securely intrenched. The uncouth but on the whole effective movements of the invaders greatly perplexed the garrison, and appear from their strangeness to have in a measure unnerved them.[1]

[1] Parkman, *Half-Century of Conflict*, II., 125.

The besieged—consisting of fifty-six regulars in bad condition and distrusted by their officers, and thirteen or fourteen hundred rustics, fishermen, and half-breeds who served as an irregular militia—acted throughout as though taken unawares. Yet some of the neighboring Indians had been in Boston during Shirley's preparations, and brought home early news of the impending crusade. The commandant, Chevalier Duchambon, was, however, of too weak a character for an emergency such as this. "We lost precious moments in useless deliberations and resolutions no sooner made than broken," petulantly writes a Louisburg diarist of the siege,[1] with the result that when the English arrived nothing had been done to withstand them. Within two days a small party of invaders, practically unhampered, occupied the formidable Grand Battery, with its thirty guns, which the panic-stricken French had precipitately deserted on their approach. This work, commanding the inner harbor as well as the fortress, was an important acquisition.[2]

A profuse cannonading now ensued on both sides, the French gunners being as a rule better marksmen than their enemies. Occasionally the garrison would make a sortie; but the officers, apparently not daring to trust either their own men or their considerable force of Indian allies, would not allow them to venture far beyond the walls. On May 19 a French

---

[1] *Lettre d'un Habitant de Louisbourg*, in *ibid.*, App., 288, 299.
[2] *Ibid.*, 116, 117; Bourinot, *Cape Breton*, 45, 46.

vessel was captured, laden with ammunition and provisions, which were quite as essential for the besiegers as for the besieged; for the colonial army soon ran short of stores of every description, and during the final three weeks was threadbare, while shoes were at a premium. Camp diseases also harried the provincials, and once (May 28) but twenty-one hundred men out of the four thousand were fit for duty.[1]

Fresh arrivals from time to time increased Warren's fleet to eleven ships, with an aggregate of five hundred and twenty-four guns,[2] now quite sufficient effectively to aid in the bombardment, which by the middle of June had laid the town in ruins, it being calculated that nine thousand cannon-balls and six hundred bombs had been planted within the walls. In due time Lighthouse Point was gained by the English, and then the Island Battery succumbed. Finally, overcome by terror, the inhabitants compelled the garrison to surrender, which it did June 16, with the stipulation that the troops should march out with arms and colors, but that all within the fortress, soldier or civilian, should take oath not again to bear arms against King George or his allies during the ensuing twelvemonth.[3] On the following day War-

---

[1] Parkman, *Half-Century of Conflict*, II., 131.

[2] Douglass, *Summary of the British Settlements*, I., 351.

[3] Text of correspondence and capitulation, in Parsons, *Pepperrell*, 95–99; *Collection de documents relatifs à l'histoire de la Nouvelle-France*, III., 221–226.

ren's ships entered the harbor and Pepperrell's
ragged crew marched in by the south gate.

The easy terms of capitulation created much
dissatisfaction among the colonial troops, who had
fondly anticipated rich loot in the sacking of Louisburg. It was impossible wholly to prevent thievery
or to curb the iconoclasm of the religious fanatics,
who hacked away at the Catholic altars as though the
breastworks of Satan. But the marauders found
that the walled town, far from being a store of
wealth, possessed little worthy the cupidity of even
a rustic militiaman whose wardrobe had been worn
to shreds.

There was much controversy in New England over
the relative degrees of credit to be awarded Pepperrell and his troops and Warren and his marines. It
was useless, however, to attempt a decision. Each
branch of the service was essential to the other.
New England dash and recklessness, based on
provincial self - conceit, were responsible for the
crusade, and accounted for the fine spirit which
throughout characterized this extraordinary performance; yet without the co-operation of the navy
it is difficult to see how the downfall of Louisburg
could have been secured. Indeed, good - luck was
accountable for not a small share of the victory,
for had not Louisburg been so wretchedly officered,
and had not a long chain of contributive events
otherwise weakened the French defence, the outcome might readily have been quite a different story.

Boston received the news by an express boat, early in the morning of July 3. The townspeople were at once awakened by booming cannon and clanging bells, and a noisy day was succeeded by a night of bonfires, fireworks, and window illumination, followed in due course by the usual day of thanksgiving. New York and Philadelphia in turn celebrated in like manner, and England was as vociferous as over the victories of Vernon and Anson. Warren was made an admiral, Pepperrell, who had spent £10,000 of his own fortune, largely in entertaining his brother-officers at camp, was created a baronet and made colonel of a fresh regiment to be raised among his doughty followers, who by this time had earned the standing of regulars; while Shirley also was remembered with a similar colonelcy. Massachusetts, having spent £183,469 on the expedition, in time had that sum returned from Whitehall, the reimbursement being promptly and wisely devoted to the redemption of her wretchedly depreciated paper currency. The other contributing colonies were not forgotten in the general enthusiasm, and also secured the rebate of their expenditures.

Pepperrell had left at Louisburg a garrison of twenty-five hundred men. The fort was in so foul a state after the siege that a pestilence broke out during the winter, which swept off nearly nine hundred of the men,[1] while by spring the majority of

[1] Shirley to Newcastle, May 10, 1746, cited in Parkman, *Half-Century of Conflict*, II., 167.

the survivors were in hospital.   The Duke of Newcastle, then prime - minister, had assured them of
early and ample reinforcements, both military and
naval.   In part fulfilment of this promise, three
British regiments arrived in April (1746).   Warren
was commissioned as governor, and the forlorn but
exultant colonists were sent to their homes.[1]

A general campaign against Canada was now
planned upon lines which soon became familiar.
A joint British and colonial army was to be transported up the St. Lawrence to attack Quebec, while
a combined land force was to strike Montreal by
way of Lake Champlain.   Seven provinces, eager
for the fray, promptly raised their quota of a force
of forty - three hundred militia, but Newcastle's
regiments failed to appear.   At a time when British
troops were sorely needed both in Flanders and
America, the regiments destined for the Canadian
campaign were used in a vain and feeble descent on
l'Orient, the port in Brittany where the French
East India Company kept its stores.[2]

Learning that Newcastle was breaking faith with
his colonies, Shirley determined on an independent
attack on Crown Point.   Just at this juncture,
however, came an alarming report that a great
French armada was on the eve of an attempt to re-
take Acadia and Louisburg and destroy Boston by
fire.   Crown Point was forgotten in the wild scramble

[1] Parkman, *Half-Century of Conflict*, II., 167.
[2] Fortescue, *British Army*, II., 259.

to defend the coast.   The armada had, indeed, reached
American waters; but, as if in answer to the combined
prayers of the New England churches, it was dispersed by a tempest off the coast of Nova Scotia, its
half-starved crews returning crestfallen to France.[1]

The next year (1747) a new French fleet was assembled for vengeance on the English colonies in
America; but Admirals Anson and Warren engaged
the squadron off Rochelle and utterly vanquished it.[2]
This fresh display of superiority of sea-power probably alone saved the colonists, for Newcastle gave
them no further material assistance.   He shipped
to Annapolis three hundred soldiers, half of whom
died on shipboard, while many others deserted to
the French, who were keeping Acadia in an uproar.
Massachusetts, determined that the peninsula should
not be lost through default, sent thither a considerable reinforcement, which, by dint of some sharp
fighting with the Acadian rangers and their Indian
allies, maintained English supremacy.[3]

[1] Douglass, *Summary of the British Settlements;* Longfellow,
"Ballad of the French Fleet":

> "Oh, Lord! we would not advise,
>   But if in thy providence
> A tempest should arise,
>   To drive the French fleet hence,
> And scatter it far and wide,
>   Or sink it in the sea,
> We should be satisfied,
>   And thine the glory be."

[2] Clowes, *Royal Navy*, III., 124–127.
[3] Parkman, *Half-Century of Conflict*, II., 198–220; Richard,
Acadia, chaps. **xi.**, **xii.**

Meanwhile, a spasmodic but grewsome conflict was in progress all along the international frontier. Local chronicles abound in the details of raids and counter-raids between French and English partisans, both sides being freely assisted by savages, whose ingenious cruelty greatly added to the ordinary horrors of warfare. In one of the incursions from Canada, which had penetrated to within sight of Albany, French and Indians attacked (November 28, 1745) the outpost of Saratoga, a small stockaded Dutch settlement; thirty persons were killed and a hundred taken prisoners.[1] This irregular contest, in which the aborigines played so large and ferocious a part, did much to develop the fighting capacity and forest diplomacy of the backwoodsmen, and thus train them for still greater encounters. While Frenchmen were generally superior in the art of tactfully handling the tribesmen and playing them against each other in the white man's interest, at least one British citizen so benefited by his training on the Iroquois border that he attained a capacity in this direction rivalling the shrewdest of the French. This was a nephew of Admiral Warren, William Johnson, a young Irish landholder on the Mohawk River, to whose remarkable influence over the Iroquois was due an important share of the success of British arms and diplomacy throughout the remainder of the protracted

[1] N. Y. Docs. Rel. to Col. Hist., VI., 228; Schuyler, New York, II., 113–124.

struggle with France for the mastery of the continent.[1]

In the northwest the Hudson's Bay Company was prepared for the worst. Each agent was instructed vigorously to defend his post against the French, and in the event of defeat to "destroy everything that be of service to the enemy, and make the best retreat you can."[2] Their vessel, the *Prince Rupert* (one hundred and eighty tons), was given letters of marque against both French and Spanish shipping, and strict watch was kept on Davis Straits for vessels of the allies. But the fall of Louisburg saved the company from further apprehension; for thenceforth England's superiority on the high seas was evident, and no French craft could be spared for such northern waters.

Weary of the long, exhaustive, and apparently futile conflict, which had been so destructive of life and treasure, France and England agreed to desist, in July, 1748, and in the following October signed the peace of Aix-la-Chapelle.[3] By this agreement all conquests were mutually restored. The news of the surrender of Louisburg, which had been won and for two years retained chiefly by New England valor and blood, caused intense dissatisfaction throughout the colonies, and tended still further to

[1] Lives by Stone and Buell.

[2] Instructions to council at Albany Fort, May 10, 1744, in Willson, *Great Company*, 258.

[3] Text in Chalmers, *Treaties*, I., 424–442; extracts in MacDonald, *Select Charters*, 251–253.

strain their relations with the mother-land, which by this time were none too pleasant.

At Whitehall it was not considered that the war had been quite in vain, for France had been brought almost to the verge of collapse; and while her own cost had been great, England's command of the ocean had been strengthened and her colonists better fitted for the giant struggle yet to come. There were, however, those who read aright the spirit of these independent and somewhat captious Englishmen over-seas, and felt that their growing strength but hastened their emancipation from leading-strings.

CHAPTER VIII

THE PEOPLE OF NEW FRANCE

(1750)

BEFORE entering upon the story of the last and fateful struggle between France and England for the mastery of the North American continent, it will be helpful briefly to study the people of the warring colonies; for the contest was not only national, it was largely a measuring of strength between social and political systems fundamentally opposed to each other and unable permanently to exist as neighbors.

The climate of Canada was not as well adapted to the purposes of seventeenth-century colonization as that wherein the English colonies had been planted. In our day of superior agricultural knowledge, methods, and utensils, a new colony might soon acquaint itself with the climate and soil conditions of the lower St. Lawrence, and by mastering the production problem become self-supporting. In the period of New France, however, even the most favorably situated European plantations in America had for several seasons practically to be maintained from the mother-land, and starvation was

often imminent in the midst of abundant natural resources which the settlers knew not how to utilize.
The English colonists, soon left by their government largely to shift for themselves, were forced to
starve or to dig, and after some bitter experiences
in due time found themselves; but to New France the
harsh climate and stubborn soil of the north were
more serious obstacles, which her people, paternally
nurtured, and thus lacking initiative, were long in
overcoming.

While in many ways the situation of Quebec was
a source of strength,[1] time came when there were
seen to be certain disadvantages in centring the
colony at such distance from the sea-coast.   The
entrance to the Gulf of St. Lawrence is so far northward that storms and ice-floes endanger navigation
during half the year.   Colonial possessions over-seas
cannot successfully be maintained unless the mother-
country possesses the means of easy and frequent
communication with them; and their importance to
the latter is largely dependent on their value as
naval bases.   With the loss of Newfoundland, Cape
Breton, and Acadia, France was left with slight
hold upon the North American coast; the St.
Lawrence afforded her but a slender naval base
compared with the fine shore dominated by the
English colonies to the south.

The fisheries of New France were important; although, quite unlike the New-Englanders, perhaps

[1] See chap. i., above.

most of the deep-sea fishers required government
assistance. Characteristically unwilling to leave
their homes for inhospitable foreign shores, it was
found necessary artificially to stimulate the industry,[1] and many harsh measures seemed essential, to
make the situation unpleasant for English poachers;
yet the latter were often able clandestinely to sell
their cargoes to the enterprising French.[2] Sometimes Frenchmen, however, would put in their nets
as far south as Cape Cod; and conflicts between
rival fishing fleets were not infrequent incidents,
tending to keep alive the long-smouldering sparks of
racial hostility.[3]

The fur - trade was the most important of the
French colonial interests, and practically a government monopoly. The great river flowing past their
doors, which drained an immense and unknown area
of forested wilderness, peopled with strange tribes
of wild men, fired the imagination of the men of
New France. In an age of exploration, and themselves among the most inquisitive and adventurous
people of Europe, Frenchmen—led by Champlain
himself, who had the *wanderlust* within his veins—
pushed their way in birch canoes up the St. Lawrence and its great affluents, the Saguenay, the
Ottawa, the Richelieu, and their wide-stretching
drainage systems. Soon they discovered, in the

[1] Marmette, in *Canadian Archives*, 1888, cxxxvii.
[2] Bourinot, *Cape Breton*, 31; Murdoch, *Nova Scotia*, 430.
[3] Parkman, *Half-Century of Conflict*, I., 106–108.

heart of the continent, the interlocking systems of the Ohio, the Mississippi, the Winnipeg, and the Saskatchewan; and these led them still farther and farther afield through endless chains and ramifications of glistening waterways.

Eastern Canada was not rich in peltries; the growing wariness of the wild animals soon led both white and savage hunters ever westward, into the darkest recesses of the wilderness, where were abundantly found the finest furs yet seen by Europeans. The up-stream movement of trade and settlement was amazingly rapid. We have seen that it was not long before New France held all the wild interior between the Rockies and the Alleghanies, and the Saskatchewan and New Orleans, with a thin line of small, fur-trade stockades and the Jesuit missions which formed so important an element in her plan of conquest. North of New York and New England, the international boundary was much as it is to-day, save for Acadia, which was still undefined and but nominally under British rule.

But though New France had soon spread ambitiously throughout the heart of the continent, in sharp distinction to the compact and slowly expanding growth of the English colonies, her resources and her population were far inferior. From the first, the court at Versailles made strenuous efforts to people the colony. The early commercial monopolies, which dominated New France until it was made a royal province in 1663, were under

bonds to induce migration thither.[1] Unlike the
English, however, the French have never been fond
of colonizing. A complete satisfaction with home
conditions, rendering them unwilling to look abroad,
is even in our day deprecated by many wise Frenchmen as a serious national weakness. Bounties to
immigrants, importation of unmarried women to
wed the superabundant bachelors, ostracism for the
unmarried of either sex, official rewards for large
families—all these measures were freely and persistently adopted by the French colonial officials.
And yet, after nearly a century and a half, but
eighty thousand whites constituted the semi-depen-
dent and unprogressive population of Canada and
Louisiana, over a stretch of territory above two
thousand miles in length, against the million and a
quarter of self-supporting English colonists, who for
the most part were, from Georgia to New Hampshire,
massed on the narrow coast between the Appalachians and the sea.

The government of New France was that of an
autocracy, continually subject to direction from
Versailles, where a fickle-minded monarch and a
corrupt court played fast and loose with their often
misguided colony.[2] The colony was governed quite

[1] Biggar, *Early Trading Companies of New France*, 95, 115,
136.
[2] For general survey, see Garneau, *Canada* (Bell's trans.), I.,
book III., chap. iii.; Parkman, *Old Régime*, chap. xvi.; Bourinot,
in *Const. Hist. of Canada*, 7–11, and "Local Government in
Canada," in *Johns Hopkins University Studies*, V., 10–20.

similarly to a province in France. The governor, generally both a soldier as well as a statesman, and as a rule carefully selected, was in control of both the civil and military administration—although we shall see that a military commander was sometimes introduced as a coadjutor—and reported directly to his sovereign. With the governor were associated the intendant and the bishop; the former a legal and financial officer intrusted with the public expenditures, exercising certain judicial functions, presiding over the council, and confidentially reporting to the king, being regarded as a check upon the governor, with whom his relations were, as a matter of course, often strained. The bishop saw to it that the interests of the church were constantly considered, and had a large body of supporters in the parish priests, who on their part exercised a powerful local influence.

These three autocrats, who were the actual rulers, save when interfered with from Versailles, had associated with them a body of resident councillors—at first five, later twelve—appointed by the crown, usually for life, upon the nomination of the governor and intendant. The three chief officials, who of course dominated the body, united with these men in forming the superior council, which exercised executive, legislative, and judicial powers, the only appeal from their decisions being to the home government. There were local governors at Montreal and Three Rivers, with but little authority or dignity,

for even warrants for fines and imprisonments must
be issued from Quebec; and subordinate courts, established by an attorney-general who was stationed
at the capital, were to be found at all important
villages. The officers of justice were appointed
without regard to their legal qualifications, being
chosen by favor from among the military men or
the prominent inhabitants.

Local government was absolutely unknown. No
public meetings for any purpose whatsoever, even
to discuss the pettiest affairs of the parish or the
market, were permitted unless special license be
granted by the intendant, a document seldom even
applied for. "Not merely was [the Canadian col-
onist] allowed no voice in the government of his
Province, or the choice of his rulers, but he was not
even permitted to associate with his neighbors for
the regulation of those municipal affairs which the
central authority neglected under the pretext of
managing." [1] Absolutism and centralization could
not have been more securely intrenched.

In order that nothing might be lacking in this
autocratic system, there was created by Richelieu,
in the charter of the Hundred Associates (1627), an
order of nobility. None was needed in so raw a
colony, where poverty was the rule, and democ-
racy more nearly fitted the needs of the situation;

---

[1] Earl of Durham, *Report on the Affairs of British North America* (January 31, 1839), 16. See also Parkman, *Old Régime*, 280,
281.

but the French could not then conceive of a state of society without its *noblesse*, therefore one was artificially produced.[1]   Many of the military officers who came out with their regiments belonged to the minor *noblesse* of France; and, as an inducement to stay in New France when their terms expired, they were given as seigniories large tracts of land along the river and lake fronts.   Sometimes the seigniories were uninhabited save by Indians and wild animals; while upon others were peasants (*habitants*), whose log-houses, whitewashed and dormer-windowed, lined the common highway perhaps a half-mile back from the water's edge, down to which sloped the fields of the seignior's tenants— narrow, ribbon-like strips, generally somewhat less than eight hundred feet wide, for these light-hearted people were gregarious and loved to be near their neighbors both on the highway and the waterway. Beyond the road the strips, while sometimes specified in the grants as being ten times their width (or nearly a mile and a half long), by custom continued as far back into the hinterland as proved convenient for pasturage or for crude agriculture.[2]   Villages of this attenuated character often stretched for miles along the shore—densely for a mile or so on either side of a parish church, and then thinning out in the midway

---

[1] Parkman, *Old Régime*, chap. xv.

[2] The usual grant was four arpents frontage on the water by ten arpents deep, the arpent being equivalent to one hundred and ninety-two English linear feet.

spaces.   The traveller of to-day sees upon the lower
St. Lawrence, on the Saguenay, and in picturesque
Gaspé, many scores of communities of this sort,
survivals of the French régime.

Now and then a seignior was comparatively prosperous, as when given a district with fishing rights,
assuring him toll upon his tenants' catch; but the
lord was often quite as poor as his *habitants*,
and continually subject to arbitrary official interference of every sort, even as to agreements between
himself and his tenants (*censitaires*).   Unless the
seignior cleared his land within a stated time it
was forfeited; and when he sold it a fifth of the
price obtained was due, although not always paid,
to his feudal superior.   The rents obtainable from
his tenants were generally in kind, and apt to be
trifling — from four to sixteen francs annually for
an ordinary holding.   On his part, the tenant was
supposed to patronize his seignior's grist-mill, to
bake his bread (for a consideration) in the seigniorial
oven, to do manual labor for him during a few days
each year, and for the privilege of fishing before
his own door to present the seignior with one fish
in every eleven.   But these duties were more nominal
than real, and often the tenant's obligation was
satisfied upon the annual performance of some petty
act of ceremony—thus did they with serious aspect
play at feudalism and satisfy the pride of the
lords of the manor.   But the seignior had no more
voice in public affairs than his tenant—both were

equally ignored, save when some powerful rustic
lord won recognition sufficient to secure his ap-
pointment to the council. He might not work
at a trade, yet occasionally there were seigniors
who tilled their own soil and whose wives and
daughters labored by their side; and there are instances where these threadbare noblemen, chancing
to be in favor, were actually provisioned by the
king.[1]

Unable otherwise to exist, the nobleman generally
took kindly to the fur-trade, which meant a roving
life, wherein much gayety was mingled with the
roughest sort of adventure. When unable or unwilling to secure a government license, he became
a *coureur de bois*, or illegal trader, a practice sub-
jecting him to the penalty of outlawry; but the
extreme punishment was seldom meted out.   These
gentlemen wanderers were of hardy stock, took
kindly to the wild, uncouth life of the forest, readily fraternized with the savages, whose dress and
manners they often affected, and, seldom possessing
refined sentiments, frequently led Indian war-parties
in bloody forays upon the frontiers of the detested
English — disguised by grease - paint, breech - clout,
and feathers, and outdoing their followers in cruelty.
Each was an experienced partisan leader, with a
small body of devoted retainers, who propelled his
boats, kept his camp, defended his property and
person, rallied around him on his raids, and were

[1] Parkman, *Old Régime*, 257–260.

as solicitous as he himself of the dignity of his
caste.[1]

A full third of the population was engaged in the
fur - trade.   From it the peasants, boatmen (*voy-
ageurs*), trading-post clerks, and trappers won but
the barest subsistence; many of the seigniors made
heavy gains, although others, of an extremely adventurous type, like La Salle and Vérendrye, were
swamped by the enormous expenses of the exploring
expeditions which they undertook in the effort both
to extend their own fields of operation and the
sphere of French influence.   The military officers at
the wilderness outposts dabbled largely in this commerce; indeed, many of them, like Vérendrye, were
given the trade monopoly of a considerable district
as their only compensation.   There are numerous
instances of such officials amassing comfortable fortunes for that day, and retiring to France to spend
them; although often their fur-trade, legitimate or
illegitimate, was less responsible for such results than
the peculation in which nearly all of them were engaged.

For corruption, especially during the closing years,
was rampant throughout New France.   The govern-
or and ecclesiastics were seldom under the ban of
suspicion; but the intendant was quite apt to be a
rare rascal, and from him down to the commandant
of the most far-away stockade extended a graded,

---

[1] Lahontan, *Voyages*, gives graphic pictures of the life of the
colonial *noblesse*.

well-organized system, whereby public moneys and
supplies from France were unconscionably preyed
upon.   Not even was the bench free from this stain.
It was said of a certain judge of the admiralty, who
was also judge of the inferior court of justice on
Cape Breton: "This magistrate and the others of
subordinate jurisdiction grew extremely rich, since
they are interested in different branches of commerce, particularly the contraband." [1]

Smuggling was everywhere practised, and as
freely winked at by interested officials.   It has already been stated that both French and English
governments sought to confine their colonial commerce to vessels flying their own flags; but, despite
severe laws, there was much clandestine trade.   We
have seen that Louisburg merchants maintained a
considerable commerce with Boston, an irregularity
overlooked by the garrison commandant because
thence came a large share of his supplies.   As early
as 1725 Louisburg was becoming a considerable port
of call for French vessels engaged in the West-Indian
trade, and ships from England and her colonies were
often in the harbor.   It was thus natural that
sugar, coffee, and tobacco from the French West
Indies, and wine and brandy from France, should be
exchanged with New England fishermen for codfish;
and brick, lumber, meal, rum, and many other New
England commodities found their way into New
France.

[1] Pichon, *Memoirs*, quoted in Bourinot, *Cape Breton*, 30.

Even the French fur-trade was confronted by this demoralizing practice. It has been shown that their forest merchants were unable to offer as high prices for furs, in barter, as the English, owing to the greater cost of obtaining goods suitable for the Indian trade through the monopoly which hung over them as a pall; whereas Englishmen enjoyed free trade and open competition.[1] Wherever English traders could penetrate—into the Cherokee country, into the Ohio Valley, along the lower Great Lakes, on the Kennebec border, and upon the New York and New Hampshire frontier—the savages, keen at a bargain, would make long journeys to reach them with their pelts. The French inflamed the natural hatred of their allies for the English as a people, and resorted to bullying and often to force to prevent this diversion of custom, but often without avail.

Ecclesiastical affairs occupied a large share of popular attention in New France.[2] The bishop and his priests ruled not only in matters spiritual, but in most of those temporal concerns that came nearest to the daily life of the people, being, indeed, "fathers" to their flocks. No community, whether of fishers, *habitants*, fur-traders, or soldiers was without either its secular priest or its missionary friar. The chapel or the church was the nucleus of every village. Being generally the only educated

[1] See chaps. iii., vi., above.
[2] Parkman, *Old Régime*, chap. xix.

man in the parish, the curé was the local school-
master, often also served as physician, and in every
walk of life accompanied and guided his "children"
from the cradle to the grave. The French colonists,
naturally an obedient people, were deeply religious;
they implicitly submitted to the father because they
honored him as a counsellor and revered him as a
man of God. Many of the ecclesiastics were bigoted,
fanatical men, in political as well as in religious life;
such as Rale were perhaps better fitted for partisan
captains than spiritual leaders. But everywhere
it was an age of bigotry and fanaticism; the annals
of neither Old nor New England are spotless in this
respect.

Take them by and large, in comparison with the
religious of their time in other lands, and the priests
and missionaries of New France will not suffer in
the examination, either intellectually or spiritually.
Indeed, the fascinating history of their remarkable
and wide-spread Indian missions, particularly those
of the Jesuits—although much might also be said in
praise of the less strenuous Recollects, Sulpitians,
and Capuchins—furnishes some of the most brilliant
examples on record of self-sacrificing and heroic
devotion to an exalted cause. The career of a village curé was less spectacular, but his work among
the simple *habitants* was even more important in the
spiritual life of the people; and although seldom alluded to in history, was not barren of incidents which
called for a high degree of physical as well as of

moral courage. It is not necessary to be a Catholic, nor is it essential that from the stand-point of the twentieth century we should endorse the wisdom of its every act in the eighteenth, most profoundly to admire the work of the Church of Rome both among whites and savages in New France. American history would lose much of its welcome color were there blotted from its pages the picturesque and often thrilling story of the curés and friars of Canada in the French régime.

The one great mistake of the church, which all can now recognize, was the barring-out of the Huguenots from New France, after the revocation of the Edict of Nantes, thereby driving to rival English settlements a considerable share of the brains and brawn of France, thus building up the rival at the expense of Canada.[1]

Practically there were no manufactures in New France. Many of the vessels engaged in interior commerce were smuggled through from New England ship-yards. The fisheries were, as we have seen, to some extent artificially fostered. Agriculture was neglected, beyond the mere necessities of subsistence. Arms, hunting, and the fur-trade were the only callings that prospered among these mercurial, imaginative, and obedient folk, who were the victims of a paternal and military government that had not trained them to work without leading-strings. They were distinctly a people who needed,

[1] See chap. i., above.

so long as this policy continued, the constant support of a power that could keep in continual touch with them, one that could dominate the lanes of the intervening sea; and to this great task France was quite unequal.

Theoretically, every male in New France between the ages of sixteen and sixty was a soldier. It will be shown in a later chapter[1] that in 1756 there were perhaps fifteen thousand of them, nearly half of these engaged in callings, such as fishing or the fur - trade, that had accustomed them to the use of arms. There were, however, in garrison but twenty-five hundred regular troops of the colonial marine,[2] from France, together with a few troops of the line, increased under Montcalm to four thousand.

There were also available, either for harrying the English borders or upon regular campaigns, a considerable number of Indians, but how many, it would be idle to estimate, for no statistics have come down to us. Most of the tribes of the Algonquian stock between the Mississippi and the sea could be relied on as allies; but the five tribes of the masterly Iroquois[3] might generally be considered as enemies, although there was ever an element of uncertainty in their policy, dependent both on the

---

[1] See chap. xii., below.
[2] French colonies were governed through the Department of Marine.
[3] Greene, *Provincial America* (*Am. Nation*, VI.), chap. vii.

presence or absence of grievances with their English patrons and on the plausibility of French diplomacy, which was ever busy among these astute warriors.

With the exception, chiefly, of the Iroquois and the Foxes, the tribesmen entertained a real affection for the French, who, greatly desiring their trade, cultivated their alliance and treated them as friends and equals; an attitude far different from that of the English, who for the most part dealt with them honestly as customers, but could not conceal either their dislike of an inferior people or the fact that they were looked upon as subjects. French traders, explorers, and adventurers lived among the savages, took Indian women for their consorts, reared half-breed families, and, although representatives of the most polished nation of Europe, for the time being acted as though to the forest born.

French missionaries succeeded in the Indian villages as no Protestant Englishman, with his cold type of Christianity, has ever done. The French father lived with the brown people, shared their privations and burdens, and ministered with loving and sacrificing zeal both to their spiritual and their physical wants. Moreover, the Catholic church, with its combination of mysticism and ritualistic pomp, its banners and processions and symbolic images and pictures, strongly appealed to the barbarians. If not really Christianized—and there is room seriously to doubt whether more than the

merest handful of North American Indians have
ever really been converted to the creed of the
Nazarene—they at least came in large numbers to
adopt the forms of Catholicism, deeming a "medi-
cine" so efficacious among white people worthy of
respectful attention.

We have seen that the people of New France had
little individual enterprise; free association among
them was discouraged; their manufactures and commerce were limited; lack of sea-power had resulted
in neglect on the part of the mother-land; the
colony's sparse population was thinly scattered over
a vast area, and was poor in resources. It might
have been, and doubtless was, thought by astute
European observers that in Canada's death-struggle
with the rival colonies to the south the end would
soon be reached and would be inevitable.

But the contest was not to prove so one-sided
as this. The autocratic polity of New France enabled her leaders to act as a unit; whereas against
her were arrayed thirteen distinct provinces, with
governors who had little authority and legislatures
which debated and wrangled with painful deliberateness, trading on the presence of a grave public
danger to gain concessions from the representatives
of the crown. Such an enemy found it difficult to
act in unison. The French colonists were poor, but
they were intensely loyal to church and king, were
trained to childlike obedience, were supremely contented under a paternalism that would have sorely

fretted Englishmen, had enjoyed a fine schooling in the hardy and adventurous life of the forest, and were warlike and quick in action. Whereas their English rivals had been reared to trade, to love peace, to deliberate before they acted, to count the cost, and to resent dictation. The English system was more favorable to peaceful growth; the French autocracy was better suited for war. New France was but a pygmy, but she certainly had a good fighting chance.

CHAPTER IX

BASIS OF THE FINAL STRUGGLE
(1748–1752)

WE have seen that at the middle of the eighteenth century France was well intrenched at
both ends of the great mid-continental drainage
trough: commanding from the rock of Quebec the
St. Lawrence, the Great Lakes, and the far northwest; and from the island of Orleans, the far-
stretching Mississippi. Superficial observers in Europe were doubtless of the opinion that she held
in her hands the destinies of all the cultivable area
of North America, save the narrow Appalachian
slope over which England was in undisputed control. But closer inspection would have revealed
a different picture: New England was now pressing upon the Acadian border; New York was controlling the dread Iroquois, and Virginia and Pennsylvania were making claims to the upper western
slope of the mountains and even to the lower lands
as far as the Ohio; now and then daring Carolina
traders found their way among the generally hostile
Cherokee, in intervals between the blows which the
latter dealt upon the white settlements. The most

serious danger of all, to New France, lay in the fact
that the hunters, trappers, fur-traders, and cattlemen of Pennsylvania, Virginia, the Carolinas, and
Georgia were at last venturing by scores through
the passes of the Blue Ridge and the Alleghanies,
and appropriating lands and forest trade upon
westering waters, which France had long considered
quite her own.

The thirteen colonies were almost as isolated from
one another as they were from Europe.   Outside of
the New England group, few persons undertook to
journey from one to the other, and those were
generally either officials or occasional tourists from
Europe—save seamen, who conducted a considerable intercolonial commerce.   Coasting vessels transported most of the travellers, for water was an
easier highway than land, the rough wagon-roads
and rude bridle-paths often leading through dense
forests, with infrequent bridges.

Had there been no differences of race, creed, and
ideals, the result of this isolation would of itself
naturally breed jealousy and distrust.   The New-
Englander seldom even saw his compatriot from
the middle colonies or the south.   Men in self-
governing communities, thus dwelling apart, were
largely taken up with their petty local village or
plantation interests; only the broader-minded few
gave a thought to the affairs of their own province;
and still more rare was the colonist who cared to
know what was doing beyond his provincial borders.

They were a hard - working, self - centred people,
engaged in the daily toil of what was in all sections
essentially a frontier life, differing only in degree;
and they had but a narrow horizon.

The New England provinces and New York,
having as yet no outlet to the west, were forced
northward in search of new lands, and in consequence possessed an intimate knowledge of their
French and Indian opponents.   South of the Hudson
the sea-coast dwellers had by the middle of the
eighteenth century largely forgotten the early Indian wars, and to them the reports about French intrigues west of the mountains meant little.   On the
uplands of Pennsylvania, Maryland, Virginia, the
Carolinas, and Georgia the adventurous borderers
—cattlemen, hunters, and fur-traders by turn—well
understood the situation; but these men on the
firing-line were as yet relatively few, and their appeals
to the low country often fell on unheeding ears.

The middle colonies and the south presented an
Indian frontier over six hundred miles in length.
During the border wars the advance agents of
British occupation, the itinerant English and Scotch-
Irish fur-traders, were obliged in large measure to
suspend their operations in the camps of the aborigines and to fall back upon the border - line of
settlement.   The frontier between civilization and
savagery was often characterized by two or three
distinctive belts of white occupation.   The farthest
outposts were the rude huts, generally many miles

apart, of borderers who existed directly upon the
resources of the forest, game and fish being their
principal food, while the skins of the deer and the
elk constituted the greater part of their clothing.
Often, for the first few seasons, the outpost settler
grew no crops, either because—graceless, untutored,
fretting under any form of restraint—he detested
plodding employment, or because his aboriginal but
scarcely more savage neighbors resented his presence
on their hunting-grounds and occasionally drove
him back towards the older settlements.   Perhaps
twenty-five or more miles farther eastward was the
second border-line, distinguished by the log-cabins
of men who were raising horses, cattle, sheep, and
hogs, which grazed at will upon the corrugated uplands of the western Carolinas or on the broad
slopes of the valley of Virginia.   Life among these
range - men resembled that experienced upon the
ranches of our own Far West, if we allow for the
differences wrought by the social changes of a
century and a half, the proximity of railroads, and
the substitution of the plains for the forest.   The
annual round-up, the branding of young stock, the
sometimes deadly disputes between herdsmen, and
the autumnal drive to market are features in common.   Still eastward, another fifty miles or so, were
the small, rough holdings of the border farmers,
separated by long stretches of forest from the more
thickly settled and prosperous country which a
generation or two before had itself been the border.

Nearly all of the frontiersmen, clad in a primitive costume in part borrowed from the Indians, were rough in manners and in speech. Not all were heroes, for among them were many who had fled from the coast settlements because no longer to be tolerated in a law-abiding community. The fur-traders, who kept in constant touch with their homes upon the border, being indeed sometimes forced back to them by their savage customers, were not seldom mean, brutal fellows; and there were others whose innate badness had in this untram-melled society developed into wickedness. Every man was a law unto himself, and education was con-fined to a few. In almost every community of these crude, unlettered folk, however, dwelt some who, of much superior caliber, in times of great public need naturally assumed leadership and exercised an elevating influence on their fellows. The history of the American border, while disgraced by many pages of lawlessness and brutality, contains quite as many telling of lofty purpose and sterling deeds.

The colonial population of about one million three hundred and seventy thousand souls had largely sprung from the middle and lower classes of the mother-land. In 1750 it was still for the most part English, especially in New England; but there were in the other colonies representatives from nearly every European land, particularly Ger-many; while perhaps a fifth or sixth of the whole were negro slaves, these varying in proportion in

the various colonies, but most numerous, because
most profitable, in the south.   During the first half
of the eighteenth century, about a hundred thousand
Scotch-Irish emigrated from northeast Ireland to
North America.   Landing upon the sea-coast all
the way from Pennsylvania to the Carolinas and
Georgia, this sturdy people—whose ancestors had
been taken from Scotland to subdue Catholic Ulster,
but who were now under royal displeasure—at once
sought new and cheap lands.   They found these
towards the frontier, which was then not far from
tide-water.

Gradually, as the pressure upon available land
became greater, the younger generations of Pennsylvania Scotch-Irish moved southwestward through
the troughs of the Alleghanies, either tarrying on the
upper waters of the Potomac or pressing on to the
deep and fertile valleys of southwest Virginia and
North Carolina.   The South Carolina and Georgia
Scotch-Irish on their part spread northwestward,
because the easy southern trails to the west, where
the Alleghanies degenerate into the gulf plain,
were savagely guarded by English-hating Cherokee.
We shall see that these Ulster bordermen, easily
developing into expert Indian fighters, formed with
the English colonial adventurers and Protestant
Germans who commingled with them a highly important factor in the coming battles for English
supremacy in the still newer land beyond the
mountains.

The contentious attitude of the assemblies towards
their governors rendered it difficult for the latter
to induce them to raise, feed, and pay military
forces. Promptness was impossible under such circumstances. There were instances where the frontier seriously suffered from French and Indian raids
before succor could be sent. In Pennsylvania, the
Quakers refused to fight, and sometimes declined
in any manner to aid in the public defence, which
added another and very serious obstacle to the
placing of the colonies on a war footing.

Moreover, the democratic social system was a
disadvantage in such emergencies. Not only were
there lacking that cohesion, precision, and promptness which are the chief merits of an autocracy, but
the officers were chosen by the men whom they
were to lead; and while this was not seriously prej-
udicial in bush-ranging, it was inimical to good
work in protracted campaigns. Special conditions
were also often attached to enlistments, such as
freedom from service beyond the colonial boundaries;
and the men were particularly tenacious of their
privilege of returning home when their term of
service had expired. Serious results sometimes
occurred, because of this captious spirit, both in the
coming French and Indian and in the Revolutionary
wars. The attitude is comprehensible, however,
when we take into account the wide-spread jealousy,
then prevalent in the colonies, of the slightest infringement by those in authority upon the personal

liberty of the subject. Massachusetts was always
the strongest military colony and the most willing
to contribute to warlike enterprises, with Connecticut a close second; this largely because their assemblies, long trained in public affairs, had themselves well in hand, and consequently entertained
less fear of royal usurpation of privilege.

As to the soldierly quality of the English provincials, when once in the field, there can be but one
judgment. Hampered by their numerous and perplexing separatist tendencies, and their sometimes
painful and unmilitary striving after personal independence, they were numerous and possessed of
enormous material resources; they came of some
of the toughest fighting stock in Europe, and at
nearly every vantage-point in the wide and diversi-
fied field of operations which we are now to survey
in some detail, they acquitted themselves in a manner
of which their descendants may well feel proud;
though in all combined operations the inefficiency
of the diffuse colonial administration, for purposes
of war, was painfully manifest.

Under the treaty of Utrecht (1713), France had
acknowledged the suzerainty of the British king over
the Iroquois confederacy. This important admis-
sion had for thirty years been held in abeyance.
In June, 1744, it bore fruit. In a great council held
with the Iroquois at the Pennsylvania outpost of
Lancaster, the latter were bribed and cajoled into
formally granting to their English overlords entire

control of the Ohio Valley north of the river, under
the plea that the Iroquois had in various encounters
conquered the Shawnee of that region and were
therefore entitled to it.[1]   It is obvious that this was
a shallow pretext, but it served to strengthen the
English contention, by giving them something tangible to fight about; indeed, it was, so long as England held her colonies, accounted the corner-stone
on which they based their pretensions to the West.
As the war - paths of the Iroquois had extended
from the Ottawa River on the north to the Carolinas
on the south, and from the Mississippi to New England, the claim of their suzerain was almost as broad
as that of New France.

No sooner had they made pretence of giving to
the English that which they did not own than the
fickle Iroquois renewed negotiations with New
France; and five years later (1749) admitted through
the Chautauqua gateway another French reconnaissance in force.   Its commandant, Céleron de
Bienville,[2] was charged with the double purpose
of formally "taking possession" by the usual means
of planting at the mouth of principal streams leaden
plates[3] graven with the French claim, and of driving
out English traders.   The latter were found swarming into the country, and, although he imprisoned

[1] Detailed report in *Pa. Colonial Records*, IV., 698-737.
[2] Parkman, *Montcalm and Wolfe*, I., 36–62.
[3] Facsimiles of two of these plates in Hildreth, *Ohio Valley*,
20–23; De Hass, *Western Virginia*, 50; and *N. Y. Docs. Rel. to
Col. Hist.*, VI., 611.

four,[1] Céleron's report was discouraging. Governor Galissonière, of New France, accompanied this document by a plea for the shipment of ten thousand French peasants to settle the region before English agricultural pioneers could reach it; but the government at Versailles was just then indifferent to the colony, and the settlers were not sent.

The backwoodsmen of Virginia were not idle, however. Several of them had already explored, hunted, and made land claims in Kentucky. But more important than these was the fact that in 1748, the year preceding Céleron's vain endeavor to drive English traders out of the Ohio Valley, a little group of agricultural frontiersmen from the neighboring valley of Virginia settled permanently at Draper's Meadows, upon New (Greenbrier) River, thus planting the first stake for England upon west-flowing waters.[2]

In the very year of Céleron's expedition, there was chartered by the British king the Ohio Company, formed for fur-trading and colonizing purposes to the west of the mountains. It was a Virginia enterprise, designed in large part slyly to checkmate Pennsylvania, which, owing to internal dissensions, was tardy in taking steps to settle the Ohio basin. In this corporation were several provincials of social and political influence — among

[1] N. Y. Docs. Rel. to Col. Hist., X., 248.
[2] On the date of this settlement, see De Hass, *Western Virginia*, 41; Hale, *Trans-Allegheny Pioneers*, 16, 17.

them Washington's two brothers, Lawrence and
Augustine—together with a like group of English
gentlemen, chief of whom was John Hanbury, a
wealthy London merchant. The charter granted
to the company (May 19, 1749) a half-million acres
south of and along the Ohio River—"which lands
are his Majesty's undoubted right by the treaty of
Lancaster and subsequent treaties at Logstown"
(on the upper Ohio).[1] They were, in return for
this grant, to build a fort on the Ohio, and to plant
on their lands a hundred families within seven
years. Such was England's reply to the now freely
circulated rumor that France was proposing to con-
struct a line of posts along the Ohio, from its forks
(now Pittsburg) to its mouth.

Christopher Gist, widely known on the frontier
as a brave, intelligent, and tactful man, with long
experience among the western Indians, was promptly despatched (1750) to explore the country as far
down as the Falls of the Ohio (now Louisville), and
to select lands for the company, as well as to bear
friendly messages to the Shawnee, still dominant in
that region. He was instructed to select only "good
level land"; for, wrote the company's officers to
him, "we had rather go quite down to the Mississippi
than take mean, broken land." During this and the
following year, Gist explored within what are now
the states of Ohio, Kentucky, and West Virginia,
besides portions of western Maryland and south-

[1] *Dinwiddie Papers*, I., 72.

western Pennsylvania. He met many Scotch-Irish traders, whose centre of operations was at Picka-willany, an Indian village on the upper Miami, at Logstown, on the Ohio, eighteen miles below the forks, and at Venango, on the Alleghany; and for the benefit of posterity he kept an interesting journal of his expedition.[1] His favorable report greatly stimulated English interest in the west.

Meanwhile, the company constructed a fortified trading - house at Wills Creek (now Cumberland, Maryland), near the head of the Potomac; and by the aid of a prominent frontiersman, Colonel Thomas Cresap, and an Indian named Nemacolin, blazed a trail sixty miles long over the picturesque water - shed of the Laurel Hills, to the mouth of Redstone Creek (now Brownsville, Pennsylvania), on the Monongahela, where was built another stockade (1752). This path, which, with some later deflections, was destined to become famous in western history as "Nemacolin's Path," "Gist's Trace," "Washington's Road," "Braddock's Road," and "Cumberland Pike," successively, was at once followed by a few daring Virginia settlers, who planted themselves upon its western terminus.[2]

There had never been any commonly recognized boundaries between the North American colonies of

---

[1] First published in 1776, in Pownall, *Topographical Description of North America.* See Darlington, *Christopher Gist's Journals.*

[2] For details, see Lowdermilk, *Cumberland;* Crumrine, *Washington County* (Pa.); Hulbert, *Historic Highways*, III., IV.

France and England. The territorial claims of
neither nation had at any time previous to the war
been stated with definiteness by officials authorized
to do so. Claims fluctuated from time to time,
according to the policy of the hour or the temperament of the person making the contention. We
have seen[1] how variable were the French contentions regarding the extent of Acadia. The English
colonial charters included, at least by inference, all
of the interior westward to the Pacific. In general
it may be stated that France, during the greater part
of the half-century preceding the final struggle, was
willing to allow the English only the Atlantic slope
below the Kennebec and the height of land rimming
in the St. Lawrence to the south, and the region
north of the Spanish claims in eastern Louisiana.
Practically, the pretensions of the French were the
basin of the St. Lawrence and Great Lakes, and
the Winnipeg and Saskatchewan drainage systems,
and to the southward all of the continental interior
between the Appalachians and the Cordilleras, so
far as this region was not already occupied by the
Spanish of the southwest.[2]

Early in 1758, however, Montcalm made to the
department of war a definite and apparently careful
official statement of the territorial claims of New
France as follows—and this we may properly accept

[1] See chap. ii., above.
[2] See *Northern and Western Boundaries of Ontario*, 53–56, for
unofficial statements of ancient boundaries of Canada.

as a clear outline of the French contention at the
height of the war: " France must have at least possession of what England calls Acadia as far as the
Isthmus, and re-take Beauséjour; she must have the
River St. John; at least leave the River St. John in
the joint occupation of the Abenaqui and Mikmak
Indians.   Lake St. Sacrement to France, at least
neutral, not to be at liberty to erect forts on Wood
creek.   England will never renounce Fort Lydius
[Edward].   I believe it to be on her territory; to
engage her to do so, Carillon [Ticonderoga] must
be abandoned.   Lake Ontario, Lake Erie to France;
the English cannot erect forts on these lakes, nor
on any rivers emptying therein.   The height of
land, the natural boundary between France and
England as far as the Ohio; thereby the Apalachies
become the boundary for England; the Ohio to
belong to France, as well as Fort Duquesne, unless
a better fort can be made, and one better lo-
cated, for Fort Duquesne is good for nothing and
is falling.   To maintain the Five Nations independent and the Indians towards the River Sus-
quehanna called Delawares (*Loups*), and that neither
France nor England have power to erect forts
among those people." [1]

[1] Montcalm to De Paulmy, February 23, 1758, in *N. Y. Docs.
Rel. to Col. Hist.*, X., 690.

CHAPTER X

OUTBREAK OF WAR

(1752–1754)

BOTH French and English were awake to the immense strategic importance of the junction of the Monongahela and Alleghany Rivers — the "Forks of the Ohio," as it was then called. The former recognized in the Ohio Company's operations the unmistakable determination of their rivals forcibly and at once to occupy the great valley, under claims based upon the sea-to-sea provisions of the colonial charters. A report to the government made by Dumas, one of the frontier captains, declared that "all the resources of the state will never preserve Canada, if the English are once settled at the heads of these western rivers." [1]

In the spring of 1753 the French, anticipating the dilatory movements of the Virginians, who as usual lost much time in debating, built a stout log stockade, Fort le Bœuf, upon French Creek, a northern tributary of the Alleghany. This was intended to protect the woodland portage route from their newly constructed fort at Presq'isle, to

[1] Winsor, *Mississippi Basin,* 251.

be followed by another outpost at the Forks of the Ohio, one hundred and twenty miles to the south. Sickness in the camp had, however, prevented so extended an advance that season. The English trading-post of Venango, at the junction of French Creek and the Alleghany, was, nevertheless, seized and occupied by a small detachment from Le Bœuf.

In November the governor of Virginia, Dinwiddie, despatched Major George Washington, adjutant-general of the colonial militia, guided by Gist, to remonstrate with the French against occupying a district "so notoriously known to be the property of the Crown of Great Britain."[1] Washington was then a land surveyor, only twenty-one years of age, and represented one of the foremost of the Virginia families. After a dreary and hazardous winter journey over mountains and through tangled forests, Washington and his small party of attendants arrived late in November, first at Venango and then at Le Bœuf. The latter's commandant received the envoy with marked politeness, but returned word to Dinwiddie that he should remain on the ground and await the orders of his superior, the Marquis Duquesne, then governor of Canada.

The Ohio Company, in whose particular interest this mission had been undertaken, was not popular with the Virginia assembly, just then engaged in a quarrel with the governor over land-patent fees.

[1] *N. Y. Docs. Rel. to Col. Hist.*, X., 258.

But several of the court party were privately concerned in the project as an investment; and although France and England were at peace, Dinwiddie and his council decided to force matters by a measure which bore a decidedly warlike appearance. Late in 1753, after the usual haggling with his assembly, the governor, in behalf of the company, despatched a party of men under Captain William Trent to build a log fort at the forks. In January the governor wrote to his friend Lord Fairfax that he had further decided, with consent of the council, "to send immediately out 200 Men to protect those already sent by the Ohio Comp' to build a Fort, and to resist any Attempts on them. I have Commission'd Major George Washington, the Bearer hereof, to command." In order to stimulate enlistment, which owing to popular indifference was extremely slow, the governor offered two hundred thousand acres of land on the Ohio to be divided among the men and officers of the expedition[1]—a part of the three million acres of western lands to which at various times up to 1757 Virginia assumed to give title.

Dinwiddie found it difficult to induce the deputies to vote supplies for this enterprise, but finally they were, in February, 1754, persuaded to grant him the slender allowance of £10,000. Of the other colonies interested, North Carolina alone offered aid, her grant being sufficient to maintain three or four hundred men in the field; while the home govern-

---

[1] *Journal of Washington* (Toner's ed.), 5.

ment allowed the use of regulars from New York and the Carolinas. But none of these arrived on the scene until after the crash in July. On the last day of March, disappointed at the non-arrival of the Carolina troops, and hearing nothing from New York, Washington, now a lieutenant - colonel, felt impelled to set forth with his three hundred Virginia frontiersmen, "towards the Ohio, there to help Captain Trent to build Forts, and to defend the possessions of his Majesty against the attempts and hostilities of the French." [1] His orders were "to be on the Defensive, but if oppos'd by the Enemy, to desire them to retire; if they sh'd still persist, to repel Force by Force." [2]

Meanwhile, Trent's little company of thirty-three men had in January commenced a stockade at the forks. But in April a force of French and Indians, aggregating more than twenty times their number, aided by eighteen pieces of light artillery, swept down the Alleghany in sixty bateaux and many canoes, and on April 17 compelled the fort-builders to surrender. The prisoners were promptly released without harm, and allowed to retreat to Wills Creek, where Washington met them. Both he and Dinwiddie took the attitude that the forcible expulsion of British troops from British territory was essentially an act of war. The mission to the Forks of the Ohio had now taken on a very dan-

[1] *Journal of Washington* (Toner's ed.), 7.
[2] *Pa. Colonial Records*, VI., 32.

gerous aspect; but notwithstanding the non-arrival
of the promised reinforcements from New York
and North Carolina, Colonel Washington set forth
with his little army upon the over-mountain path,
determined to succeed where Trent had failed.

Along Nemacolin's Path over the undulating
Laurel Hills were two treeless, springy valleys—
the Little and Great Meadows—where the pack-
trains of fur-traders in their trans-Alleghany trips
would unlimber, that the horses might be refreshed
upon the sweet grasses of these natural pastures.
In the last week of May, Washington arrived at
Great Meadows, within a few days' march of the
forks, and selected this as his military base.

The French had, in the interval, rapidly pushed
to completion and extended Trent's work, calling
their stronghold Fort Duquesne. Here had been
gathered a considerable force of Canadians, regulars, and Indian allies, a detachment from which,
led by Coulon de Jumonville, persistently dogged
Nemacolin's Path and kept Washington well in
sight. Upon May 28, at the head of a scouting
party, the latter stumbled upon Jumonville, who
was in hiding. Suspecting the intentions of an
enemy who had already captured a British fort in
time of nominal peace between the two nations,
and was now suspiciously haunting his path, the
Virginia colonel promptly attacked. "The action,"
laconically writes Washington in his journal, "only
lasted a quarter of an hour before the enemy was

routed." In this brief time had been fired a train which led at once to a general conflagration. Washington had discharged the first shot in the French and Indian War, for the Trent affair had been bloodless.[1]

The Virginians lost but one killed and two wounded, but of the French ten were killed, one wounded, and twenty-one taken prisoners. Among the French dead was Jumonville. His compatriots at once worked themselves into a frenzy over what they called his "assassination," claiming that he was but bearing to Washington peaceful despatches. There appears to be small basis for such a contention —judicious peace messengers do not hide for days on the flanks of the enemy and act like spies.[2]

On receipt of the news, Coulon de Villiers, the brother of Jumonville, set out from Fort Duquesne at the head of an avenging expedition, which proceeded in boats up the Monongahela to Redstone Creek; whereupon Washington withdrew to Great Meadows, where he erected a "fort with small palisades." The place was unfit for defence, for on three sides higher ground, heavily forested, approached closely to the stockade. But the Virginians were by this time sorely distressed for provisions, ammunition, and other supplies, and

[1] Washington's "Journal," in *Writings* (Ford's ed.), I., 74, 75, 88, 90. See also Toner's edition, with notes by French authorities.

[2] *Ibid.*, 77–90; correspondence between Druillon and Dinwiddie, in *Va. Hist. Collections*, I., 225–228.

did not deem it wise to retreat farther; hence the stockade was, in token of their desperate stage, called Fort Necessity.

Here, on July 3, from eleven in the morning until eight o'clock of a dark, rainy night, the ragged little band stood siege at the hands of a skilled and desperate enemy, whites and savages, aggregating double their number and enjoying the advantage of natural cover. It was useless longer to contend against such odds, and Washington signed articles of capitulation[1] in the midst of a storm so fierce that it was with difficulty that the candle, brought to illumine the pages, could be kept lighted.

In this document, which was written in French, Villiers played a petty trick by inserting a phrase in which Jumonville was said to have been "assassinated" by the English. None of the Virginia officers being able to read French, a Dutch colleague named Van Braam, who had conducted the negotiations for them, essayed a verbal translation, which in the midst of the tempest was necessarily a brief summary. Whether Van Braam so rendered it or not, the officers understood him to state that the killing of Jumonville was referred to in the paper as either a "death" or a "loss." Washington himself afterwards indignantly wrote that, "we were wilfully or ignorantly deceived by our interpreter in regard to the word *assassination*." The French, on their part, were much elated over the signatures of the Vir-

---

[1] Text in *Pa. Archives*, II., 145, 146.

ginians "confessing," even unwittingly, to the truth
of the former's allegation.[1]

The number of French and Indians engaged in this
affair is unknown.   Their loss was stated by Villiers
as two killed — one Frenchman and one Indian;
seriously wounded—fifteen French and two Indians;
besides many others slightly hurt.   Of Washington's
three hundred men, he tells us in his " Journal "
that twelve were killed and forty-three wounded.

At daybreak of July 4 the "buckskin general"
—as the French sneeringly called him—marched
out over Nemacolin's Path towards Wills Creek,
a toilsome journey of fifty miles across the mountains, the heart - sick officers and men bearing
their baggage on their backs and their wounded on
stretchers.   They were suffered to carry one swivel
with them, for defence from the savages who hung
upon their flanks, and to spike the eight left behind
them in the fort.

The expedition had failed, but through no fault
of Washington.   An expert frontiersman and Indian
fighter, despite his youth, his own part had been
well played throughout, with a proper admixture
of dash, bravery, and caution, and his men had
conducted themselves with commendable coolness.
The delay of the Virginia deputies had caused his

[1] Villiers's "Journal," cited in Parkman, *Montcalm and Wolfe*,
I., 158, and II., App., 421–423.   Synopsized, without reference
to the "confession," in *N. Y. Docs. Rel. to Col. Hist.*, X, 260–
262.

arrival on the scene too late for effective action; a month earlier, and the result would probably have been quite a different story. As Dinwiddie, nettled at being outmanœuvred by the French, but not blaming his little army, wrote: "If the assembly had voted the money in November which they did in February, the post would have been built and garrisoned before the French approached." [1]

As for the two companies of regulars from New York, they arrived on the scene after it was all over, undisciplined, lacking ammunition, tents, and supplies of every sort, and generally useless. The North Carolina militia, still less competent, mutinied en route and scattered to their homes without ever reaching Wills Creek. [2]

Upon news of Washington's defeat, practically all of the British traders and pioneers in the country beyond the mountains withdrew to the older settlements. After the middle of July, New France was once more in complete possession of the west. The gravity of the situation appealed more strongly to Dinwiddie than to any other of the provincial governors, save of course Shirley, of Massachusetts, who as a close student of American affairs had a keen perception of the crisis now at hand. These two leaders commenced a campaign for a concerted intercolonial movement against the French, whom Dinwiddie stigmatized as "troublesome people and

[1] Fortescue, *British Army*, 266.
[2] *Ibid.*, 267; Parkman, *Montcalm and Wolfe*, I., 162.

enemies of mankind," who had invaded "the undoubted limits of His Majesty's dominion."

None of the assemblies, outside of Virginia and
New England, rose to the necessities of the case.
Even the Virginia burgesses, seeking to gain concessions from the governor, at first persisted in at-
taching riders to the grants which were requested
from them, until Dinwiddie cried in desperation,
"A governor is really to be pitied in the discharge
of his duty to his king and country, in having to
do with such obstinate, self - conceited people."[1]
However, after a protracted wrangle they finally
voted him sufficient for his needs.   Governor Hamilton, in Pennsylvania, quarrelled all summer with
his obstinate assembly, composed in the main of
Quaker shop - keepers, whose religious principles
were opposed to war, and of peace-loving, thrifty
Germans, who wanted but to till their acres, and
concerned themselves little whether Frenchmen or
Englishmen were their political masters.   They told
the governor that they were willing to give him
£20,000, but on conditions which he could not
accept and be faithful to either his proprietors
or his king; moreover, some of the members in-
timated that they did not propose to assist Virginia
in pulling her chestnuts from the fire.[2]   The New

[1] Dinwiddie to Hamilton, September 6, 1754, and to J. Aber-
crombie, September 1, 1754, MSS. in British Record Office.
[2] *Pa. Colonial Records*, VI., 168, 178, 184 – 186, 299, 300;
Olden Time, II., 225.

York assembly, having little knowledge of or concern in a country so far away as the Ohio, at first
refused to believe that the French had actually invaded English territory; but at last they voted a
tardy grant of £5000. New Jersey, having no Indian frontier to protect, with selfish bluntness declined to take part. Maryland contributed £6000.
New England alone, controlled by Massachusetts,
was really eager and willing to enter the strife;
everywhere else the bulk of the people were sluggish-
ly indifferent.

While these scant preparations went forward in
the provinces, Dinwiddie was persistently appealing
for assistance to the home authorities, who slowly
awakened to some sense of the importance of helping
their colonists regain the country back from France,
and in general asserting the right of Great Britain
to the west. But the Duke of Newcastle, then
prime-minister, was of stuff too weak for a national
crisis, and his propositions to Parliament were quite
inadequate. The net result of his aid was the
shipment to Virginia of £10,000 in specie, two thousand stand of arms, and two Irish regiments of
five hundred men each, the design being to increase
them to the standard numbers by American enlistments. The Duke of Cumberland, commander-in-
chief of the army, selected as the leader of this force
General Edward Braddock, "an officer of forty-five
years' service, rough, brutal, and insolent, a martinet
of the narrowest type, but wanting neither spirit nor

ability, and brave as a lion." [1]   It was also ordered
that two new regiments of the line be raised in
America, with a thousand men each, under the
colonelcies of Shirley and Pepperrell—the former,
it will be remembered, having sponsored and the
latter commanded the expedition against Louisburg
in 1745. [2]

A few wise men had long favored some form of
union to secure intercolonial action in great public emergencies.   The New England Confederation
(1643–1684), which sought to bind together the four
northern colonies in "a firm and perpetual league
of friendship and amity for offence and defence,
mutual advice and succor, upon all just occasions,"
was little more than a committee of public safety. [3]
The first continental conference, held at Albany in
1690, for treating with the Iroquois against the
common enemy, has already been alluded to. [4]   It
was, however, the government party which usually
urged formal unions, and consequently they were
unkindly looked upon as a possible vehicle for royal control.   Several times during the Indian wars
there were held informal neighborhood congresses,
chiefly to negotiate with the tribesmen or for common defence; these were principally attended by
the official class, and attracted little popular atten-

---

[1] Fortescue, *British Army*, 268.   [2] See chap. vii., above.
[3] Tyler, *England in America* (*Am. Nation*, V.), chap. xviii.
[4] Frothingham, *Rise of the Republic*, 89–93; see also chap. ii.,
above.

tion, although they served in a measure to accustom the people to the spectacle of colonial union for matters of common interest.

The first really significant colonial congress was held in 1754 at Albany, then a palisaded frontier village of twenty-six hundred people. The previous August, Lord Holdernesse, British secretary of state, addressed a note to the governors urging them to resist French territorial encroachments, even to the use of armed force. This was followed in September by a letter to the governors from the Lords of Trade, directing them to hold a convention to treat with the Iroquois — just then being tampered with by the French—and if not possible to secure their alliance, at least to obtain a promise of neutrality. The governors were to "take care that all the provinces be comprised, if practicable, in one great treaty." The provinces were also urged to adopt "articles of union and confederation with each other for the mutual defence of his Majesty's subjects and interests in North America, as well in time of peace as war."

The congress met at Albany on June 19, being presided over by Lieutenant - Governor Delancy, of New York. Massachusetts and New York each sent five commissioners, New Hampshire and Pennsylvania four each, Connecticut three, and Rhode Island and Maryland each two—twenty-five in all. Among them were some of the most prominent men in the English colonies, those best known

in our day being Thomas Hutchinson of Massachusetts, Stephen Hopkins of Rhode Island, William
Johnson of New York, and Benjamin Franklin of
Pennsylvania. Hutchinson and Franklin were respectively the strongest types of the aristocratic
and popular parties.

In the last week of June the commissioners met a
hundred and fifty Iroquois chiefs in council. Hen-
drick, a Mohawk sachem, dominated his fellows,
and was not slow to taunt the English with the
feeble character of their occupation of the country. "Look at the French: they are men; they are
fortifying everywhere. But you are all like women,
bare and open, without fortifications." The conference was in this regard without tangible results.
The chiefs were loaded with presents; but the
commissioners not having the power to grant all of
the numerous native demands, the tribesmen returned home obviously dissatisfied.

Meanwhile a committee of seven of the ablest men
in the congress considered at length a plan of union.
This was finally draughted by Franklin upon July
10, and tentatively adopted the same day. Only
the New England members were authorized to enter
into a definite agreement relative to confederation.
It was necessary that the plan be laid before the
provinces, and later transmitted to Whitehall for
ratification. The scheme provided for the appoint-
ment and support by the crown of a president-
general, and the formation of a grand, or federal,

council composed of representatives from each province, and to meet once a year. The president-general was to possess the veto power over the council's acts, the right of nominating military officers and commissioning all officials, and, in conjunction with the council, to have the management of Indian affairs. The council was to elect a speaker, make treaties with the Indians, control public lands, enact laws, levy taxes, nominate civil officers, jointly control all expenditures, raise and pay soldiers, build forts, and appoint not only a federal treasurer, but one in each province; and unless its laws were disapproved by the king within three years they should remain in force. Local colonial administration was not to be interfered with.[1]

The congress had attracted but small attention from the general public, and each of the assemblies promptly rejected the plan, even Massachusetts men not being "inclined to part with so great a share of power as was to be given to this general government."[2] The Privy Council took no action, and the Lords of Trade thought it un-English. Franklin thus summarized the causes of opposition: "The Crown disapproved of it, as having too much weight

---

[1] Text in Franklin, *Writings* (Sparks's ed.), III., 36–55; see also *N. Y. Docs. Rel. to Col. Hist.*, VI., for documents appertaining to the congress; *Journal of Proceedings*, in Mass. Hist. Soc., *Collections*, 3d series, V.; general discussion in Frothingham, *Rise of the Republic*, 134–149; Foster, "Hopkins," in *R. I. Hist. Tracts*, XIX., chap. vi.

[2] Hutchinson, *Hist. of Mass. Bay*, III., 23.

in the democratic form of the constitution, and every assembly as having allowed too much to prerogative."[1] No further attempts at formal colonial union were made, until out of the stress of the Revolution was evolved the Continental Congress which signed the Declaration of Independence.

[1] *Carey's American Museum* (1789), V., 368; Frothingham, *Rise of the Republic*, 149.

CHAPTER XI

A YEAR OF DISASTER

(1755)

GENERAL BRADDOCK arrived at Alexandria with his two regiments towards the end of March (1755), and at his camp was held (April 14) a conference between the governors of Virginia, Massachusetts, New York, Pennsylvania, and Maryland. Shirley, although without military experience in the field, had already planned a campaign, and his ideas were in the main adopted by the general. Four expeditions were determined upon: Braddock and his column were to undertake an offensive campaign against Fort Duquesne; Shirley, with Pepperrell second in command, was with the two freshly recruited regiments to attack the French fort at Niagara, and thus seize upon the lake route to the west; William Johnson, not a military man, but possessed of immense influence over the Iroquois and other tribes allied with the English, was to lead the provincial militia from New England and New York against Crown Point, on Lake Champlain, with the design of checking the French advance from the north and furnishing a base for an ultimate British

173

expedition against Montreal; and, lastly, Lieutenant-
Colonel Robert Monckton was to proceed to the
isthmus connecting the Nova-Scotian peninsula with
the continent, and by reducing Fort Beauséjour and
its dependent stockades to cut off Acadia from
New France and render it possible to subdue this
hotbed of French-Indian forays against the New
England borders.

Military critics now consider that it was a mis-
taken policy to divide the attack on the French
centre by sending expeditions against both Fort
Duquesne and Fort Niagara, and that better results
might have been obtained had the English assault
been concentrated upon the latter.   Another undoubtedly just criticism is that Braddock committed
a fatal blunder in following Washington's wilderness
road to the Ohio, and making Fort Cumberland
his principal base.   It was a circuitous, rough, and
unsettled route, lacking in forage and transport, and
affording abundant cover for his foes; whereas, had
he proceeded westward from Philadelphia, he would
have had the advantage, much of the way, of a
settled country abounding in supplies and the means
of transport.[1]

Virginia was poorly supplied with wagons and
horses, for rivers and bays were her principal routes
of commerce, so that these had to be obtained in
Pennsylvania, where Franklin's prestige alone succeeded in wheedling them out of the reluctant

[1] Fortescue, *British Army*, 270.

people. Braddock wrote (June 5) to the secretary of state for the colonies: "I desired Mr. B. Franklin, post master of Pennsylvania, who has great credit in that province, to hire me one hundred and fifty waggons and the number of horses necessary, which he did with so much goodness and readiness, that it is almost the first instance of integrity, address and ability that I have seen in all these provinces." [1]

All this occasioned great delay, which was not decreased by the bad blood soon evident between Braddock and the provincial militia, whom he and his officers treated with insufferable arrogance. However, he invited Washington to be of his staff, with rank of major, which indicated that the general was not altogether insensible to the value of local knowledge and methods. On his part, the young major appears to have developed a certain fondness for the brave but blustering veteran of Fontenoy, who must not be overblamed, for he himself was the victim of Newcastle's weakness in being sent out with insufficient and unsuitable men and equipment suddenly to face conditions never before confronted by a British general.

On May 10 the column reached Fort Cumberland. The two regular regiments had now been recruited up to seven hundred men each; there were a few artillerymen and "handy" marines; the Virginia militia numbered four hundred and fifty picked Indian fighters, who knew the rules of the game and proved

[1] *Olden Time*, II., 237.

the backbone of the expedition, although these buckskin-clad backwoods settlers, who obeyed only their own popularly elected officers—and those none too well — were as yet held in contempt by the veteran regulars; and fifty Indians, gay in warpaint and feathers, served as scouts, much to the amazement of Tommy Atkins, who was not accustomed to serving with such outlandish allies.[1]

Braddock well understood European tactics, and had a fine reputation at home; but he was now amid conditions heretofore undreamed of by him; moreover, he was not an organizer. He wasted just a month waiting for his cannon, so that it was June 10 before he started to cross the divide. Washington's road had to be widened for the artillery and transport wagons. Three hundred axemen cleared the way, but progress was so slow that in eight days only thirty miles had been covered, and men and horses were worn out and ailing. Braddock's deliberateness—for he stopped "to level every molehill and to throw a bridge over every brook"[2]—was exasperating to the provincials, who realized that haste was necessary.

Sixteen days out from Fort Cumberland, news came that the French had taken advantage of the English delay to throw an additional force into Fort Duquesne, and that a détachment therefrom was awaiting them on the path. On Washington's advice,

---

[1] Parkman, *Montcalm and Wolfe*, I., 263.
[2] Fortescue, *British Army*, 273.

Braddock selected twelve hundred men, with a few cannon, wagons, and pack-horses, and pushed forward to meet the enemy. Colonel Dunbar was to follow at a slower pace, in charge of the heavy baggage and the reserves. On July 8, 1755, at the mouth of Turtle Creek, an affluent of the Monongahela, eight miles from Fort Duquesne, Braddock's way led through a "wide and bushy ravine." The road was filled with the wagons and artillery, the soldiers marched through the woods on either side, and flanking parties and Indian scouts ranged still farther afield. There was certainly no lack of caution.

The commandant of the fort, Contrecœur, had now in garrison a few companies of seasoned French regulars, a large body of Canadian militia, every man of them familiar with the tactics of bushranging, and some nine hundred Indians gathered from the Ohio River and points as far west as Michigan and Wisconsin.[1] He detached Captain Beaujeu, with 70 regulars, 150 Canadians, and 650 Indians, to meet Braddock's advance. For several days previous to reaching the fatal ravine, where were stationed Beaujeu and his main party, the column had suffered slightly from individual Indian attacks upon its flanks, and, as the march proceeded, signs of the hovering enemy multiplied.

It was long believed that Beaujeu ambushed

---

[1] There is a tradition, not verifiable, that Pontiac, afterwards famous in our annals, headed the Ottawa from eastern Michigan.

Braddock. This is not so; what occurred was a regulation forest fight, in which the French and their allies flanked the British on either side, drove them in towards the road, and, from behind the trees or fallen trunks, poured into the struggling, disordered mass of men and horses a withering fire, while they themselves were completely hidden.

Had Braddock left his men to their own devices, it is possible that the day might even here have been saved. The Virginians, as a matter of course, adopted the Indian method of seeking individual cover, and—to use a term now familiar to us, as a product of the British-Boer war—"sniping" the assailants. Many of the British soldiers, no longer contemptuous of the border sharp-shooters, attempted to follow their example; but Braddock, with an utter disregard of self, rode to and fro—four horses being shot under him—deriding his men as "cowardly curs," and driving them with the flat of his sword back into the ranks. Here, in their bright scarlet coats, they were not only mowed down by the enemy like a field of poppies, but their own blind volleys were disastrous to the provincials in front of them. Washington indignantly wrote to Dinwiddie that only thirty Virginians were left alive out of three companies, "while the dastardly behavior of the English soldiers exposed all those who were inclined to do their duty to almost certain death. . . . Two thirds of both killed and wounded received

their shots from our own cowardly dogs of soldiers."[1]

Beaujeu was killed early in the fray, whereupon
his men fled precipitately; but his second, Dumas,
rallied them to a fresh attack. The honors of the
day, however, such as they were, lay largely with
Charles de Langlade, a Wisconsin fur-trader, who,
independently of Dumas, headed his savage band of
Chippewa, Menominee, Potawatomi, Ottawa, and
Huron from the upper lakes, in the final assault
which at the end of two hours of hideous tumult
shattered the British column.[2]

" — Down the long trail, from the Fort to the ford,
  Naked and streaked, plunge a moccasin'd horde:
  Huron and Wyandot, hot for the bout;
  Shawnee and Ottawa, barring him out!

" 'Twixt the pit and the crest, 'twixt the rocks and the
        grass,
  Where the bush hides the foe and the foe holds the
        pass,
  Beaujeu and Pontiac, striving amain;
  Huron and Wyandot, jeering the slain!"[3]

Braddock himself was pierced through an arm
and the lungs just as the break occurred, and it
fell to Major Washington, whose uniform was riddled

---

[1] Washington, *Writings* (Ford's ed.), I., 173–175.
[2] *Wis. Hist. Collections*, III., 212–215, VII., 130–135; Lowdermilk, *Cumberland*, 176–178; Parkman, *Montcalm and Wolfe*,
II., App., 425, 426.
[3] John Williamson Palmer, "Ned Braddock," in *Yale Alumni
Weekly*, October 28, 1903.

with bullets and who had performed many feats of valor upon the field, to conduct the retreat to Christopher Gist's "plantation" near by, after failing to rally the panic-stricken horde. As for Dunbar, with the heavy reserves, he had (July 2) gone into camp high up on the Laurel Hills. When news came of the cruel disaster in the ravine, panic at once overcame him and his men. Assistance to Braddock was unthought of, ammunition and stores were destroyed by wholesale,[1] and a disgraceful and disorderly flight ensued all the way back to Fort Cumberland.[2] Among the fleeing wagoners in this sorry rout, riding one of his horses whose traces he had cut, was young Daniel Boone, then a borderer on the uplands of North Carolina.[3]

Nothing was now left for the decimated advance but to follow the cowardly reserves, which they did in a far more orderly and leisurely fashion; for it was evident that, contrary to the reports of frenzied stragglers, the French and Indians were not pursuing them. Indeed, the latter had, when contemplating the frightful slaughter wrought in the defile, themselves become panic-stricken in their fear of vengeance, and were flying northward almost as fast as the British were scurrying back over the ill-fated path of Nemacolin. July 10, while upon the sad march, Braddock died from his wounds, his last words being, "Another time we shall know better

---

[1] Orme's account in Lowdermilk, *Cumberland*, 181.
[2] *Ibid.*, 183.   [3] Thwaites, *Daniel Boone*, 21.

how to deal with them." He had learned his lesson, but too late to apply it.[1] On the 17th the last
of the dismal train arrived under shelter of Fort
Cumberland.

The disaster was complete. Fort Duquesne had
not been taken, and much ground had been lost,
in territory as well as prestige. Probably not a
British settler or trader now remained west of the
mountains. The French continued in absolute control of the trans-Alleghany country, and now even
held sway eastward of the Laurel Hills, to within
sight of Fort Cumberland, a condition of affairs
destined to last through three years to come. Large
stores of costly ammunition, supplies, and transport had ruthlessly been destroyed; and of the force
of nineteen hundred men sent into the field less
than five hundred were unharmed, against a loss to
the allied enemy of about twenty-five.

The expedition against Crown Point, under William Johnson, comprised three thousand raw provincials from New England and some three hundred Indians. Provincial jealousies and faulty organization caused the usual delay, so that it was
well into July before camp was formed at Albany,
which had been selected as the base. About the
middle of August the column moved leisurely up

[1] Sargeant, *Braddock's Expedition*, 233–237. For description
of Jumonville's camp, the site of Fort Necessity, Braddock's
grave, and Dunbar's camp, as they appear to-day, see Thwaites.
"A Day on Braddock's Road," in *How George Rogers Clark
Won the Northwest*, etc.

the Hudson to the "great carrying place" between
that river and Lake George, and here Fort Edward
(at first called Fort Lyman), a stockaded storehouse,
was commenced.   Five hundred men being kept
here to complete the work and guard it, a provok-
ingly slow advance was made along the fourteen-
mile portage to the lake.

While the provincials were thus wasting time, the
French were active.   Duquesne had been replaced
as governor of New France by the Marquis de
Vaudreuil, who in the spring (1755) sailed for
Canada in company with Baron Dieskau as com-
mander-in-chief and several battalions of regulars.
Documents found on the field of Braddock's defeat had given ample information of the English
plans of campaign, so that Johnson discovered
Dieskau awaiting him near the end of the path with
3573 regulars, Canadians, and savages.   Several
skirmishes ensued, in one of which five hundred of
the English were caught and crushed in an ambuscade, and in another Dieskau was not only defeated but himself wounded and taken prisoner.
This advantage, however, Johnson failed to follow up,
and, pleading illness, scarcity of food and ammunition, and the undoubted lack of discipline and harmony among his troops, he frittered away his time
until the close of November.   He built Fort William
Henry at the foot of Lake George, but left Crown
Point untouched.   The expedition was a failure;
nevertheless, the home government, probably in

view of his Iroquois ascendency, made him a baronet and obtained for him a parliamentary grant of
£5000.[1]

Despite his planning of the Louisburg campaign
eleven years before, Governor Shirley was unfitted
to command the enterprise of reducing Fort Niagara. His colleague, Pepperrell, had gained some
experience during the Cape Breton affair, but was
likewise unequal to the present emergency. Their
two regiments of gayly uniformed but undisciplined
provincial recruits of the line—in "silver-laced hat,"
"fine scarlet broadcloth," and "hair or wigs pow-
dered"[2]—were joined by a militia regiment from
New Jersey, the column aggregating twenty-five
hundred men.

Rendezvousing at Albany in July, the party ascended the Mohawk in bateaux to the great portage (at Rome), and crossing through the dense
forest over to Wood Creek, with their boats on
sledges, thence descended to Fort Ontario, at
Oswego. But the French, of course now quite
aware of all the English plans, had thrown a large
reinforcement into Fort Frontenac (the present
Kingston), which served completely to checkmate
Shirley; for that officer at once realized that he
must now first reduce Kingston, else as soon as he

[1] *N. Y. Docs. Rel. to Col. Hist.*, VII., 158; Stone, *Sir William
Johnson*, I., 526, 554.
[2] Letter of Sergeant James Gray, in Parkman, *Montcalm and
Wolfe*, I., 321.

was embarked on the lake for Niagara the former garrison would cross over and capture his base. Lacking in supplies, which failed to follow him in season—the commissariat and transportation were generally weak, on the English side, through lack of organization—Shirley deemed it inadvisable to attempt this double task, and therefore left for home at the close of October. The only result of his venture was the leaving of a garrison of seven hundred men at Oswego, as a menace to French operations on the Great Lakes.[1]

Monckton's expedition against Fort Beauséjour, on the Acadian isthmus, was the only successful enterprise of the season.   We have already referred[2] to the sad condition of the *habitants* and fishermen of Acadia.   The treaty of Utrecht (1713) had given them "liberty to remove themselves within a year to any other place, as they shall think fit, with all their movable effects."   But although they were anxious to betake themselves to Cape Breton and Prince Edward Island, various obstacles were placed in their path by Lieutenant - Governor Vetch, who represented to the authorities in London that their removal would "wholly strip and Ruine Nova Scotia," and "at once make Cape Brittoun a populous and well stocked Colony" of France.[3]   Forced,

---

[1] *N. Y. Docs. Rel. to Col. Hist.*, VI., 953–959, 994–996; *Pa. Archives*, II., 338, 348, 381, 402, 413–437; *N. H. Provincial Papers*, VI., 432.   [2] See chap. vi., above.
[3] Documents in Richard, *Acadia*, I., 73–98.

therefore, against their will to remain under the English flag, it is not unnatural that the majority of them, especially when so advised by their priests, should decline to take the oath of allegiance to the British king, whom they execrated as a heretic and whose race they despised. They were, indeed, kept in a constant ferment of disaffection by the French military and ecclesiastical agents who circulated freely among them. Not only was this spirit preventing Great Britain from developing the Nova Scotia peninsula, but British authority actually extended no farther than could be seen from the walls of the few forts erected by the conquerors—chief among them being Annapolis and Halifax.

These posts were weak, and geographically isolated from the other colonies, so that the garrisons lived in perpetual fear of being overwhelmed by the settlers and their aboriginal friends, who were equally of a warlike disposition; for Acadia, which for a full century past had been a centre for French and Indian forays against New England, could now muster on occasion two thousand experienced French bush-rangers and a much larger contingent of savage and half-breed allies. When the present troubles arose, the French had converted Fort Beauséjour into a formidable stronghold, which controlled the entire neck of connecting land, and many of the most active Acadian hotheads had removed to its neighborhood. The majority of the *habitants*, however, remained peacefully but stub-

bornly upon their diked fields in the long and adjacent tidal basins of Annapolis and Mines, which
were then, as they still are, the "garden" of Nova
Scotia.[1]

The situation was uncomfortable for all concerned.
The French authorities, with small regard for the
welfare of the Acadians, were using them merely as
pawns in the international game. Proceeding on
the contention, which was certainly admissible under the clumsy phrasing of the treaty of Utrecht—
although long usage was to the contrary — that
Acadia meant simply Annapolis and its immediate
neighborhood, New France was now claiming the
greater part of Nova Scotia. Fort Beauséjour and
two or three outlying posts constituted the opening
wedge of occupation. The French were using every
possible means to inflame the Acadians to attack
the Kennebec border while New England was busy
in the west, and plans were hatching to concentrate
troops at Louisburg for this purpose.[2] It therefore
seemed to the British of the utmost importance that
a blow should be struck at Beauséjour, and the
threatened inroad prevented. Moreover, from the
naval point of view, with Acadia lost, Great Britain's
hold upon the Gulf of St. Lawrence, the chief gateway to New France, would be greatly weakened;

[1] Richard, *Acadia*, chaps. xix.–xxvi.
[2] Shirley's correspondence with the British ministry, in
1754–1755, the originals of which are in the Record Office at
London, and are cited by Parkman, *Montcalm and Wolfe*, give
ample evidence of this.

and this it was necessary to maintain for the great and final struggle for continental mastery which could not much longer be postponed.

Monckton's force consisted of a few regulars and two thousand untrained New England volunteers, who, sailing up the Bay of Fundy, arrived before Fort Beauséjour on June 1.[1] The commandant of the fortress was Duchambon de Vergor, a rascally fellow, who, under the patronage of the notorious Intendant Bigot, had enriched himself by wholesale peculation. With him was associated Le Loutre, a fanatical missionary who had been prominent in the work of securing the Acadians to the French and who took a large part in the present defence. After a fortnight's siege the fort was surrendered; and word coming from Louisburg that no assistance could be rendered because British ships were blockading that harbor, Acadia was at the mercy of Monckton.

There was now committed by him and his assistants an act of harshness which doubtless was sanctioned by the stern necessities of war, for by its operation Acadia ceased thenceforth to be a problem to the military authorities of England. But the result was wide-spread misery; and when it is considered that this unhappy people had in the previous generation, forty years before, been kept in the country against their will, we may well consider this event one of the most lamentable in the history of the British advance in America.

[1] Parkman, *Montcalm and Wolfe*, I., 241–247.

Allowed one last opportunity to take the oath of allegiance, the Acadians, inspired by their priests, once more deliberately refused. Thereupon their houses, lands, and cattle were peremptorily confiscated, and nearly seven thousand of them—somewhat less than a half of the population of the entire peninsula—were in October packed aboard transports, with little regard for their comfort or health, and unloaded as houseless paupers at various English settlements along the coast, all the way from Massachusetts to Georgia. For the most part they suffered untold hardships before adapting themselves to their new surroundings. Many settled in France, and in Santo Domingo and other West India islands; but nearly all of these eventually (1784–1787), after thirty years of "suffering all the heart-burnings of separation, exile, death, misery in all its multitudinous forms," found an asylum among the people of their own speech and blood in the then Spanish-dominated province of Louisiana, where their descendants form to-day a distinct agricultural population. Others, upon the return of peace, crept back "in a long and dolorous pilgrimage" to their beloved and once-happy Acadia, to find men of another tongue and race in possession of their homes and flocks and fields, and they themselves compelled to seek shelter elsewhere and begin life anew. The majority, however, were permanently absorbed by the English provinces.[1]

[1] Richard, *Acadia*, II., 341, 342, discusses their destination.

CHAPTER XII

GUARDING THE WESTERN FRONTIER
(1755–1756)

THE news of Braddock's defeat spread throughout the west like a forest fire. Dunbar's disgraceful withdrawal of the reserves was followed by
his complete abandonment of the frontier; despite
the frantic appeals of the Virginians, he left them
in the lurch and marched to Philadelphia. Dinwiddie wrote to Captain Orme of the regulars:
"Your great colonel has gone to a peaceful colony,
and left our frontiers open. . . . The whole conduct
of Colonel Dunbar appears to me monstrous. . . .
To march off all the regulars, and leave the fort
[Cumberland] and frontiers to be defended by four
hundred sick and wounded, and the poor remains
of our provincial forces, appears to me absurd."[1]
Unwonted activity at once ensued on the part of
the French. Dumas, succeeding Contrecœur at
Fort Duquesne, despatched runners among the
Shawnee, Delawares, and Mingo, former friends of
the English, bearing the message that the latter
were soon to be driven into the sea, and inducing

[1] *Dinwiddie Papers*, IV., 148.

them to take up the hatchet against the decadent red-coats; while it was not difficult once more to egg on the old allies of the French, the painted tribes of the Great Lakes and Canada, whose repre-sentatives had revelled in the loot of Braddock's field.[1]

Braddock's road, laboriously cleaved through the wilderness to reach the French and the Indians, now proved equally convenient to the latter as a path-way to the English border. Dumas had often six or seven savage war-parties out at a time, "always accompanied by Frenchmen"; and while provincial troops were being massed upon the Niagara and Lake George frontiers, and in far-off Acadia, the summer and autumn of 1755 brought rare misery to the neglected frontiersmen of the middle and southern colonies. In July the commandant at Fort Du-quesne could exultantly write to Versailles: " I have succeeded in ruining the three adjacent prov-inces, Pennsylvania, Maryland, and Virginia, driv-ing off the inhabitants, and totally destroying the settlements over a tract of country thirty leagues wide, reckoning from the line of Fort Cumberland. . . . The Indian villages are full of prisoners of every age and sex. The enemy has lost far more since the battle than on the day of his defeat." [2]

Undoubtedly, Dumas did his best to repress the

[1] *Wis. Hist. Collections*, III., 214, 215, VII., 132.
[2] Dumas to the minister, July 24, 1755, original letter in British Record Office.

savagery of his naked allies by continually counsel-
ling them to refrain from assaulting women and tort-
uring prisoners. Documents of the period prove that
he was far from being the blood-thirsty ogre which
American border historians have generally painted
him. But his efforts at humanity were in vain;
the phials of wrath had been opened, and pillage,
arson, and violence of every sort, culminating with
the unspeakable horrors of the stake, were now the
almost daily experiences of the British frontier.

One of the most flagrant acts of the French
partisan leaders was to disguise themselves as warriors, and, thus accoutred, often to outdo their companions in acts of savagery. This practice was,
to their credit, deprecated by the authorities at
Versailles, who once wrote to Duquesne concerning
it: "It appears merely proper to enjoin on him
expressly to prevent the French painting or dress-
ing themselves like Indians, in order to assault the
English. 'Tis a flagrant treachery which must not
be permitted even in time of war."[1] Like the
British authorities with their own colonists, French
ministers, however, had but slight hold upon their
kinsmen fighting in the unseen wilderness of America,
and the practice was never seriously checked.

Amid all this frightful din, one man alone stands
out as the guardian of the west. Washington, at
first with a thousand Virginia militiamen, but

---

[1] "Minute of instructions to be given to M. Duquesne," April,
1752, in *N. Y. Docs. Rel. to Col. Hist.*, X., 205.

later with fifteen hundred, did what he could to protect three hundred and fifty miles of open border. His command contained many expert riflemen, who understood the art of forest warfare. But they were a turbulent and undisciplined soldiery, electing their own officers, fixing their own terms of enlistment, and proudly disdaining all manifestations of authority that did not appeal to their individual judgments.[1] There was, of course, no attempt among them to uniform, the officers in no wise being distinguished from their men, save Washington himself, who appears seldom to have forgotten the essential insignia of rank, although he declared that the ideal costume for both men and officers was Indian dress.[2] Attired in fringed buckskin hunting-shirts, leggings and moccasins of the same, and either broad-brimmed felt hats or coon-skin caps, and carrying long, home-made flint-lock rifles, with powder-horn, tomahawk, and scalping-knife dependent from the belt, they probably presented much the appearance of the cowboy scouts of our later Indian wars, save in the crudity of their weapons.

Had the colonies been left alone to defend themselves, without hope of royal aid or direction, no doubt they would have felt forced to unite, and might in time have brought together a creditable

---

[1] Concerning methods of frontier militia, see Thwaites and Kellogg, *Documentary History of Dunmore's War.*

[2] Washington to Bouquet, July 3, 1758, in Washington, *Writings* (Ford's ed.), II., 39-43.

colonial army, such as was developed, less than a quarter of a century later, during the Revolutionary war.   But instead there was a deal of foolishness displayed both in London and in the provinces. After Braddock's defeat the provincials hastily concluded that the regulars were useless material.   On their part the regulars felt the utmost contempt for the ununiformed and undisciplined horde of colonial militiamen.   For instance, Wolfe, at Halifax, dubbed them "la canaille," and spoke scornfully of "the dirtiest, most contemptible cowardly dogs. . . . Such rascals as these are rather an encumbrance than any real strength to an army."[1] It is small wonder that, although both were in their own way efficient, the two branches of the service grew apart; consequently, in the presence of a united and determined foe, the provinces suffered severely.

Washington's task, which lasted throughout the war, was a most onerous and thankless one.   Dinwiddie now disliked him; the Virginia assembly was irritable, jealous of the military, and granted stores and men with tardiness and insufficiency.   It was with great difficulty that even the small quotas voted by the assembly could be raised; the frontiersmen themselves had to be fairly driven into the unpopular service by means of the draft.[2]   There was constant apprehension of a slave uprising, and

[1] Wood, *Fight for Canada*, 40, 41.
[2] Washington, *Writings* (Sparks's ed.), II., 135, 137, 138, 141, 142, 154.

Virginians in consequence feared to be long absent
from home.   Desertions were so frequent as often
seriously to cripple the little army of defence; and
among the rangers in the field it was almost impossible to maintain discipline.   One of his officers
wrote: "If we talk of obliging men to serve their
country, we are sure to hear a fellow mumble over
the words 'liberty' and 'poverty' a thousand times." [1]

Washington, however, although only twenty-four
years of age, was accounted perhaps the most
accomplished Indian fighter of his time, as he
certainly was the most prominent, and to him the
colony looked for the defence of its western frontier.
He felt strongly this great obligation resting upon
his young shoulders, and fairly pelted the governor,
the assembly, and other influential men with letters
appealing for necessary assistance.   "I am little
acquainted, Sir," he wrote on April 22, 1756, to
Dinwiddie, "with pathetic language to attempt a
description of the people's distresses, though I have
a generous soul, sensible of wrongs, and swelling
for redress.   But what can I do?   I see their
situation, know their danger, and participate their
sufferings, without having it in my power to give
them further relief, than uncertain promises. . . .
The supplicating tears of the women, and moving
petitions of the men, melt me into such deadly
sorrow, that I solemnly declare, if I know my own

[1] Extracts in Washington, *Writings* (Sparks's ed.), II., 145,
154, 159.

mind, I could offer myself a willing sacrifice to the butchering enemy, provided that would contribute to the people's ease."[1]

Although her frontier was at first quite unprotected, for the reason that her tribes had hitherto been friendly, Pennsylvania would for a long time grant no assistance. The governor and his legislature were in a deadlock over the question of taxing proprietary lands in levies for military purposes; and we have seen[2] that the Quakers and Germans were opposed on principle to voting money for fighting Indians. At last, after large districts had been laid waste by the savages, and hundreds of Pennsylvania pioneers had been slaughtered in their homes, infuriated backwoodsmen, bearing to the very door of the assembly ghastly portions of the mutilated bodies of their neighbors, threatened to besiege the capital and compel official protection. The affrighted legislature now yielded its point; but the military measures it undertook were ridiculously inadequate. Indeed, taking hope from Pennsylvania's weakness and indifference, the latter occasioned in part by its large quota of foreign settlers, the French were a few months later found to be considering measures for turning the province into a recruiting-ground for their own side.[3]

---

[1] Extracts in Washington, *Writings* (Sparks's ed.), II., 143, 144.   [2] See chap. ix., above.

[3] Intercepted letter of March, 1756, MS. in Public Record Office, *Colonial Papers*, LXXXI.

Early in the French and Indian raids, and continuing through several ensuing years (1755-1759), the Virginia and Carolina borderers, under Washington's skilful supervision, erected in the principal mountain - passes or at other vantage - points on either side of the divide a line of stockaded blockhouses a hundred to a hundred and fifty miles beyond the main settlements. These were garrisoned by the westernmost fringe of frontiersmen, who in the intervals of raids worked their outlying fields as best they might. Fort Ligonier, on the Loyalhanna, a branch of the Alleghany, was the northernmost; Fort Cumberland, on the upper Potomac, came next, with its memories of Dumas's rout; then Fort Chiswell, on the gentle slopes of the valley of Virginia; Fort Byrd, on Long Island, in the upper Holston, a favorite Indian rendezvous; and finally Fort Loudoun, on the Little Tennessee. Around these several log strongholds, all of them famous in border story, there spasmodically raged throughout the long contest a fierce and bloody warfare, to which, however, we shall hereafter find few occasions to refer. None the less must it be remembered that all the while the larger operations of the war were being waged in the north and northeast. Washington, with his motley but generally efficient corps of riflemen, was hurling back the warparties of French-guided savages which almost continually sought to break his cordon. His task was quite as important as any, although less heralded,

for at the back-door of the British provinces he
was striving to retain the Ohio Valley, and that
was really the key to the situation. So long as
France held this noble waterway, Canada and
Louisiana, joining hands with their line of posts,
could shut out the English from the continental
interior and hem them to the coast; in the hands
of the latter it meant the dismemberment of New
France. Washington understood the situation; few
other Englishmen did.

In England the year abounded in political turmoil. The nation was still nominally at peace with
France, although hostilities were in full progress
between their subjects in North America. The
weakness of Newcastle and his confrères but ag-
gravated the situation. Fifty thousand sailors were
recruited, but the fleet was wretchedly handled,
the army was confused by the premier's jealousy of
Cumberland, and the king was on the continent during the summer, looking after his miserable affairs
in Hanover. England was alarmed and distracted
over the situation, fearing a threatened French invasion, while the ministry writhed under the lash
of Pitt, who unsparingly denounced the government and their works, and during the winter forced
on them plans for a more efficient war footing.
These latter, however, were not wholly to his liking;
especially an act which had passed Parliament by a
vote of three to one, authorizing the king to import Hanoverians and Prussians for the defence of

the island, and to grant commissions to foreign
Protestants in America; Pitt stoutly held that only
British soldiers should be employed to fight British
battles.[1]

Hostilities were finally proclaimed between France
and England May 18, 1756, a full year after they
had openly commenced. In Europe the contest is
called the Seven Years' War, and grew out of the
alliance of France, Russia, Austria, and Poland to
check the aggressive designs of Frederick the Great
of Prussia. England was allied with Frederick, and
felt especial enmity against France because the
latter was trying to oust her from India and was
not a comfortable neighbor in America. The final
struggle between France and England for American
supremacy is known in our history as the French
and Indian War.

It was at last intended by the government at
Whitehall, spurred on by the minority, under Pitt,
to organize vigorous campaigns, both in the Old
World and the New. The Mediterranean fleet
was supposedly strengthened, under Admiral Byng;
and a defence fund of £115,000 and several regiments of regulars were ordered sent out to Lord
Loudoun, the new British military commander in
America. The French, less dilatory, struck first,
by attacking Port Mahon in Minorca, which was
insufficiently garrisoned and supplied. The defence
was stubborn; but the French were in better order,

[1] Green, *William Pitt*, 36, 37.

and Byng's belated ships were so ill-manned that he recognized the difficulty of assisting, and disgracefully retreated, for which cowardice he later suffered death. Port Mahon fell (June 28) after a siege of seventy days, and Englishmen were enraged at the incompetence of the government. Popular discontent became fury when, later in the season, French diplomacy acquired Corsica from the republic of Genoa, and for the time being English interests ceased to control the Mediterranean, save that Gibraltar guarded its entrance.[1]

As for Loudoun's reinforcements, they did not arrive until June and July, and the season was lost through inaction, induced by camp diseases, the inefficiency of the general, the inexperience of provincial commanders, and the usual dilatory attitude of the colonial legislatures, several of which utterly refused aid; while even those at last voting men and supplies imposed conditions inconsistent with good military management.

The French autocracy had, of course, no troubles of this character to contend with, but were not without serious difficulties of their own. The Marquis de Montcalm, an able, energetic, if somewhat impetuous officer, deputed by the king to conduct his military operations in America, arrived at Quebec the middle of May. Governor Vaudreuil, a native of Canada, was jealous of this intrusion from France. He was still nominally in supreme control,

[1] Clowes, *Royal Navy*, III., 146–160.

and had desired to take command in the field; this was, however, denied him by the ministry, and thenceforth there was a sharp antagonism between the two, accentuated by the fact that they were of quite opposite temperaments.

Montcalm had had a brilliant European career; he was scholarly in tastes, entertained noble sentiments, and appears to have been a Christian gentleman. Vaudreuil was said by the general to be "slow and irresolute,"[1] but he generally meant well. His was a petty mind, prone to take offence at trifles, egotistical, wedded to bureaucratic methods, and morbidly distrustful of the officers from France, whom he constantly disparaged in his voluminous letters to the ministry at Versailles. Moreover, he was not above the practice of petty peculation, although more honest than many of his colleagues. To add to the difficulty, the Intendant Bigot, whose real power, as keeper of the public funds, surpassed that of either Vaudreuil or the general, was a vicious rascal, who plundered right and left, and saw no good in those whom he could not use as tools. Poor in purse as he was proud in spirit, inclined to lavish entertainment in the face of growing debt, and at times indiscreetly irascible, Montcalm had a sorry time of it under the thumb of these resident officials, who united only against

[1] Montcalm to the minister, June 19, 1756, cited in Parkman, *Montcalm and Wolfe*, I., 377; incorrectly synopsized in *N. Y. Docs. Rel. to Col. Hist.*, X., 421.

him.   His sole confidants in America appear to have
been his lieutenants, Lévis and Bourlamaque, but
he found a vent for his opinions in numerous letters to his wife, his mother, and other relatives
and friends in France.   These missives were de-
lightfully full and unreserved, generally playful
in tone, yet exhibiting pent-up emotion.   They
afford rich material for the inside history of New
France during the great struggle.   "What a country," he wrote to one of his correspondents, "where
knaves grow rich and honest men are ruined." [1]
And on another occasion the impatient soldier ex-
claimed: "Forgive the confusion of this letter; I
have not slept all night with thinking of the rob-
beries and mismanagement and folly.   *Pauvre Roi,
pauvre France, cara patria.*" [2]   This miserable and
untimely dissension in the little government at
Quebec materially weakened New France, and was
almost as serious in its way as the divided councils
of the English colonies.

Montcalm's army consisted of nearly four thousand regulars from France (*troupes de terre*), nearly
twenty-five hundred colonial regulars (*troupes de la
marine*), and some five thousand colonial militia, to
which branch of the service all able-bodied men
in the colony, say fifteen thousand in all, were lia-
ble to be called.   In addition there were irregular

---

[1] Parkman, *Montcalm and Wolfe*, II., 172.
[2] *Ibid.*, 169; for account of Montcalm's correspondence in
general, *ibid.*, App., 426–428.

bands of allied Indians from the valleys of the St.
Lawrence and the Mississippi, the warriors fluctuat-
ing in number from time to time—from the six
hundred and fifty at Braddock's defeat to the
eighteen hundred or more before Fort William
Henry, while probably not over a thousand served
at the siege of Quebec. At the height of the war,
Montcalm had a nominal command over possibly
about twenty thousand men in field, garrison, and
reserve; while as many more were supposed to be
engaged in irregularly defending the attenuated
cordon of log outposts and missionary hamlets
stretching between Canada and Louisiana. The
actual fighting strength of New France was, however, far less than indicated on the rolls.

We have seen that the British campaign of this
year was marked by weakness, induced by governmental delays, provincial dissensions, and the
military incompetence of Lord Loudoun. The
movements of Montcalm and Vaudreuil, however
—for the time being they acted in common—
were characterized by considerable energy and
tactical skill. While the British were slowly preparing to reinforce Fort Ontario, at Oswego, Montcalm, with a force of three thousand, quickly swooped down upon this important key to the Indian
trade of the Great Lakes, and forced it to surrender
(August 14) after three days' siege, with its three
thousand men and considerable supplies. The relief column, pursuing a leisurely journey thither,

was thereupon forced hurriedly to retreat; while Montcalm burned his prize and retired first to Montreal, but later to Ticonderoga, where, with a garrison of five thousand, behind strengthened defences, he was for the time being secure against dislodgement.[1]

Thus the season of 1756 ended for the British with Hanover in imminent danger of attack, Minorca fallen, the navy in sad repute, Loudoun discredited, and the west abandoned; and finally, while the people were mourning because of the humiliations to which their shambling government had brought them, there was speeding on the way to England, as fast as sail could bring it, fully as distressful news from far-off India—the loss of Calcutta at the hands of young Surajah Dowlah (June 20) and the frightful tragedy of the Black Hole Prison.

[1] Parkman, *Montcalm and Wolfe*, II., 410–416.

CHAPTER XIII

A YEAR OF HUMILIATION

(1757)

UNABLE to withstand the general outcry against his mismanagement, the Duke of Newcastle retired in November, 1756, to be succeeded by the Duke of Devonshire. But William Pitt, now forty-eight years of age, was the strong man of the new cabinet, and with his accession as one of the two secretaries of state an entirely different spirit prevailed in the official as well as the popular attitude towards the war. Parliament met early in December. The continental troops imported to assist in British defence were promptly sent home, the militia were strengthened to over thirty-two thousand men, the artillery and the marines were heavily increased, and the island was put in condition to defend itself. Squadrons were despatched to India and the West Indies; nineteen thousand troops, including two thousand Highlanders under their clan leaders—former foes, now for the first time taken into the British service — were ordered to America; and the somewhat fantastic regiments of

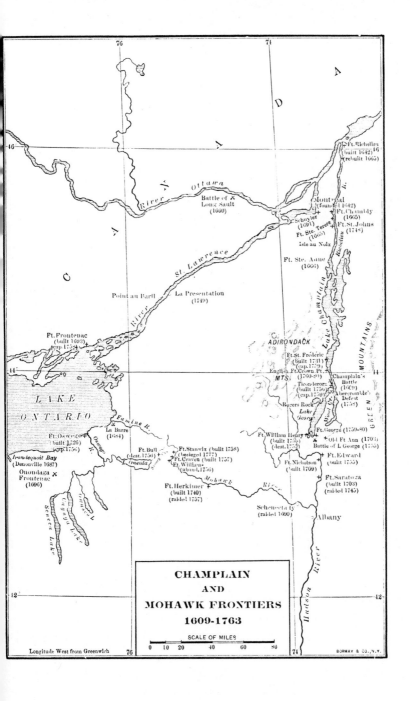

CHAMPLAIN
AND
MOHAWK FRONTIERS
1609-1763

SCALE OF MILES

0   10   20   40   60   80

Longitude West from Greenwich   76   74   BORMAY & CO., N.Y.

Shirley and Pepperrell were disbanded, in order to make room for the kilted braves.[1]

Pitt, more clearly than any other statesman of his time, recognized the path to British greatness. France had made some gains in the Mediterranean, yet her sea-power was relatively weak. Her navy in 1756 consisted of but sixty-three ships of the line, of which only forty-five need be reckoned with; while her possible naval ally, Spain, could muster only forty-six, and few of those were seriously to be considered as fighting machines. The British fleet aggregated a hundred and thirty men-of-war, nearly all in fair condition.[2] France was also so closely and needlessly entangled in continental politics, as an ally of Austria against Frederick of Prussia, that she could not concentrate her strength against England. Pitt perceived that the latter's advantage lay in looking chiefly to the sea and her colonies, hence he made a side issue of the national alliance with Frederick, who was assisted only sufficiently to enable him to engage the attention of France, whose land forces alone were powerful. Under Pitt's inspiring leadership the nation glowed with military enthusiasm. On every hand, men were eager to join the army and the fleet, and the war office became the centre of unwonted action.

Meanwhile, in the colonies, the winter was distinguished by a characteristic dispute over the

[1] Fortescue, *British Army*, 300.
[2] Mahan, *Influence of Sea Power*, 291.

quartering of the British regulars. The provincial
troops, enlisted only for particular campaigns, were
disbanded and returned to their homes at the opening of winter, necessitating fresh levies the ensuing spring; but the regulars could not be disposed
of in this fashion. Lord Loudoun billeted his
men upon the inhabitants—the bulk of them in
Boston, New York, and Philadelphia. With that
watchful jealousy of the exercise of arbitrary power, which has ever been a leading characteristic of
the English people, perhaps not unmingled in this
case with a penuriousness common to the colonists,
Loudoun's billets at once aroused opposition. It
was argued by the general that billeting was a usage
prevalent in England in time of war, and that the
troops were here for nothing else than to defend
the provinces; moreover, an act of Parliament
sanctioned his demand. New York and Philadelphia yielded under pressure of threats, but Boston was settled by the sort of "Britons who never
will be slaves," and obstinately stood out on principle. The Massachusetts assembly finally com-
promised the matter by passing a special act authorizing billeting, thus by implication denying
that an act of Parliament could be binding upon
them.[1]

Devonshire's ministry was high in public favor,
but it could not command a parliamentary majority, and at court it had no friends. The king,

[1] Mass. Bay, *Acts and Resolves*, IV., chap. xvi., 47, 48.

who disliked Pitt, complained that "the secretary made him long speeches, which possibly might be very fine, but were greatly beyond his comprehension; and that his letters were affected, formal, and pedantic."[1] Suddenly, early in April (1757), his majesty peremptorily dismissed the objectionable minister, in order to please the Duke of Cumberland; the king wished the duke to command a column to be sent to the defence of Hanover against the French, and the latter petulantly declared he would not take orders from Pitt.   But the popular indignation was so great throughout the island, and it was so plainly seen that none but the great commoner could conduct the government in the present crisis, that his majesty with ill grace recalled him late in June as secretary of state for war and foreign affairs— the virtual head of a reorganized ministry, based on a convenient although undignified bargain between Pitt and Newcastle, the latter being still in control of the parliamentary majority.   Newcastle thereby regained his premiership and the civil and ecclesiastical patronage which his vulgar ambition craved, while to Pitt were given the reins of real power, an arrangement which he described as "borrowing the Duke of Newcastle's majority to carry on the business of the country."   The new master, who never lacked self-confidence, is credited with declaring, "I am sure that I can save this country, and that no one else can,"[2] a boast borne out by the facts.

[1] Waldegrave, *Memoirs*, 95.   [2] Walpole, *Memoirs*, III., 84.

But Pitt's dismissal had for eleven weeks practically disorganized the governmental machinery
and consequently delayed all military operations,
so that much of the energy characterizing the winter and early spring was dissipated for the present
season.   In America, Loudoun had early received
(January, 1757) one new regiment from a former
Newcastle assignment, but there passed many long
and weary months before instructions and additional reinforcements reached him.   Seven battalions supposed to have been shipped to America in
March had at first loitered and then been harassed
by ocean storms, so that it was the middle of July
before they straggled into Halifax harbor, the proposed rendezvous.

It had been Pitt's intention, acting on Loudoun's
advice, to attack Louisburg, and thus again obtain
control of the Gulf of St. Lawrence.   For this enterprise, the time for which was not yet ripe, the
general had unwisely withdrawn the majority of his
troops from the northern border, and tarried long at
New York ready for embarkation, embarrassed as to
his proper course.   News reached him of a great
French fleet patrolling the Nova Scotian coast; but
finally he ventured late in June to start for Halifax, reaching there with his twelve thousand men
after a ten days' voyage, without sighting a hostile
sail. The long-promised co-operating squadron from
England, under Admiral Holbourne, arrived a fortnight later.

It was soon learned, however (August 4), that the French had reinforced the Louisburg garrison, so that now there were seven thousand well-trained troops behind its formidable bastions, while twenty-two ships of the line crowded the harbor. Thereupon Loudoun, quite lacking in the spirit which animated the dare-devil New England rustics who had carried Louisburg by their clumsy assault a dozen years before, quickly returned with his forces to New York. The admiral, with truer British grit, remained behind to challenge his naval enemy, who, however, seemed loath to accept. But there now arose a fierce September gale, that wrought sad havoc with his ships, and Louisburg was spared for another year.[1]

Loudoun's weakening of the British frontier defence afforded a fine opportunity for Montcalm, of which he was not slow to take advantage. With Oswego destroyed, western communications were opened, so that his attention could be concentrated on the threatened British advance from the south by way of the now familiar route of lakes George and Champlain. In Fort Edward, at the Hudson River end of the portage, Colonel Daniel Webb was stationed with a garrison of thirty-six hundred. The Lake George terminus of the road, fourteen miles to the eastward, was guarded by the outpost of Fort William Henry, commanded by

[1] See Bourinot, *Cape Breton*, 154, for detailed list of authorities on this expedition.

Lieutenant-Colonel Monro, with a force of twenty-two hundred. The French held Crown Point and Ticonderoga; while protecting their base towards Montreal were two other strongholds, forts St. John and Chambly, on the Richelieu.

Late in July, Montcalm assembled at Ticonderoga a formidable war-party of three thousand regulars, a like number of militia, and nearly two thousand Indians — the latter gathered from a wide stretch of territory, extending even to and beyond the Mississippi. The untamed western tribes surprised the officers from France with their "brute paganism," their music "strongly resembling the cries and howlings of wolves," and their "decoration with every ornament most fitted to disfigure, in European eyes, their physiognomies. Vermilion, white, green, yellow, and black made from soot or scrapings of the pots; on a single face are seen united all these different colors."[1]

Accompanied by this motley throng, the general suddenly appeared before Monro's camp, and by holding the portage path prevented Webb from coming to the rescue. After suffering three days' heavy bombardment, with no hope of relief, Monro surrendered on August 9, his casualties having aggregated three hundred, while small-pox had broken out among his men.

Montcalm had pledged his Indian allies to desist

[1] Father P. J. A. Ribaud, in Thwaites, *Jesuit Relations*, LXX., 95.

from worrying the prisoners, and fearing to excite them had forbidden liquor to be doled out to the tribesmen until the British were at a safe distance. The latter had been "granted the right of going out of the fort with all the honors of war," but on parole "of not serving against His Most Christian Majesty for eighteen months," and of "restoring liberty to all Canadians taken in this war."[1]

After another night in the intrenchments, during which they were robbed and frequently assaulted by pillaging savages who crept through the ruined casemates, the English troops prepared to march out, early in the morning of August 10. Yielding to the importunities of the "ferocious beasts" who now crowded about them with threatening gestures, "The English dispossessed and despoiled themselves, and reduced to nothing, that they might buy at least life by this general renunciation."[2] Unfortunately, among the peace-offerings thus tendered was a quantity of spirits, which on being passed around among them roused the savages to fury. The little guard of four hundred French troops, detailed to "protect the retreat of the enemy," soon arrived; but as the English, among whom were several women, defiled into the open, their protectors were rudely thrust aside, and, indeed, some of them killed outright, and an orgy of human butchery commenced.

[1] These quotations are from Ribaud's account, in Thwaites, *Jesuit Relations*, LXX., 95.   [2] *Ibid.*, 179

Montcalm and his fellow-officers, encamped at a considerable distance, rushed into the mêlée at the risk of their lives, and by dint of "prayers, menaces, promises and at last force" succeeded in restoring order.   But in the course of the brief turmoil about fifty of the English had been killed and scalped, and some four or five hundred kidnapped by the Indians.[1] The remainder found refuge in the tents of the French, and a few days later, "to the number of nearly five hundred," were, this time under adequate guard, safely forwarded to Fort Edward.   The captives were eventually ransomed by Montcalm "at great expense," and carried to Quebec, where they took ship for Boston.

There is no ground whatever for suspecting the French of complicity in this shocking affair; indeed, Father Ribaud's report, which bears the stamp of accuracy, seems sufficient evidence to the contrary. "The Savages," he declares, "are alone responsible for the infringement of the law of nations; and it is only to their insatiable ferocity and their independence that the cause of it can be ascribed." Nevertheless, none better than the French knew the characteristics of these demi-demons; with a force of six thousand regulars and militia at hand, a more efficient safeguard should have been given to the unfortunate prisoners.

[1] On casualty statistics see Parkman, *Montcalm and Wolfe*, I., 514. We follow Ribaud, in Thwaites, *Jesuit Relations*, LXX., 183–199.

It was part of Montcalm's plan to cross over to
Fort Edward and either capture or drive out Webb.
But he had suffered a considerable loss in dead and
wounded, his militiamen were leaving for home to
look after their harvests, and the Indians were slink-
ing away with loot and captives.   He was soon reduced to his three thousand regulars, whom he did
not care to pit against the forty-five hundred now
at Fort Edward; moreover, transport facilities were
meagre and provisions were running low.   He therefore burned the remains of Fort William Henry,
throwing the heaps of French, British, and savage
slain into the consuming flames, and retired to
Ticonderoga.

During the winter of 1757–1758, Vaudreuil busied
himself with letters to Versailles, accusing the general of incompetency for neglecting to finish his
task by attacking Webb.   On his part, Montcalm,
impatient of the governor's bickerings, was request-
ing the ministry to give him supreme command in
New France, an application supported by the best
of his colonial colleagues.   Doreil, in charge of the
colonial commissariat, expressed the common sentiment of unprejudiced men in Canada when he wrote
to the minister of war, Marshal Belle-Isle: "No
matter whether the war is to continue or not, if His
Majesty wants Canadian affairs put on a solid footing, let him confide the general government to the
Marquis de Montcalm." [1]

[1] Wood, *Fight for Canada*, 74.

While these events were transpiring in America,
British interests in the Old World were also suffering materially.   Among the earliest incidents con-
fronting Pitt on his resumption of power, was news
of the Duke of Cumberland's defeat at the hands of
the French in the battle of Hastenbeck (July 26),
and that commander's pusillanimous agreement to
evacuate the country, which Pitt promptly dis-
avowed.   The minister, eager to do something to
save the year from utter disaster, now allowed himself to be drawn into the enterprise of despatching
ten battalions and a powerful fleet against the
French harbor fortress of Rochefort, on the strength
of an ill-founded rumor that its defences were weak.
But on nearing their destination the officers learned that Rochefort was quite ready for them, whereupon (October 1) they discreetly withdrew to meet
an infuriated British public that throughout the
winter bombarded them with abusive pamphlets.

CHAPTER XIV

THE TURNING OF THE SCALE

(1758)

THE mass of the British people were in the depths of despondency, but now a master was in control who soon was to lead them to almost unexampled victory. The elements of success were present; they simply needed organization and direction, and this was the great service which in the present crisis William Pitt rendered to his country.

Of the historical figures that trod the stage of British politics during the eighteenth century, he was by all odds the most striking. Of good family, and fairly well educated, although of narrow means, Pitt first entered the army as a cavalry cornet, but soon sought a parliamentary career, becoming a member of the House in his twenty-seventh year. Thenceforth he was much in the public eye, for during nearly twenty - two years before he became the head of the government he was a leader of the opposition. His brilliant and powerful oratory, notable for invective and sarcasm, was always at the command of progressive measures, and awakened wide-spread popular applause. "In him the people

first felt their power.   He was essentially their representative, and he gloried in avowing it."[1]   But
this fact, emphasized by his caustic jibes and often
violent attacks on incapacity in high places, rendered him obnoxious to king and court.

His "figure was tall and imposing, with the eyes
of a hawk, a little head, a thin face, and a long
aquiline nose ";[2] his carriage was graceful and dig-
nified, and he was exact in his attire.   If we may
accept the judgment of his contemporaries—for it
was previous to the introduction of modern stenog-
raphy, and we have only synoptical reports of his
speeches, and reminiscences of their effect upon his
public—he must be ranked with the greatest orators
of all times.   His style was impassioned; his utter-
ance "was both full and clear; his lowest whisper
was distinctly heard; his middle tones were sweet,
rich, and beautifully varied; when he elevated his
voice to its highest pitch, the house was completely
filled with the volume of sound."[3]

Pitt was without doubt possessed of foibles and
weaknesses; his vanity was monumental; he seldom
took counsel of his colleagues; there was "a degree
of pedantry in his conversation "; his manner, both
in private and public life, was peremptory, impetuous, and often theatrical; his reading was limited,
and he knew few subjects thoroughly; frequently,

[1] Lecky, *England*, II., 516.
[2] Barker, in *Dict. National Biog.*, XLV., 365, art. Pitt.
[3] Butler, *Reminiscences*, I., 139.

he was inconsistent in his political attitude; and he was much too fond of war, apparently recking little of its cost in treasure, pain, and blood. But his private life was exemplary; no suspicion of corruption attached to him, in an age when official malfeasance was almost universal. His own military plans were not always well formulated or successful, yet he knew how to select good commanders, and generally was wise enough to leave details to them. He personally created the enginery of war, and was largely responsible for originating the campaign that thrust France from the path of British imperialism. He was fertile in resources, was bold and ardent, possessed tremendous energy and indomitable courage, and had the rare power of infusing the nation with the same leonine spirit with which he himself was imbued. France must not only be ousted from North America, but must be so crippled both on land and sea as to render her henceforth incapable of adequate revenge; to this end, with incomparable genius, he aroused the British people to the highest pitch of patriotic endeavor. As a result, "at the end of seven years the kingdom of Great Britain had become the British Empire." [1]

With Newcastle's substantial parliamentary majority quite at his command, Pitt spent the winter of 1757–1758 in organizing and equipping his dogs of war. Realizing that in a struggle for colonial supremacy his chief reliance must be the navy, he

[1] Mahan, *Influence of Sea Power*, 291.

exhausted every resource in making it, under the
splendid management of Admiral Anson, unques-
tionably the greatest fighting machine of his day.
The sea power of France had, in the previous years
of contest, been relatively weaker; and now it fast
retrograded, not because of failure in marine archi-
tecture or in equipment—for her vessels were generally built on better lines, had stouter rigging, and
were more amply supplied than those of England[1]
—but largely from inferior seamanship. The British people, insular in situation and dependent on a
wide-spread commerce for the very necessaries of
life, contained the largest body of commercial sailors
on earth, which constituted a splendid recruiting-field
for the ever-expanding navy. In the nature of
things, the latter's carefully selected personnel was
much superior to that of its competitors, who,
failing in skill but not at all in courage, had at
their command a much smaller nursery of competent seamen.

For the men themselves, the British naval service was far from a primrose path. The majority
of the sailors were recruited by the rude methods of
impressment, which made their employment a sort
of slavery. Conditions afloat were as unwholesome
physically as they often were morally. The work
was of the hardest, and the standard of accomplish-
ment exacting. Deaths from illness occasioned by
unsanitary surroundings were far more numerous

[1] Wood, *Fight for Canada*, 95.

than in actual battle;[1] but the loss from desertions was greater than either of the other two causes combined. Yet there were instances of common sailors serving over sixty years at their rude calling, and high patriotic sentiment was general among them; although there was also in the service a large sprinkling of foreigners, who were the merest hirelings. In the popular mind the navy was accounted England's "wooden walls," and sea power was exalted above all other. At the close of the Seven Years' War, the official rolls carried seventy thousand seamen, many of them with a fine record for steadfast bravery under fire.

France, her energies chiefly directed toward land wars in Europe—harrying Frederick, who, although financially aided by England, with difficulty held his own against the allies — begrudged the money spent on her inferior navy. In India the British regained Calcutta and won Bengal through Clive's brilliant victory at Plassey (June 23, 1757), the news of which reached London in November following; but the British did not yet recognize that their empire was born. Desperate at these reverses, the French began preparations for invading England, but Pitt and Anson made ready for them by centring a series of great naval operations in the Channel and along the shores of France: (1) A squadron was set to watch the French Atlantic ports, especially

[1] Statistics in Wood, *Fight for Canada*, 106; Clowes, *Royal Navy*, III., 21–23.

Brest, to prevent their ships from getting out to
sea; (2) flying squadrons attacked several minor
Channel and Atlantic ports and landed marauding
parties—a movement intended to keep French
troops at home, and thus divert them from Frederick's territory; (3) a fleet in the Mediterranean,
near Gibraltar, was designed to prevent the escape
to the Atlantic of the French fleet at Toulon; (4)
small expeditions were despatched against French
colonies in the West Indies and along the African
coast; while a squadron in East-Indian waters interrupted communication between France and her
Indian possessions.[1] The immediate domestic result of this wide-spread naval activity, by means of
which the ships of France were unable to get to
sea while her colonies were being battered and her
ocean commerce destroyed, was the postponement
of the French invasion project for another year.

On her part, New France could hope but for few
reinforcements from the mother-land. Domestic
affairs were at their worst. Vaudreuil and Bigot
continued their cabal against Montcalm, whom the
short-sighted ministry should have placed in complete control, but would not. The avaricious
Bigot, correctly interpreting the handwriting on
the wall, tightened his hold upon the avenues of
peculation, by elaborating to the utmost a system
of official thievery which extended from Vaudreuil
himself down to the commandant of the farthest

[1] Clowes, *Royal Navy*, III., 172.

military and trading outpost. Supplies sent out
from France for colonial relief were intercepted
and sold to the colonial government at exorbitant
prices — sometimes twice over, through collusion
between receipting and auditing officials; supplies
bought in the colony for the king's service were
paid for at excessive rates and in short measure; Indian presents forwarded by the home government were privately utilized in the purchase of
furs for the confederates; military stores were boldly confiscated, the soldiers in the field being maintained in rags and on short rations; even the out-
cast and destitute Acadians, for whom the ministry
contributed food, fell victims to this organized ra-
pacity, aid intended for them going but to swell
the warehouses of Bigot's heartless crew; and, in
order to complete their rascality, grain and other
provisions were "cornered" at statutory prices, ostensibly for the public service, and then doled out
to the people at rates far beyond purchase figures.
Fraud entered into every branch of public service,
while extortion, gambling, and other forms of private
vice thrived at Montreal and Quebec as never before.[1]

Montcalm, himself untainted and the scope of
his authority uncertain, occupied an exceedingly
difficult and delicate position. Overwhelmed with
dismay, and foreseeing nothing but disaster as the
fruit of this riot of chicanery in the face of a strength-

[1] See Parkman, *Montcalm and Wolfe*, II., 37, for list of MS.
sources for studying Bigot's career.

ening foe, he privately, but persistently and unre-
servedly, reported the rascals to the minister of
war. "It seems," he wrote, "as if they were all
hastening to make their fortunes before the loss of
the colony; which many of them perhaps desire as
a veil to their conduct." [1] Convinced at last, for
the evidence adduced by Montcalm was complete,
that the king and his unfortunate colonists were,
in a period of grave public danger, being ruthlessly
robbed by the governor and intendant, who had corrupted the official life of New France to its core,[2]
the government at Versailles now pelted them with
threatening letters—a futile procedure, for the mis-
chief had been done and the end was near.

Meanwhile, the "tyrants of the sea," as the
British were dubbed by continental powers, did not
neglect their land forces. The army, now com-
prising a hundred thousand men, was infused with
vigor. Loudoun, detested by Pitt, was recalled
from America, which was henceforth to be the
centre of British military operations; but his successor, General James Abercromby, was an unfortunate choice. Colonel Jeffrey Amherst, fresh from
service in Germany, was also ordered to the colonies with the new rank of major-general, his special
task being the siege of Louisburg.[3]

[1] Montcalm to Belle-Isle, April 12, 1759.
[2] See Doughty and Parmelee, *Siege of Quebec*, II., 35–44, for
details of Bigot's rascality and his ultimate trial.
[3] Royal instructions to Amherst, March 3, 1758, MS. in Public Record Office.

The number of provincial troops made ready for
the field was twenty thousand, several times in excess of any previous levy.   The agreement with Pitt
was that the provinces should raise, clothe, and pay
these men—the suggestion being thrown out that a
portion of the cost might eventually be reimbursed
by Parliament[1]—while the government directly supplied tents, arms, ammunition, and provisions, and
promised that the regulars should thenceforth recognize the commissions of militia officers.   As a matter of fact, the new generals and their colleagues
gladly co-operated with the provincials and treated
them with frank consideration, the result being that
the latter at once awakened to enthusiasm, and the
assemblies no longer failed in their duties.   The day
of the arrogant martinets who looked with contempt on the "buckskins" was at an end; so also
vanished, in this era of good feeling which Pitt had
inspired, the foolish American prejudice which long
had held against the regulars.   The English colonies were at last united, and found in this union a
strength which certain far-seeing statesmen in the
mother-country viewed with prophetic misgivings.

In Montcalm's long and attenuated line of defence, his left flank consisted of the river and gulf of
St. Lawrence, guarded by the fortress of Louisburg,
on the eastern shore of Cape Breton Island; his right,
Lake Ontario, held chiefly by Fort Frontenac, and

---

[1] Pitt to the provincial governors, December 30, 1757, MS.
in Public Record Office.

the Ohio Valley, with Fort Duquesne as its key; while the Lake Champlain trough was his centre. Louisburg was as well garrisoned as possible, but its chief weakness lay in the lack of strong naval support from France; for Fort Duquesne nothing could be done with the limited means at the general's command; he was, therefore, obliged to concentrate his defence on the centre, his stronghold and base being Ticonderoga, which he occupied in June with thirty-eight hundred well-seasoned regulars.

The British plans of offence were, as usual, three-fold: Brigadier John Forbes, with nineteen hundred regulars and five thousand provincials, was ordered to recapture Fort Duquesne and repair the loss occasioned by Braddock's tragic failure; the centre was to be attacked by Abercromby, ostensibly aided but in reality directed by Brigadier-General Lord Howe, with the relatively enormous force of six thousand regulars and nine thousand provincials; while Amherst, aided by Brigadier-Generals Charles Lawrence, Edward Whitmore, and James Wolfe, was to lead fourteen thousand regulars to the reduction of Louisburg.

Pitt had desired that the siege of Louisburg should not commence later than April 20. But although Admiral Edward Boscawen set sail with the army on February 19, in a fleet strong enough to overpower any possible French squadron in American waters, it was May 9 before his flag-ship reached Halifax, and the 28th before the vessel carrying Amherst put in an appearance. Immediately on Amherst's arrival, Boscawen set out for the fortress, with a hundred and fifty-seven sail transporting twelve thousand troops, and on June 2 arrived in Gabarus Bay, immediately westward of Louisburg harbor—the latter a landlocked basin some seven miles in circumference.[1]

It will be remembered[2] that the famous fortress, which had been greatly strengthened since the siege of 1744, and was now the stoutest military stronghold in North America, lay at the base of an undulating, rocky tongue of land half encircling the harbor upon the south. The seaward side was in large measure protected by a wide marsh, precluding approach from that quarter. Between this morass and the harbor to the north and eastward the walls of the fortification extended for twelve hundred yards, protected by the Princess's, the Queen's, the King's, and the Dauphin's bastions. The entire length of the walls was somewhat over a mile and a half, within them lying a town of between three and four thousand inhabitants and a territory of a hundred acres. In either direction are leagues of craggy shores, whose bases are swept by angry surf and boiling tides. The tortuous mouth of the harbor is strewn with reefs and islets, on one of

[1] For a naval account of the expedition, see Clowes, *Royal Navy*, III., 182–186. For lists of vessels and troops, see Bourinot, *Cape Breton*, 68, 69, and Brown, *Cape Breton*, 295.

[2] See chapter vii., above.

which was the Island Battery, while on the harbor
main-land were several outlying batteries of considerable strength—chiefly the Grand, on high land
westward, and Lighthouse Point, the northern shore
of the inlet.[1]

The fortress walls were surmounted by two hundred and eighteen cannon and seventeen mortars;
the garrison, under the Chevalier Drucour, comprised thirty-four hundred regulars, seven hundred
island militia, and three hundred Indians, besides the
inhabitants of the town; and within the harbor were
fourteen vessels carrying five hundred and sixty-
two guns and manned by crews aggregating three
thousand men.   As less than ten thousand of the
British force were at any time fit for duty, the
fighting strength of the besiegers was about twice
that of the garrison.

Strong as Louisburg undoubtedly was, experience
had already shown the weak spots in her armor.
High land, with fair cover of stunted firs and shallow
ravines, closely approached the Dauphin's bastion
upon the northwest corner, close to the harbor; it
was also possible to approach from the eastward,
under cover of a projecting ledge which had served
as a quarry in the construction of the fort; and from
the south, where some firm ground lay between
Princess's bastion and the sea; while the French

[1] See plans and details in Bourinot, *Cape Breton;* also list of
authorities on the siege, cited in Parkman, *Montcalm and Wolfe*,
II., 81, 82.

found Lighthouse Point untenable. There were also
three possible landing-places within easy distance
along the southwest sea-shore, towards Gabarus Bay,
and to these the brigadiers were speedily ordered—
Wolfe to Freshwater Cove, four miles from the fort;
Whitmore to Flat Point, three miles away; and Lawrence to White Point, but a mile distant. All of the
landings were strongly guarded by Drucour's men;
but after five days of baffling fog and surf, Wolfe—
although suffering much from sea - sickness — first
succeeded, effecting a lodgement in the face of a hot
fire, each side sustaining in the skirmish somewhat
over a hundred casualties. More than a hundred
boats were also stove in during the landing of the
forces. It will be curious to note how closely the
plans and many of the incidents of the second
siege, conducted by skilled seamen and generals,
followed those adopted and experienced fourteen
years previous by the irregular colonial assailants
under the doughty Pepperrell.

Grand Battery was at once destroyed by the
French, and soon thereafter they abandoned Lighthouse Point. Wolfe, with twelve hundred men, being sent to the latter vantage-point, soon silenced
Island Battery and drove the French ships to take
refuge under the guns of the fortress. This left the
harbor mouth open to the British; but six large
French ships were at once sunk in the channel, with
a view of " bottling " the entrance. Meanwhile,
Amherst was slowly approaching the Dauphin's

bastion by regular trenches; and Wolfe, in addition
to his north - side duties, and his assistance to
Amherst, was pushing parallels towards the southern
end of the walls, opposite Princess's bastion.   On
July 16 this omnipresent officer made a bold dash
which effected an intrenched lodgement on high
ground within three hundred yards of the Dauphin's,
from which he could not be driven by the furious
cannonading that at once greeted him.

On July 21 a shell fell upon and lighted one of
the French men-of-war, which, drifting, set fire to
two others, all three being burned to the water's
edge.   The two now left were attacked a few nights
later by six hundred British sailors—among whom
was a petty officer later world-renowned as Captain
James Cook, the marine explorer—who boldly rowed
out into the harbor under a storm of shells from the
French batteries, captured the crews, and sought to
tow the vessels to the outer sea.   One of them
grounded and was burned by her captors, but the
other — the sole remaining ship in the original
French fleet of fourteen—was successfully removed.

Gradually the coil of British parallels encircling
the great fortress was drawn closer and closer.
Amherst's redoubts had badly shattered the bastions,
the citadel, the hospital, the barracks, and most of
the other principal buildings; while within, the walls
were now crumbling under their own fire, several
of the batteries being thereby silenced.   On the
26th, with scarcely more than a dozen of his

cannon available, with great breaches showing in
the principal bastions, the inhabitants insisting that
further resistance meant useless waste of life, and
the British preparing for a general and supposedly
final assault, Drucour, who had conducted a brave
and even skilful defence, sued for capitulation.
Amherst and Boscawen, whose naval co-operation
had of course been of the greatest service, would
offer no better terms than to accept the besieged,
now six thousand in number, as prisoners of war,
to be taken to England; and on the following morning the victors triumphantly marched in by the
west gate. The British loss had been but five
hundred and twenty-one killed and wounded; the
French casualties were doubtless greater, especially
from camp diseases—possibly a thousand all told.[1]

Amherst was now anxious that Boscawen should
take the army to Quebec and endeavor by the same
tactics to conquer that stronghold. But the admiral,
although a tenacious fighter, thought the time not
ripe for so daring an enterprise. The general accordingly detailed four battalions as a garrison for
Louisburg, and sent Monckton, Wolfe, and Lord
Rollo in separate commands to complete the
subjugation of Prince Edward's Island, the Gulf
of St. Lawrence, and the Bay of Fundy; the French

[1] Amherst's report (July 27, 1758) "of the guns, mortars,
shot, shell, etc., found in the Town of Louisburg upon its surrender this day," cited in Parkman, *Montcalm and Wolfe*,
II., 75.

having, with the fortress, agreed to surrender all
their possessions in land, garrisons, and stores upon
and around the great gulf.   This unwelcome task
accomplished, Wolfe, who was quite the hero of the
siege, departed for home on sick-leave.   Amherst,
meanwhile, sailed with five battalions for Boston,
where they were received (September 14) with such
boisterous enthusiasm that the general complained,
"I could not prevent the men from being filled with
rum by the inhabitants." [1]

As for Louisburg, the inhabitants—chiefly merchants and fishermen, with their families — were
eventually removed to the French port of La
Rochelle; and two years later (1760) the majestic
walls were overturned, for the neighboring British
stronghold at Halifax was sufficient for that quarter
of the world.   To-day the site of this once formidable fortress, which bulks so largely upon the pages
of our colonial history, is occupied by a small hamlet
of Scotch and Irish fishermen; these eke out their
slender incomes by guiding summer tourists among
the grass-grown ridges and mounds which—after
nearly a century and a half of spoliation, for this
cyclopean mass of cut stone is still the quarry of a
neighborhood with bounds extending to Halifax—
are about all that now remain of the walls and
buildings of "the Dunkirk of America"; while under
the crumbling arches of those shell-wracked bastions

[1] Amherst to Pitt, September 18, 1758, MS. in Public Record
Office.

that have survived the tooth of time, sheep are
safely folded from the ocean tempests which frequently sweep across this rugged little peninsula.

The lateness of the season when Amherst and
Boscawen found it possible to begin the siege, combined with the obstinacy of the French defence,
rendered it impracticable for Amherst to carry out
his programme of assistance to Abercromby, upon
whom had devolved the duty of attacking Montcalm's centre.   Early in June—after long and vexatious delays in assembling and training provincial
troops and forwarding supplies up the Hudson to
Fort Edward — the British general assembled his
fifteen thousand regulars and—provincials at the
head of Lake George.   A political appointee, with
but small ability, Abercromby depended chiefly
upon his brilliant lieutenant, Brigadier Lord Howe,
whom Wolfe declared to be " the noblest Englishman
that has appeared in my time, and the best soldier
in the British army," and whom Pitt described as " a
character of ancient times; a complete model of
military virtue."   The campaign had to this point
been in every detail directed by Howe, selected by
Pitt because he possessed the qualities in which
Abercromby was conspicuously lacking.[1]

July 4, 1758, the army advanced against Ticonderoga in a brilliant line six miles in length.   The
following day they were suddenly attacked in the
depth of the forest by their bush-ranging foe, and

[1] Chesterfield, *Letters* (Mahon's ed.), IV., 260.

it was with difficulty that a panic akin to Braddock's Field was averted. In the course of the skirmish, wherein the enemy were seldom seen, Howe was killed, to the genuine sorrow of every man in the column, for he was universally popular. As for the French, they were caught between two fires, and precipitately fled with considerable loss. With the fall of their real commander, however, the British rapidly became demoralized, for Abercromby could not take Howe's place. "With his death the whole soul of the army expired."[1]

Throughout July 8, from nine in the morning until twilight, a furious battle raged in front of Ticonderoga and its outlying breastworks and formidable abattis of fallen trees. Both British and French fought with the utmost spirit and bravery, the contest being compared by experts to Malplaquet and Badajoz. But the British were without a leader, and struck wildly; while the cool and calculating Montcalm, admirably intrenched, and aided by his two best lieutenants, Lévis and Bourlamaque, was everywhere, and never to better effect. Under cover of darkness, the blundering and now disheartened Abercromby withdrew with his thirteen thousand men without attempting another attack. His loss had been nineteen hundred and forty-four in killed, wounded, and missing, while the French reported but three hundred and seventy-seven.[2]

[1] Fortescue, *British Army*, 326.
[2] Parkman, *Montcalm and Wolfe*, II., App., 431-433.

Montcalm wrote to his wife, exultantly and with
some measure of overstatement: "Without Indians,
almost without Canadians or colony troops—I had
only four hundred — alone with Lévis and Bourlamaque and the troops of the line, thirty-one hundred fighting men, I have beaten an army of
twenty-five thousand. They repassed the lake precipitately, with a loss of at least five thousand."
In the same strain, he wrote to another: "What a
day for France! If I had had two hundred Indians
to send out at the head of a thousand picked men
under the Chevalier de Lévis, not many would have
escaped. Ah, my dear Doreil, what soldiers are
ours! I never saw the like. Why were they not
at Louisburg?" [1]

In his elation Montcalm was cautious. He was
content with having given to New France another
year of life, and did nothing further than to im-
prove the defences of Ticonderoga, and with his
bush-rangers to haunt the road which lay between
Lake George and Fort Edward. On his part,
Abercromby remained supinely in camp at the
head of Lake Champlain through the remainder of
the season. In October, Amherst arrived, but it
was then too late to accomplish any result, and the
army prepared to spend the winter on the spot.

Lieutenant - Colonel John Bradstreet, of Abercromby's command, a dashing and accomplished
officer, had long wished to lead an expedition

[1] Parkman, *Montcalm and Wolfe*, II., App., iii, 112.

against Fort Frontenac (the modern town of Kingston, Ontario), which lay at the outlet of Lake
Ontario. It had been an important vantage-point
for the French from the old days of La Salle, and
commanded Oswego, Niagara, and thus the lake
route to the west. Loudoun had favored the scheme,
but Abercromby overruled it; his endorsement was,
however, forced by a council of war, held soon after
the battle of Ticonderoga.

With twenty-five hundred men, Bradstreet dodged
the enemy on the portage trail, returned to Albany,
ascended by the Mohawk route to Oswego, crossed
the lake, and on August 25 arrived before Fort
Frontenac. That stronghold was garrisoned by
only a hundred men, while nine small vessels were
in the harbor. These fell an easy prize to the adventurous colonel (August 27), who destroyed the
fort and all but two of the ships, and returned to
Albany exultant.

He had reason to be, for his success was by all
means the most important strategical accomplish-
ment of the year: Lake Ontario, one of the two important gateways to the west, was now entirely under British control. Thus Fort Niagara was isolated,
and the French could no longer communicate with
the Ohio River. Fort Duquesne lay at the mercy
of the British advance, which speedily followed.
Brigadier Forbes, a Scotch veteran charged with
the Duquesne expedition, had arrived in Philadelphia in April, but found no army awaiting him,

although troops had been promised from Pennsylvania, Maryland, Virginia, and North Carolina. June was nearly ended before he could march. His force aggregated between six and seven thousand men, among whom were twelve hundred Highlanders under Colonel Montgomery, and a battalion of the Sixtieth Royal Americans commanded by Colonel Henry Bouquet, a brave and ingenious Swiss officer who had invented a forest drill which included the most effective of Indian tactics. The Virginians, clad in fringed leather hunting-shirts, and now a well-trained body of fighters, were headed by Colonel Washington, whose judgment was frequently asked by his fellow-officers.

Much time was spent over deciding which road to take—Braddock's, from Virginia, or a new trail to be struck out through the dense forests of Pennsylvania. The latter was selected, after much display of provincial jealousy, for each colony was desirous both of the prestige and the profit to be derived from the presence of the troops. Forbes's plan of moving forward by easy stages, and leaving behind him a line of block-houses as a continuous base, was safe, and it had the advantage of being slow. Aware that the French commander had gathered at Fort Duquesne the usual crew of breech-clouted Indian allies from the upper Great Lakes, and knowing their lack of patience, Forbes thought to weary the waiting savages until they should, in disgust at the non-appearance of the

English, return to their homes[1]—which is exactly
what happened. Meanwhile, the brigadier upon
his leisurely progress called a convention of Iroquois, Delaware, Mingo, and Shawnee, which met
at Easton in October, and those powerful tribes
gave in their adherence to the English.[2]

The advancing column met with some reverses
at the hands of French bush-rangers, but the capture of Fort Frontenac had really decided the situation. The Indians deserted Fort Duquesne, the
Canadian militia returned home for the winter, and
De Ligneris, the commandant, was left with a garrison of but four or five hundred. When (November 25, 1758) Forbes's advance guard reached the
fortress, they discovered nothing but blackened
ruins—the walls having been blown up the previous night, and barracks and stores burned; while
the defenders had scattered by land and water,
some down the Ohio to Fort Massac, others to
Presq'isle, and the commander with a small body-
guard to Fort Machault, the Venango of former
years. With Lake Ontario possessed by the enemy,
retreat to Canada was now impracticable.

Montcalm's right flank had thus not only been
shattered at two points, but its extremity had been
driven into the interior, and, through the loss of

[1] Forbes to Bouquet, August 18, 1758, *Bouquet and Haldimand
Papers*, MSS. in British Museum.

[2] See journals of Charles Frederick Post, in Thwaites, *Early
Western Travels*, I., 185–291; this missionary was the principal
go-between in the British-Indian negotiations of 1758–1759.

Fort Frontenac, entirely cut off from its base on
the St. Lawrence. His left flank had been sadly
maimed, through the fall of Louisburg, but there
was still left a fighting chance for communication
with the sea. His centre was still intact, however,
and with consummate courage he awaited another
year, hoping for the best but fearing the end.

Despite the jubilant tone adopted in his letters
to Marquise Montcalm and his friends, he really
found small encouragement in the Ticonderoga incident, and was despondent over the future. Folly
in the enemy's plan had alone saved the French
from being hemmed in to the St. Lawrence. Partly
because of neglect by the Versailles government,
partly owing to the British naval blockade, partly
because Vaudreuil and Bigot were interested in sup-
pressing news of the actual condition of affairs, but
in large measure because troops were being poured
into Germany by the hundred thousand and few
were left for Canada, New France was at last on the
brink of ruin. The military levies took so many
men from the fields that an insufficient crop had
been garnered. The dissensions between the governor and the general now reached a point almost
unbearable, the civil and military establishments
being wellnigh at a deadlock.

Montcalm sought to resign, but the fall of Duquesne and Louisburg caused him to withdraw his
request and resolve to stand by the colony. His
appeal to Vaudreuil for harmony (August 23) was

useless. Dissatisfaction and official debauchery were rampant, for Bigot and his fellows were lining their nests in anticipation of the crash that should destroy the evidences of their evil deeds; the fur-trade had been ruined; a financial crisis was at hand. But outside the governmental cabal the people of New France were firm against the common foe; although hard pressed, and with divided councils, civilians and soldiers were willing to contend for their king and their religion to the last.

Marshal Belle-Isle, the French war minister, feared the worst, but admonished Montcalm to at least retain some footing upon North America: "However small soever the space you are able to hold may be, it is indispensable to keep a foothold in North America; for, if we once lose the country entirely, its recovery will be almost impossible." To which the general—the one admirable character in the public life of New France, in these its closing months—replied, "I shall do everything to save this unhappy colony, or die." As for the English, eager and pressing, they were not at all disheartened by the disaster at Ticonderoga. The causes of the failure were patent: Abercromby had stupidly blundered; and it was resolved to avoid his mistakes in another, and it was hoped final, attempt.

CHAPTER XV

THE FALL OF QUEBEC
(1759)

THE British Parliament met late in November,
1758, at a time when the nation was aglow
with enthusiasm over the successes of the year—
Louisburg and Frontenac in North America, and
the driving of the French from the Guinea coast as
the result of battles at Sénégal (May) and Gorée
(November).[1] The war was proving far more costly
than had been anticipated, yet Pitt rigidly held the
country to the task; but not against its will, and the
necessary funds were freely voted. Walpole wrote
to a friend: " Our unanimity is prodigious. You
would as soon hear 'No' from an old maid as from
the House of Commons." The preparations for the
new year were on a much larger scale than before;
both by land and sea France was to be pushed to
the uttermost, and the warlike spirit of Great Britain seemed wrought to the highest pitch.

The new French premier, Choiseul, was himself
not lacking in activity. He renewed with vigor the
project of invading Great Britain, preparations

[1] Clowes, *Royal Navy*, III., 186–189.

therefor being evident quite early in the year 1759. Fifty thousand men were to land in England, and twelve thousand in Scotland, where the Stuart cause still lingered. But as usual the effort came to naught. The Toulon squadron was to cooperate with one from Brest; Boscawen, who now commanded the Mediterranean fleet, apprehended the former while trying to escape through the Straits of Gibraltar in a thick haze (August 17), and after destroying several of the ships dispersed the others; while Sir Edward Hawke annihilated the Brest fleet in a brilliant sea-fight off Quiberon Bay (November 20).[1] Relieved of the possibility of insular invasion, the Channel and Mediterranean squadrons were now free to raid French commerce, patrol French ports, and thus intercept communication with New France and to harry French — and, later, Spanish—colonies over-seas.

We have seen that in 1757 Clive had regained Calcutta and won Bengal at the famous battle of Plassey. Two years thereafter the East Indian seas were abandoned by the French after three decisive actions won by Pitt's valiant seamen, and India thus became a permanent possession of the British empire.[2] In January, 1759, also, the British captured Guadeloupe, in the West Indies.[3] Lacking sea power, it was impossible for France much longer to hold her colonies; it was but a question

---

[1] Clowes, *Royal Navy*, III., 210–214, on Boscawen's victory; 216–222, on Hawke's. [2] *Ibid.*, 196–201. [3] *Ibid.*, 201–203.

of time when the remainder should fall into the
clutches of the mistress of the ocean.

Notwithstanding all this naval activity, Pitt's
principal operations were really centred against
Canada. The movement thither was to be along
two lines, which eventually were to meet in co-
operation. First, a direct attack was to be made
upon Quebec, headed by Wolfe, who was to be
convoyed and assisted by a fleet under the command
of Admiral Saunders; second, Amherst—now commander - in - chief in America, Abercromby having
been recalled — was to penetrate Canada by way
of lakes George and Champlain. He was to join
Wolfe at Quebec, but was authorized to make such
diversions as he found practicable — principally to
re-establish Oswego and to relieve Pittsburg (Fort
Duquesne) with reinforcements and supplies.

Wolfe's selection as leader of the Quebec expedition occasioned general surprise in England.
Yet it was in the natural course of events. He
had been the life of the Louisburg campaign of the
year before, and when Amherst was expressing the
desire of attacking Quebec after the reduction of
Cape Breton he wrote to the latter: "An offensive,
daring kind of war will awe the Indians and ruin
the French. Block-houses and a trembling defensive encourage the meanest scoundrels to attack
us. If you will attempt to cut up New France by
the roots, I will come with pleasure to assist." [1]

---

[1] Parkman, *Montcalm and Wolfe*, II., 80.

Wolfe, whose family enjoyed some influence, had attained a captaincy at the age of seventeen and became a major at twenty. He was now thirty-two, a major-general, and with an excellent fighting record both in Flanders and America. Quiet and modest in demeanor, although occasionally using excitable and ill-guarded language, he was a refined and educated gentleman, careful of and beloved by his troops, yet a stern disciplinarian; and although frail in body, and often overcome by rheumatism and other ailments, capable of great strain when buoyed by the zeal which was one of his characteristics. The majority of his portraits represent a tall, lank, ungainly form, with a singularly weak facial profile; but it is likely that these belie him, for he had an indubitable spirit, a profound mind, quick intuition, a charming manner, and was much thought of by women. Indeed, just before sailing, he had become engaged to the beautiful and charming Katharine Lowther, sister of Lord Lonsdale, and afterwards the Duchess of Bolton.[1]

On February 17, Wolfe departed with Saunders's fleet of twenty-one sail, bearing the king's secret instructions to "carry into execution the said important operation with the utmost application and vigour."[2] The voyage was protracted, and after

---

[1] For biographical details of Wolfe's early career, see Wright, *Life*, and Doughty and Parmelee, *Siege of Quebec*, I., 1–128; in *ibid.*, II., 16, is a portrait of Wolfe's fiancée.

[2] Text in Doughty and Parmelee, *Siege of Quebec*, VI., 87–90.

arrival at Louisburg he was obliged to wait long before the promised troops appeared. He had expected regiments from Guadaloupe, but these could not yet be spared, owing to their wretched condition; and the Nova Scotia garrisons had also been weakened by disease, so that of the twelve thousand agreed upon he finally could muster somewhat under nine thousand.[1] These were of the best quality of their kind; although the general still entertained a low opinion of the value of the provincials, who, it must be admitted, were, however serviceable in bush-ranging, far below the efficiency of the regulars in a campaign of this character. The force was divided into three brigades, under Monckton, Townsend, and Murray, young men of ability; although Townsend's supercilious manner—the fruit of a superior social connection—did not endear him either to his men or his colleagues.

On June 1 the fleet began to leave Louisburg. There were thirty-nine men-of-war, ten auxiliaries, seventy-six transports, and a hundred and sixty-two miscellaneous craft, which were manned by thirteen thousand naval seamen and five thousand of the mercantile marine—an aggregate of eighteen thousand, or twice as many as the landsmen under Wolfe.[2] While to the latter is commonly given credit for the result, it must not be forgotten that the victory was quite as much

[1] Lists in Doughty and Parmelee, *Siege of Quebec*, II., 22, 23.
[2] Wood, *Fight for Canada*, 166, 167, 173.

due to the skilful management of the navy as to that of the army, the expedition being in all respects a joint enterprise, into which the men of both branches of the service entered with intense enthusiasm.

The French had placed much reliance on the supposed impossibility of great battle-ships being successfully navigated up the St. Lawrence above the mouth of the Saguenay without the most careful piloting. This portion of the river, a hundred and twenty miles in length, certainly is intricate water, being streaked with perplexing currents created by the mingling of the river's strong flow with the flood and ebb of the tide; the great stream is diverted into two parallel channels by reefs and islands, and there are numerous shoals—moreover, the French had removed all lights and other aids to navigation. But British sailors laughed at difficulties such as these, and, while they managed to capture a pilot, had small use for him, preferring their own cautious methods. Preceded by a crescent of sounding-boats, officered by Captain James Cook, afterwards of glorious memory as a pathfinder, the fleet advanced slowly but safely, its approach heralded by beacons gleaming nightly to the fore, upon the rounded hill-tops overlooking the long, thin line of river-side settlement which extended eastward from Quebec to the Saguenay.[1]

[1] "Journal of the Expedition up the River St. Lawrence," by a sergeant-major of grenadiers, in Doughty and Parmelee, *Siege of Quebec*, V., 1–11.

The French had at first expected attacks only from Lake Ontario and from the south. But receiving early tidings of Wolfe's expedition, through convoys with supplies from France that had escaped Saunders's patrol of the gulf, general alarm prevailed, and Montcalm decided to make his stand at Quebec. To the last he appears to have shared in the popular delusion that British men-of-war could not ascend the river; nevertheless, he promptly summoned to the capital the greater part of the militia from all sections of Canada, save that a thousand whites and savages were left with Pouchot to defend Niagara, twelve hundred men under De la Corne to guard Lake Ontario, and Bourlamaque, with upwards of three thousand, was ordered to delay Amherst's advance and thus prevent him from joining Wolfe. The population of Canada at the time was about eighty-five thousand souls, and of these perhaps twenty-two thousand were capable of bearing arms.[1] The force now gathered in and about Quebec aggregated about seventeen thousand, of whom some ten thousand were militia, four thousand regulars of the line, and a thousand each of colonial regulars, seamen, and Indians; of these two thousand were reserved for the garrison of Quebec, under De Ramezay, while the remainder were at the disposal of Montcalm for the general defence.[2]

[1] Doughty and Parmelee, *Siege of Quebec*, II., 51–53.
[2] Wood, *Fight for Canada*, 152.

The "rock of Quebec" is the northeast end of a long, narrow, triangular promontory, to the north of which lies the valley of the St. Charles and to the south that of the St. Lawrence. The acclivity on the St. Charles side is lower and less steep than the cliffs fringing the St. Lawrence, which rise almost precipitously from two to three hundred feet above the river—the citadel cliff being three hundred and forty-five feet, almost sheer. Either side of the promontory was easily defensible from assault, the table-land being only reached by steep and narrow paths. Surmounting the cliffs, at the apex of the triangle, was Upper Town, the capital of New France. Batteries, largely manned by sailors, lined the cliff-tops within the town, and the western base, fronting the Plains of Abraham, was protected by fifteen hundred yards of insecure wall —for, after all, Quebec had, despite the money spent upon it, never been scientifically fortified, its commanders having from the first relied chiefly upon its natural position as a stronghold.

At the base of the promontory, on the St. Lawrence side, is a wide beach occupied by Lower Town, where were the market, the commercial warehouses, a large share of the business establishments, and the homes of the trading and laboring classes. A narrow strand, little more than the width of a roadway, extended along the base of the cliffs westward, communicating with the up-river country; another road led westward along the table-land above. Thus the

city obtained its supplies from the interior both by
highway and by river.

Entrance to the St. Charles side of the promontory
had been blocked by booms at the mouth of that
river, protected by strong redoubts; and off Lower
Town was a line of floating batteries.   Beyond the
St. Charles, for a distance of seven miles eastward
to the gorge of the Montmorenci, Montcalm disposed
the greater part of his forces, his position being a
plain naturally protected by a steep slope descending to the meadow and tidal flats which here margin
the St. Lawrence.   This plain rises gradually from
the St. Charles, until at the Montmorenci cataract it
attains a height of three hundred feet, and along
the summit of the slope were well-devised trenches.
The gorge furnished a strong natural defence to
the left wing, for it could be forded only in the
dense forest at a considerable distance above the
falls, and to force this approach would have been
to invite an ambuscade.   Wolfe contented himself,
therefore, with intrenching a considerable force
along the eastern bank of the gorge, and thence
issuing for frontal attacks on the Beauport Flats
—so called from the name of the village midway.
Montcalm had chosen this as the chief line of defence, on the theory that the approach by the St.
Charles would be the one selected by the invaders;
as, indeed, it long seemed to Wolfe the only possible
path to the works of Upper Town.

Westward of the city, upon the table - land,

Bougainville headed a corps of observation, supposed continually to patrol the St. Lawrence clifftops and keep communications open with the interior; but this precaution failed in the hour of need. The height of Point Lévis, across the river from the town, on the south bank, was unoccupied. Montcalm had wished to fortify this vantage-point, and thus block the river from both sides, but Vaudreuil had overruled him, and the result was fatal. Other weak points in the defence were divided command and the scarcity of food and ammunition, occasioned largely by Bigot's rapacious knavery.

On June 26 the British fleet anchored off the Isle of Orleans, thus dissipating the fond hopes of the French that some disaster might prevent its approach. Three days later Wolfe's men, now encamped on the island at a safe distance from Montcalm's guns, made an easy capture of Point Lévis, and there erected batteries which commanded the town. British ships were, in consequence, soon able to pass Quebec, under cover of the Point Lévis guns, and destroy some of the French shipping anchored in the upper basin; while landing parties harried the country to the west, forcing *habitants* to neutrality and intercepting supplies. Frequently, the British forces were, upon these various enterprises, divided into three or four isolated divisions, which might have been roughly handled by a venturesome foe. But Montcalm rigidly maintained the policy of defence, his only offensive operations being the unsuccessful despatch of fire-ships against the invading fleet.

On his part, Wolfe made several futile attacks upon the Beauport redoubts. The position was, however, too strong for him to master, and in one assault (July 31) he lost half of his landing party— nearly five hundred killed, wounded, and missing.[1] This continued ill-success fretted Wolfe and at last quite disheartened him, for the season was rapidly wearing on, and winter sets in early at Quebec; moreover, nothing had yet been heard of Amherst. There was, indeed, some talk of waiting until another season. However, more and more British ships worked their way past the fort, and, by making frequent feints of landing at widely separated points, caused Bougainville great annoyance. Montcalm was accordingly obliged to weaken his lower forces by sending reinforcements to the plains west of the city. Thus, while Wolfe was pining, French uneasiness was growing, for the British were now intercepting supplies and reinforcements from both above and below, and Bougainville's men were growing weary of constantly patrolling fifteen or twenty miles of cliffs.[2]

Meanwhile, let us see how Amherst was faring.

[1] Authorities cited in Parkman, *Montcalm and Wolfe*, II., 233, 234. For details, consult Doughty and Parmelee, *Siege of Quebec*, II., chap. vi.

[2] See Bougainville's correspondence, in Doughty and Parmelee, *Siege of Quebec*, IV., 1-141.

At the end of June the general assembled five thousand provincials and six thousand five hundred regulars at the head of Lake George. He had previously despatched Brigadier Prideaux with five thousand regulars and provincials to reduce Niagara, and Brigadier Stanwix, who had been of Bradstreet's party the year before, to succor Pittsburg, now in imminent danger from French bushrangers and Indians who were swarming at Presqu'isle, Le Bœuf, and Venango.

Amherst himself moved slowly, it being July 21 before the army started northward upon the lake. Bourlamaque, whose sole purpose was to delay the British advance, lay at Ticonderoga with three thousand five hundred men, but on the 26th he blew up the fort and retreated in good order to Crown Point. On the British approaching that post he again fell back, this time to a strong position at Isle aux Noix, at the outlet of Lake Champlain, where, wrote Bourlamaque to a friend, "we are entrenched to the teeth, and armed with a hundred pieces of cannon." [1] Amherst now deeming vessels essential, yet lacking ship-carpenters, it was the middle of September before his little navy was ready, and then he thought the season too far advanced for further operations. [2]

---

[1] September 22, 1759, quoted in Parkman, *Montcalm and Wolfe*, II., 249.

[2] Official journal of Amherst, in *London Magazine*, XXVII., 379–383.

Amherst's advance had, however, induced Montcalm to defend Montreal, Lévis having been despatched thither for this purpose.

Prideaux, advancing up the Mohawk, proceeded to Oswego, where he left half of his men to cover his retreat, and then sailed to Niagara. Slain by accident during the siege, his place was taken by Sir William Johnson, the Indian commander, who pushed the work with vigor. Suddenly confronted by a French force of thirteen hundred rangers and savages from the west, who had been deflected thither from a proposed attack on Pittsburg, with the view of recovering that fort, Johnson completely vanquished them (July 24). The discomfited crew burned their posts in that region and retreated precipitately to Detroit. The following day Niagara surrendered, and thus, with Pittsburg also saved, the west was entirely cut off from Canada, and the upper Ohio Valley was placed in British hands. The work of Stanwix having been accomplished by Johnson, the former, who had been greatly delayed by transport difficulties, advanced as promptly as possible to the Forks of the Ohio, and in the place of the old French works built the modernized stronghold of Fort Pitt. [1]

On August 20, Wolfe fell seriously ill. Both he and the army were discouraged. The casualties had thus far been over eight hundred men, and dis-

[1] Stanwix to Pitt, November 20, 1759, MS. in Public Record Office.

ease had cut a wide swath through the ranks.
Desperate, he at last accepted the counsel of his
officers, that a landing be attempted above the town,
supplies definitively cut off from Montreal, and
Montcalm forced to fight or surrender. From
September 3 to 12, Wolfe, arisen from his bed but
still weak, quietly withdrew his troops from the
Montmorenci camp and transported them in vessels
which successfully passed through a heavy cannonading from the fort to safe anchorage in the
upper basin. Reinforcements marching along the
southern bank, from Point Lévis, soon joined their
comrades aboard the ships. For several days this
portion of the fleet regularly floated up and down
the river above Quebec, with the changing tide,
thus wearing out Bougainville's men, who in
great perplexity followed the enemy along the
cliff - tops, through a beat of several leagues, until
from sheer exhaustion they at last became care-
less.

On the evening of September 12, Saunders—whose
admirable handling of the fleet deserves equal recognition with the services of Wolfe — commenced
a heavy bombardment of the Beauport lines, and
feigned a general landing at that place. Montcalm,
not knowing that the majority of the British were
by this time above the town, and deceived as to his
enemy's real intent, hurried to Beauport the bulk of
his troops, save those necessary for Bougainville's
rear guard. Meanwhile, however, Wolfe was pre-

paring for his desperate attempt several miles up the river.

Before daylight the following morning (September 13), thirty boats containing seventeen hundred picked men, with Wolfe at their head, floated down the stream under the dark shadow of the apparently insurmountable cliffs. They were challenged by sentinels along the shore; but, by pretending to be a provision convoy which had been expected from up-country, suspicion was disarmed. About two miles above Quebec they landed at an indentation then known as Anse du Foulon, but now called Wolfe's Cove. From the narrow beach a small, winding path, sighted by Wolfe two days before, led up through the trees and underbrush to the Plains of Abraham. The climbing party of twenty-four infantrymen found the path obstructed by an abattis and trenches; but, nothing daunted, they clambered up the height of two hundred feet by the aid of stunted shrubs, reached the top, overcame the weak and cowardly guard of a hundred men, made way for their comrades, and by sunrise forty-five hundred men of the British army were drawn up across the plateau before the walls of Quebec.

Montcalm, ten miles away on the other side of the St. Charles, was amazed at the daring feat, but by nine o'clock had massed his troops and confronted his enemy. The battle was brief but desperate. The intrepid Wolfe fell on the field—"the only

British general," declared Horace Walpole, "belonging to the reign of George the Second, who can be said to have earned a lasting reputation." [1] Montcalm, mortally wounded, was carried by his fleeing comrades within the city, where he died before morning. During the seven hours' battle, the British had lost fifty-eight killed and five hundred and ninety-seven wounded, about twenty per cent. of the firing-line; the French lost about twelve hundred killed, wounded, and prisoners, of whom perhaps a fourth were killed. [2]

Torn by disorder, the militia mutinous, the walls in ruins from the cannonading of the British fleet, and Vaudreuil and his fellows fleeing to the interior, the helpless garrison of Quebec surrendered, September 17, the British troops entering the following day. The English flag now floated over the citadel, and soon there was great rejoicing throughout Great Britain and her American colonies; and well there might be, for the affair on the Plains of Abraham was one of the most heroic and far-reaching achievements ever wrought by Englishmen in any land or age. [3]

[1] Doughty and Parmelee, *Siege of Quebec*, II., 237.

[2] *Ibid.*, II., 332, with detailed British returns; Wood, *Fight for Canada*, 262.

[3] For detailed description of the siege, consult Doughty and Parmelee, *Siege of Quebec*, II., III., and documents in IV.–VI.

CHAPTER XVI

CONQUEST APPROACHING

(1759–1760)

SOON after the surrender of Quebec, Brigadier Monckton, disabled by a wound, was ordered to the south for his health, leaving Townsend in charge. For a time Bougainville gave the latter some trouble, but soon was silenced. Late in October, Saunders set sail with the fleet, carrying Townsend with him to England, whom his enemies accused of hurrying unduly to gain applause at home.[1] Murray was thereupon left in command, with a few more than seven thousand British troops, to face the rigors of a Canadian winter, which proved one of the severest on record.

Such of the Canadian militia as gave up their arms and took the oath of allegiance to the British king were allowed to return to their homes, an arrangement which affected nearly all of the *habitants* below Three Rivers. Indeed, all but three thousand of the citizens of Quebec had scattered to various parts of the country. Both the walls and buildings of Upper Town were for the most

[1] Parkman, *Montcalm and Wolfe*, II., 317.

part in ruins, thievery was rampant, disorder prevailed on every hand, and the general demoralization was heightened by a shortage of provisions, for the country round about had been denuded of subsistence material. Wood-cutting was a pressing necessity, the supply coming from the forest of Ste. Foy, four miles away, whence the soldiers hauled the loaded sleighs, for no horses were to be had. The troops suffered greatly from insufficiency of clothing, lack of proper quarters, and unwonted exposure to arctic conditions; frost-bites were common, and the unsanitary conditions, combined with the almost exclusive use of salt meats, induced scurvy, dysentery, and fevers, which frequently resulted in death. By the last week of April, 1760, no more than three thousand of Murray's men were fit for duty. Of the dead there were six hundred and fifty, most of the bodies having been preserved in snow-banks, awaiting burial after the spring thaw.[1] Yet it has been asserted that of the six hundred women attached to the British garrison during this frightful experience not one had died and but few were ill.[2]

Conditions might doubtless have been softened had Murray been provided with adequate funds for the purchase of supplies from the *habitants* in the interior, many of whom were disposed to be politic

[1] Public Record Office MSS., *Return of the Forces*, April 24, 1760; Kingsford, *Canada*, IV., 362.
[2] Bradley, *Fight with France*, 360.

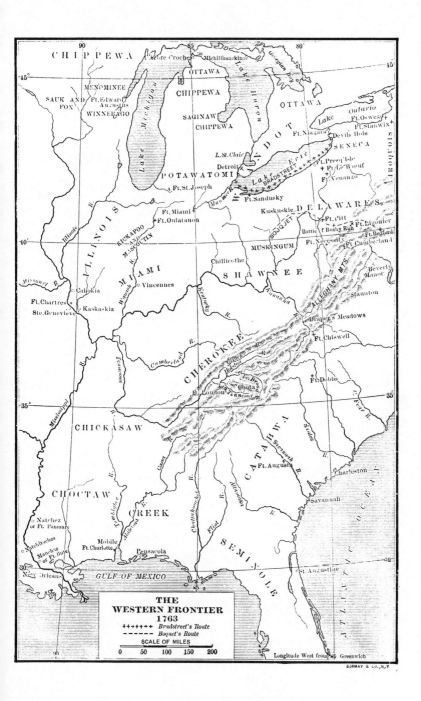

THE
WESTERN FRONTIER
1763

++++++ *Bradstreet's Route*
------- *Boquet's Route*

SCALE OF MILES

0   50   100   150   200

Longitude West from Greenwich

BORMAY & CO., N.Y

towards the invaders.   But after October 24 there
was no money even to pay the troops, the incom-
petent secretary of state for war, Lord Barrington,
having shamefully neglected to supply the military
chest in Canada, which was literally empty through
the entire winter.[1]

Meanwhile, Lévis, who had succeeded Montcalm,
was busy in the rear, towards Montreal, where
Vaudreuil commanded in person; and alarming reports of extensive preparations for attack were
frequent in Quebec.   Murray maintained outposts
at Ste. Foy and Old Lorette, and these were frequently threatened by prowling Canadian rangers,
who passed much of the winter at St. Augustine,
but two days' march from the city.   In the last
week of April, Lévis appeared before the British
outposts with eleven thousand men, mostly regulars, although with them were many of the *habitants*
who had viewed their oath too lightly, and Murray drew back to Quebec.   But on the morning of
April 28, having a good train of artillery, he sal-
lied forth with three thousand men to meet the
enemy on the Plains of Abraham.[2]   The lines of
battle were strikingly similar to those maintained
on the previous September 18, save that the respective positions were reversed.

The ground was covered with drifts of sodden

[1] Kingsford, *Canada*, IV., 361, 362.
[2] Wood, *Fight for Canada*, 337; Parkman, *Montcalm and Wolfe*, II., 442–444; Kingsford, *Canada*, IV., 369.

snow, which soon was trampled to liquid mud, wellnigh knee-deep.   The young and impetuous Murray
had been over-confident, both he and his men having under-estimated the fighting capacity of the
French; they were fairly worsted after a two hours'
fight, and obliged to leave their guns on the field,
but their retreat to the city was orderly.   The
British loss was eleven hundred and twenty-four
killed and wounded, a third of the force engaged,
while the French are supposed to have lost two
thousand.[1]

For nearly a fortnight the situation looked desperate to Murray.   Half of his twenty-four hundred men reported fit for duty were in wretched
condition, being, as one of them wrote, "half-
starved, scorbutic skeletons." [2]   But their lesson
had been learned, and they now set to work with
feverish activity to repair the defences.   In the
face of this determined attitude Lévis did not, despite his superior forces, push the attack, and in
his hesitation waited too long.   Between May 9
and 16 three frigates arrived from England, which
brought not only blessed relief to the hollow-eyed
garrison, but destroyed Lévis's ships in the river
and their cargoes of military stores.   On the
latter day, being vigorously attacked by Murray
and the entire strength of the garrison batteries,
the French precipitately retreated, leaving forty

[1] Kingsford, *Canada*, IV., 368–371.
[2] Parkman, *Montcalm and Wolfe*, II., 352.

guns, much siege material, and all their sick and wounded.[1]

The retreat of Lévis towards Montreal, and the destruction of his ships and stores, together with the burning of a flotilla of twenty-five other French vessels with their cargoes of supplies upon the Restigouche, in July,[2] left New France with no outlet to the sea. It was a mere question of time when her lingering defence could be cornered and strangled, and yet there was danger in bringing her to bay. Montreal was now her only stronghold, and upon this point Amherst, with admirable caution, proceeded to concentrate his attack. He himself was to proceed down the St. Lawrence from Lake Ontario and cut off the French retreat westward; Brigadier Haviland was to push his way through from Lake Champlain; and Murray was to sail up from Quebec—all three expeditions to unite at Montreal and force a general surrender.

The task was not as simple as appears on the map; for there were formidable rapids for Amherst and Haviland to encounter in the St. Lawrence, several French forts to overcome upon the way, and the three points of departure were widely separated, with but slight communication between them. Moreover, there was the customary vexatious delay on the part of the provincial governments, which had promised militia quotas. It required a large

[1] List of authorities, in Parkman, *Montcalm and Wolfe*, 358.
[2] Wood, *Fight for Canada*, 299.

fund of patience on the part of Amherst, and much delicate management, to bring it all about. A misstep might readily prevent the desired conjunction, and then Lévis would have had a fair chance to annihilate each column in turn.

Murray moved first. July 15 his little army of two thousand four hundred and fifty men embarked in forty boats, bateaux, and other transports, escorted by three frigates and a numerous flotilla of smaller craft,[1] followed a little later by one thousand three hundred men from the now dismantled fortress of Louisburg, under Lord Rollo. With a keen watch of scouting parties ranging the banks, and disarming the *habitants* as he went along, Murray's progress was slow. At Sorel, east of Montreal, Bourlamaque and Dumas lay intrenched on both banks with a force of four thousand, but offered no resistance. Judiciously displaying harshness towards enemies, but kindness towards non-combatants, Murray persuaded half of their men to disarm and take the oath of neutrality, the others following the fleet along the shore, hoping that when Montreal was reached the British would find themselves embarrassed between two fires. August 24 he arrived at Contrecœur, eighteen miles below Montreal, and went into camp to await his colleagues, who were not long in arriving at the island.

Haviland, whose troops had suffered greatly

[1] Clowes, *Royal Navy*, III., 227, 228; Knox, *Campaigns in North America*, II., 344, 348.

throughout the winter from cold, disease, and an insufficient commissariat, left Crown Point on August 16 with a force of about three thousand four hundred men—regulars, provincials, and Indians.[1] Bougainville was in strong position at Isle aux Noix, with nearly as many men as Haviland; but on a show of force withdrew, and many of his discouraged rangers soon deserted him. Forts St. John and Chambly were also abandoned as the British advanced both by land and water, and Haviland, on September 6, joined Amherst on the island of Montreal.

It was August 10 before Amherst, delayed by the co-operating militia, could get his little army afloat at Oswego. It consisted of about eleven thousand men, of whom less than six thousand were regulars, four thousand five hundred provincials, and seven hundred Indians under Sir William Johnson.[2] The flotilla of nearly eight hundred whale-boats and bateaux were escorted by several gun-boats. Fort La Galette (now Ogdensburg), at the head of the St. Lawrence rapids, was passed five days later, a French brig of ten guns being captured by the gun-boats. A little below, on an island in the rapids, Fort Lévis, with a garrison of three hundred, stood a siege of three days before it surrendered. But

[1] Fortescue, *British Army*, 397; Parkman, *Montcalm and Wolfe*, II., 367; Kingsford, *Canada*, IV., 396.

[2] Fortescue, *British Army*, 399; Kingsford, *Canada*, IV., 381–393.

the most dangerous experience was the descent of
the rapids, an undertaking involving great care and
bravery; as it was, sixty boats were wrecked or
damaged and eighty-four men drowned. On September 6, the very day of Haviland's arrival—so
carefully timed had been the concentrating movements of the British—the fleet glided triumphantly
to the shore of Lachine, at the head of the great
rapids, nine miles above Montreal. The troops
marched unopposed to a camp outside the western
gate of the shabby little town, whose ill-constructed
stone walls were proof against Indians, but presented a sorry defence to the attack of civilized
soldiers with artillery.

Vaudreuil, Bougainville, Bourlamaque, and Roque-
maure — the last-named the commander of Fort
St. John—were now confronted by seventeen thousand British, well supplied with cannon and stores;
while they could muster behind their weak fortifications barely two thousand five hundred—practically all of them regulars, for the militia had
deserted, but "demoralized in order, in spirit, and
in discipline."[1] There were provisions for but fifteen to twenty days,[2] the Indians had characteristically gone over to the stronger side, the Canadians were disheartened and now for the most
part disarmed and sworn to neutrality, and further struggle seemed useless.

September 7, Bougainville waited on Amherst

[1] Fortescue, *British Army*, 399.   [2] Lévis, *Journal*, 303.

with an offer of capitulation, demanding only that
the garrison be allowed to march out with the
honors of war. But the British general, charging
the French with inhumanity and particularly with
inciting the Indians against English borderers, peremptorily refused this concession, demanding that
"The whole garrison of Montreal and all other
French troops in Canada must lay down their arms,
and shall not serve during the present war." [1] Next
day, despite hot protests from the indomitable
Lévis, who wanted to fight to the last ditch, the
articles were signed as dictated by Amherst. [2] Thus
all of the vast domain of New France, with its population of about seventy-three thousand souls—allow-
ing fifty-seven thousand to Canada, ten thousand
to Acadia, and six thousand to Detroit and the Illinois, but excluding some ten thousand in the
province of Louisiana proper [3]—passed into the control of Great Britain. Robert Rogers, prominent
throughout the war as a daring and successful
leader of provincial rangers, was sent up the Great
Lakes to enforce the capitulation at the French outposts in the west; and during the winter and the
following year secured the transfer of forts Miami,
Detroit, Mackinac, and St. Joseph.

[1] *Procès verbal*, quoted in Parkman, *Montcalm and Wolfe*, II., 373.
[2] *Ibid.*, 375; French text in Kingsford, *Canada*, IV., 417–433;
no English original was made.
[3] Kingsford. *Canada*, IV., 413; Coffin, *Province of Quebec*, 280;
Com. of Canadian Archives, *Report*, 1890, p. 109; Hinsdale,
Old Northwest, 48.

In accordance with the terms of the treaty,
the prisoners of war, the chief civil officers of New
France, a great part of the Canadian *noblesse*, and
the leading merchants departed (September 13–22)
for Quebec, whence a month later they left for
France. Upon reaching Paris, Vaudreuil, Bigot,
and their rascally confederates were imprisoned in
the Bastile for fraud and malfeasance in office.
When brought to trial in December, 1761, they made
a sorry spectacle before the court, with their mutual
criminations. Vaudreuil was acquitted for lack of
legal proof; Bigot was fined one million five hundred thousand francs, his property confiscated, and
he was banished from France for life; others, a
score in number, received various sentences, their
dishonesty in the end profiting them but slightly.[1]

The Canadian peasantry, and such of the regulars
as chose Canada for their home, settled down under
their new political masters, and in time became
happier and more prosperous under the new flag
than they had ever been under the old. Amherst
had detailed General Gage to be governor of Montreal, General Ralph Burton was made governor of
Three Rivers, and Murray continued in charge of
Quebec. To them was left the administration of a
policy of kindliness to the unfortunate *habitants*, who
were protected against the Indian allies of the conquerors, allowed to conduct their own affairs with the
least possible interference, and accorded a considera-

[1] Parkman, *Montcalm and Wolfe*, II., 385.

tion in political affairs which they had not before experienced.

Within a month Amherst reported to Pitt that the soldiers and Canadians were fraternizing.[1] The general's quiet perseverance and industry had overcome formidable difficulties in the final campaign, and he was now equally strong in directing the reorganization of society in its shattered state. An eminent military critic has truthfully declared that " he was the greatest military administrator produced by England since the death of Marlborough, and remained the greatest until the rise of Wellington." [2]

[1] Amherst to Pitt, October 18, 1760, MSS. in British Public Record Office; for details of the new régime, see Kingsford, *Canada*, IV., 440–466.

[2] Fortescue, *British Army*, 405.

CHAPTER XVII

THE TREATY OF PARIS
(1760–1763)

THE war for British supremacy in North America was at last practically over. The intermittent struggle between France and England, which in India had lasted for fifteen years, was in 1760 rapidly drawing to a close, as garrison after garrison of the French throughout that great peninsula was being reduced. On the European continent the coils were gradually tightening around France. At the close of the military season of 1760, perhaps the most triumphant year thus far known to British arms, George II. passed away (October 20). With the accession of George III., who was bent on peace almost at any price, the official influence of the pugnacious Pitt began to wane, and indeed did not last a twelvemonth; although the confidence placed in "the people's minister" by Englishmen at large was unimpaired. Newcastle's power was still predominant in the cabinet; but the man of the hour, destined soon to succeed the foremost statesman of his time, was the Earl of Bute, a weak, commonplace person, who, through the favor of the princess royal, chanced to enjoy the confidence of the king's household.

In the spring of 1761, Pitt was approached by France with proposals of peace, and negotiations looking thereto were in progress during the summer. But on August 15 there had secretly been signed a Family Compact between the Bourbon kings of France and Spain, whereby they mutually declared that the enemy of the one was the enemy of the other: not in so many words an alliance against England, but obviously looking to that end.[1]

The navy of France had been utterly ruined, and the Spanish fleet numbered only fifty inferior and poorly equipped vessels; while England now had in commission, not counting her reserves, one hundred and twenty ships of the line, manned by seventy thousand seamen well seasoned in the art of war.[2] Of the few naval craft that left the ports of France in 1761 nearly all were captured, an experience to be repeated the following year. Her resources were exhausted, from a maritime point of view; and with sea power gone her colonies could, of course, no longer be held. There would seem to have been small reason, therefore, in Spain's seeking a partnership with so weak a neighbor.

Nevertheless, Charles III., aside from sentiment in behalf of his "brother and cousin," Louis XV., viewed Great Britain's colonial growth with alarm, and

[1] Text in Cantillo, *Tratados de paz*, etc., 468.
[2] Mahan, *Influence of Sea Power*, 312.

believed that Spain's over-sea dominions would suffer so soon as France had been driven from North America. Moreover, he had many specific complaints of his own; for Great Britain, in vigorously searching for enemy's property on neutral ships, had not respected the Spanish, nor indeed any other neutral flag. During 1758 "not less than 176 neutral vessels, laden with the rich produce of the French colonies, or with military and naval stores, to enable them to continue the war, rewarded the vigilance of the British Navy."[1]   The British held that contraband of war might freely be sought in neutral bottoms, and that her paper blockade of French ports was to be respected by all. This attitude was cause sufficient for the growing unpopularity of England on the continent.

Pitt was not long in discovering the existence of the Family Compact. Indignantly breaking off communications with France, he proposed at once to declare war against Spain, hoping to gain advantage from the latter's unprepared condition. But under Bute's lead the king and the cabinet refused to follow him in this extreme measure, and the great commoner therefore resigned, October 5, 1761, declaring that "he would not continue without having the direction."[2]

After three months, Spain thought herself strong enough to carry a high hand, and became so insolent

---

[1] Campbell, *Lives of British Admirals*, V., 70.
[2] Green, *William Pitt*, 185.

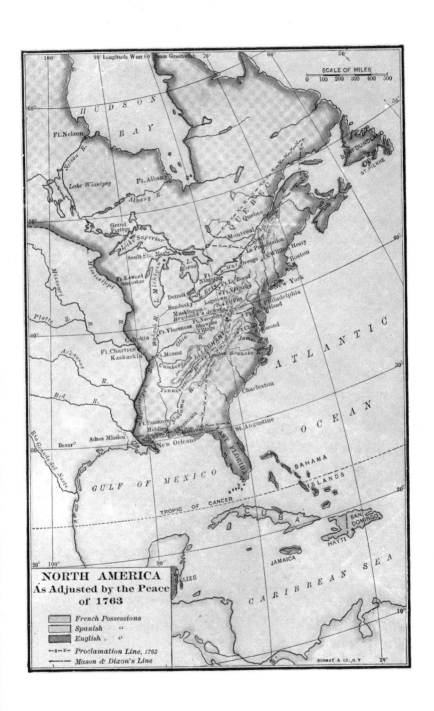

SCALE OF MILES
0   100   200   300   400   500

NORTH AMERICA
As Adjusted by the Peace
of 1763

French Possessions
Spanish   "
English   "
-x-x- Proclamation Line, 1763
--- Mason & Dixon's Line

BORMAY & CO., N.Y

in her presentation of claims that even **Bute himself**
felt obliged to declare war, January 4, 1762.   Fortunately for the government, Pitt's preparations had
been well forwarded before his retirement, and his
plans were substantially carried out.

The army now contained two hundred and fifteen thousand men, of whom sixty-five thousand
were German mercenaries.[1]   The day following
the declaration against Spain, an event not yet
heralded in the New World, Monckton sailed from
Barbadoes with fourteen thousand troops gathered
from England, Canada, and the British West Indian
islands, and on February 12 reduced Martinique,
the centre of French privateering: thereby breaking
up a nest of marauders who during the war had
captured one thousand four hundred English merchantmen in that quarter of the globe.   Grenada,
St. Lucia, and St. Vincent followed (February 26–
March 3), thus giving England control of the Wind-
ward Islands.   By this time there had arrived ad-
vices from London relative to the new Bourbon
foe.   Lord Albemarle promptly conducted fifteen
thousand five hundred men, convoyed by Admiral
Sir George Pocock, against the Spanish stronghold
of Havana, which surrendered on August 13, with
twelve ships of the line, stores, specie, and miscellaneous valuables, all aggregating a value of
$15,000,000.   But the campaign for the capture of
Cuba and the control of the gulf was accompanied

[1] Fortescue, *British Army*, 536, 537.

by frightful losses to the British—one thousand
in killed and wounded, and five thousand deaths
from illness, for the plague had broken out in the
army.   Because of this havoc in the ranks, a con-
templated attack on the French in Louisiana was
countermanded.[1]

Meanwhile, the French, taking advantage of the
withdrawal of British troops from Canada, sent out
from Brest a small squadron against Newfoundland, which was surrendered by a still weaker garrison on June 27; the island was, however, retaken
by the British on September 18.[2]   The allies had
sought to coerce Portugal into joining them, but an
English fleet and army drove them back into Spain.[3]
In the first week of October the Philippine Islands
were surrendered to an expedition which sailed from
Calcutta on September 1 and easily captured Manila
and the island of Luzon.   A ransom of $4,000,000
was promised by the Spanish for the return of
the archipelago; but as the indemnity was not
mentioned in the subsequent treaty of Paris, it was
never paid.[4]   At the same time English vessels
captured several heavily laden Spanish treasure
ships bound from the Philippines to Mexico and
Peru.   The loss of Manila meant the cutting off
of Spain from Asia, and the fall of Havana severed

[1] Fortescue, *British Army*, 536–544; Clowes, *Royal Navy*, III.,
242–250.
[2] Kingsford, *Canada*, IV., 493–495; Clowes, *Royal Navy*, III.,
250, 251.   [3] Mahan, *Influence of Sea Power*, 315, 316.
[4] *Ibid.*, 316, 498; Fortescue, *British Army*, 545.

her in large measure from America. Plucked at
every turn, and no longer able to communicate with
her most important colonies over-seas, the government at Madrid soon wearied of the Family Compact. On the continent, England's friend, Frederick
the Great of Prussia, had at last surmounted his
foes, and with the fall of Cassel (November 1) the
war ended.

Both France and Spain suffered at the hands of the
omnipresent "tyrants of the seas" enormous losses
and hardships in all parts of the world. The former
no longer possessed a single man-of-war. Her sailors,
turned privateersmen, had in 1761 captured eight
hundred and twelve of the enemy's merchantmen;
but there were still eight thousand British sail dot-
ting the seas of the world, for owing to her naval
supremacy the ocean-borne commerce of the island
had grown rapidly throughout the war. In British
jails were twenty-five thousand French prisoners of
war, against twelve hundred Britons in the prisons
of France.[1] The continental allies were far out-
classed.

On November 3, 1762, the preliminaries of peace
were signed at Fontainebleau.[2] Had Pitt's plans
been carried out to the full, and the management of
British interests at the convention been in his hands,
there is no room to doubt that they would have

[1] Mahan, *Influence of Sea Power*, 317–319.
[2] Text in *Gentleman's Magazine*, XXXII., 569–573; *American
History Leaflets*, No. 5.

been more carefully conserved. Bute and the king exhibited undue haste at peace-making. To this spirit of complacency was attributable the sur-render to the French of Gorée, Guadeloupe, and Martinique; also the grant to them of fish-drying rights on the west and north shores of Newfound-land, as under the treaty of Utrecht (1713), and the setting apart of the islands of St. Pierre and Miquelon "to serve as a shelter for the French fishermen"—although French fishers must not ap-proach within fifteen leagues of the island of Cape Breton or other English coasts.

During the peace negotiations, in the summer of 1762, the question was raised among the repre-sentatives of England whether it were worth while to hold New France, some contending that it would be more profitable to retain instead the sugar-producing island of Guadeloupe. Canada, it was argued, was valuable only for its fur trade; were it to remain in the possession of France, the English continental colonies, hemmed in to the Atlantic slope, would have a standing menace at their back door, admonishing them to remain dependent on Great Britain. England was plainly warned by foreign statesmen, who had watched the growing spirit of independence in America, that she would lose her colonies "the moment Canada should be ceded." Franklin's statement, however, that the colonies were so jealous of one another that there was "not any danger of their uniting against their own

nation "; and his demand that the settlers be relieved from the grievous necessity of constantly defending their long frontier from French and Indian
forays, at last induced the commissioners to require
the cession of New France.[1]

The manner of determining the boundary of New
France is an interesting study.[2] Spain had at first
bitterly opposed any terms by which the English
might gain a main-land footing on the Gulf of Mexico,
which she had long regarded as her own waters. But
with the humiliating fall of Havana, in August,
Charles could only regain Cuba by surrendering
either Porto Rico or Florida—the latter his main-
land holding from Mississippi eastward to the sea.
Florida was of less importance to Spain than Cuba,
but Charles's ministers chafed at the thought of
handing to the English one of the principal keys
to the gulf. France had already agreed to cede to
England all of Louisiana east of the Mississippi;
she now, with a show of consideration for her ally,
offered to the victor the portion of the province
lying west of that river—the region later comprised
in the Louisiana Purchase of 1803—if Florida might
be saved to her Bourbon cousin. But England
promptly declined, preferring Florida.[3] France,
however, was secretly tired of her colony, which she
had long neglected, and which cost her "eight hun-

[1] Parkman, *Montcalm and Wolfe*, II., 403.
[2] Developed in Shepherd, "Cession of Louisiana to Spain," in
Polit. Sci. Quarterly, XIX., 439–458.   [3] *Ibid.*, 448, 449.

dred thousand livres a year, without yielding a sou in return," and now, with an amusing air of magnanimity, proposed to turn it over to Spain.[1] But the latter claimed the territory as her own, on the ground of prior discovery, French occupation having only been "tolerated by Spain," and was not at first disposed to accept it back again as a gift—indeed, she plainly showed that she did not care for this vast and untamed wilderness.

In his generosity, however, Louis XV. overlooked this reluctance, and on the very day (November 3) when the preliminary articles with England were signed, in a personal letter solemnly conveyed Louisiana to the court of Spain, as a partial recompense for what the war had cost his beloved ally; and nine days later Charles III., apparently with some hesitation, accepted the act of cession. His Catholic majesty thought fit to explain to his Council of the Indies that in taking on this costly charge he "was inclined to accept" because the Mississippi would form an excellent natural boundary to Mexico; because smuggling from Louisiana into Mexico would now be stopped; because if Spain did not take the territory Great Britain might feel impelled to do so, and then it would be "fortified by the English at our very back"; and in general, it was not good policy to offend France.[2] This private transaction

[1] Choiseul to Ossun, September 20, 1762, in *Polit. Sci. Quarterly*, xix., 447.

[2] *Ibid.*, 455–457.

was not mentioned in the definitive treaty between
France and England, signed at Paris on February
10, 1763,[1] and it does not appear that the news
reached London until long afterwards.

By the treaty of Paris, England retained in India
all but Pondicherry and Chandernagore. In Africa,
Senegal fell to her portion. In America, France
lost Canada, Nova Scotia, Cape Breton, the Ohio
Valley, all lands eastward of the Mississippi save
the "island of Orleans," and the West Indian islands of Tobago, Dominica, Grenada, and St. Vincent; while Cuba was returned to Spain in exchange for Florida. One important and beneficent
condition was, that the British king's "new Roman
Catholic subjects may profess the worship of their
religion according to the rule of the Romish church,
as far as the laws of Great Britain permit"; and
such Canadians as wished to retire to France within
eighteen months might do so without restraint of
property or person. Eleven years later (1774) the
Quebec Act confirmed to the French in Canada
"the benefit and use of their own laws, usages, and
customs"; and this privilege the people of the province of Quebec have enjoyed unto the present day.[2]

In England the treaty was bitterly opposed by
Pitt and his followers, because of its lenient treatment of France. "By restoring her all the valu-

[1] Text in *Gentleman's Magazine*, XXXIII., 121–126.
[2] Coffin, *Province of Quebec*, 450–462; Howard, *Preliminaries of the Revolution* (*Am. Nation*, VIII.), chap. xiii.

able West Indian islands, and by our concessions in the Newfoundland fishery," said Pitt, "we have given to her the means of recovering her prodigious losses, and of becoming once more formidable at sea." [1] The unpopular compact was forced through Parliament only by a scandalous course of governmental intimidation and bribery.[2] Notwithstanding this opposition, however, England, as a result of the Seven Years' War, had in four continents made tremendous strides in imperial prestige, as well as added enormously to her realm. Her present greatness then received its principal impetus.

The contest between French and English for supremacy in North America had been inevitable. In speech, thought, and aims, the two races were widely separated. Each had aspirations of extensive empire, and one could not grow without hampering the field of the other. The struggle was long impending before it came to an issue; but in the end the race best suited to conquer the wilderness won. That the victory should have taken place before the walls of Quebec was accidental. Had not Wolfe scaled the Heights of Abraham, another leader in some later year would doubtless have led the English to success; the result was merely a question of time. Considering the circumstances, it was in the nature of things that the

[1] Green, *William Pitt*, 206.
[2] *Ibid.*, 199, 200; Mahan, *Influence of Sea Power*, 322, 323; Kingsford, *Canada*, IV., 499.

English tongue should triumph in North America over the French; that local self-government should supplant centralization and absolutism; that the farmer should succeed the forest trader, and the policy of temporizing with savagery fall before the policy of subjection. The treaty of Paris meant that civilization had taken a forward step.

Nine months after George III. had acquired from France and Spain his new possessions in North America, he issued a proclamation (October 7, 1763) [1] forming this vast territory, island and mainland, into "four distinct and separate governments, stiled and called by the names of Quebec, East Florida, West Florida, and Grenada." The province of Quebec in general terms embraced Canada and what we now know as the Old Northwest; East and West Florida divided between them the mainland south of the Atlantic coast colonies; while Grenada included the West Indian islands. In order to please the savages and to cultivate the fur trade, and perhaps also to act as a check upon the westward growth of the English coast colonies, the king commanded his "loving subjects" not to purchase or settle lands beyond the mountains "without our especial leave and license." It is needless to say that this injunction was not obeyed: the expansion of the English colonies in America

[1] Text in *Gentleman's Magazine*, XXXIII., 477–479; reprinted in *Wis. Hist. Collections*, XI., 46–52.

was irresistible; the great west was theirs, and they proceeded in due time to occupy it.

English institutions, having defeated French, were now put to another test. The western savages, unconquered allies of France, must now be pacified before the English could enter into full possession of the Ohio and the upper lakes. An uprising under Pontiac, head-chief of the Ottawa, in 1763, was the last act in the drama. The natives did not look kindly upon the treaty of Paris, and proposed to assert themselves by destroying the new masters of their ancient domain. "The English shall never come here so long as a red man lives," was the message sent by them to the Illinois French, who were nothing loath to encourage the uprising, if the Indians would do the fighting; for it was plainly foreseen by them as by the Indians that English rule meant that the wilderness was not much longer to remain a fur-trading Arcady, that the old life in the west must soon become a thing of the past. While taking no part in the war, there was no hesitation on the side of the French in hinting that their "great father," now strong again, was preparing to recapture the country, and Pontiac would but prepare the way.[1]

The conspiracy was active from Niagara and the Alleghanies on the east to Lake Superior and the Mississippi on the west. Throughout the summer

[1] Moses, *Illinois*, I., 124, 125; Parkman, *Conspiracy of Pontiac*, I., 174, *n*.

of 1763 the English forts were besieged with a
persistence almost unique among savages. Detroit
and Fort Pitt successfully withstood attacks made
upon them; but several others—notacly Mackinac,
Sandusky, St. Joseph, and Ouiatanon (near Lafayette, Indiana)—succumbed, and the garrisons were
massacred. A reign of terror existed along the
western border, hundreds of pioneer families were
murdered and scalped, outlying plantations and
towns were destroyed by fire, traders were waylaid
in the forests, and the very existence of the English
colonies was threatened. Virginia and Maryland
were fairly active against the savage foe, but Pennsylvania deserved General Amherst's anger at her
"infatuated and stupidly obstinate conduct";[1] by
this attitude she did much to justify the maintenance in America of a standing army for the regulation of colonial affairs.

As usual, the Indians in time wearied of their
confederacy and were cowed by repeated defeats.
In 1765 the French induced Pontiac to sue for
peace. Thenceforth, until the opening of the Revolutionary War, the westward expansion of the
colonies did not encounter more than customary
local opposition from the tribesmen, who jealously
guarded the passes of the Appalachians.

The unification of eastern North America was
a splendid achievement, but it marks the end of
England's greatness in America. In 1765 the Eng-

[1] Parkman, *Conspiracy of Pontiac*, II., 96.

lish North American colonies were twenty-three in number, grouping the West Indian islands as one province. Of these Newfoundland, Nova Scotia, what is now New Brunswick, Hudson Bay, and the two Floridas had but a feeble population; Quebec was French in all but government. The thirteen colonies most distinctly English in institutions and sentiment had, notwithstanding the king's proclamation restricting them to the coast, a new opportunity of territorial and industrial development. In their hands lay the future of the entire region between the Mississippi and the Atlantic.

CHAPTER XVIII

LOUISIANA UNDER SPAIN

(1762-1803)

IT remains but briefly to trace the fortunes of the French in Louisiana, which Louis XV. had on November 3, 1762, secretly ceded to his "dear and beloved cousin, the King of Spain." The news of their transfer to a new master was not broken to the residents of New Orleans until the receipt by the astonished commandant, d'Abbadie, in October, 1764, of a letter from his monarch announcing this fact, and bidding him to "deliver into the hands of the governor or any other officer appointed to that effect by the King of Spain, the said country and colony of Louisiana, and dependent posts, together with the city and the island of New Orleans." [1]   But Charles III. was in no hurry to assume charge of this white elephant, and it was two years later before he sent over his first governor.

The boundaries of the province were long disputed, being left undefined in the treaty of cession: but it is now generally agreed that they did not

[1] Text in Fortier, *Louisiana*, I., 148-150.

include Oregon or any other lands westward of the Rockies;[1] neither was Texas a part of this broad domain.[2] Spain never acknowledged that France possessed any rights in Texas, La Salle's colony in 1685 being considered but a temporary and unintentional settlement; and even after she acquired Louisiana, Texas was governed as a separate province. As for the claim of the United States to the northwest coast, it lies not in the purchase of Louisiana territory from France in 1803, but on discovery from the sea by Captain Gray (1792), the Lewis and Clark expedition (1805), the settlement of Astoria (1811), the acquisition of the rights of Spain (1819),[3] and actual colonization in later years.[4]

The population of Louisiana at the close of the great war was probably thirteen thousand whites, of whom three thousand were in the present Indiana and Illinois, and the remainder in Lower Louisiana, leaving out of account as attached to Canada the three thousand or more people in Detroit and its trading-post dependencies on the upper lakes. New Orleans, both from its position and the superior character of its people, was

[1] Marbois, *Memoirs*, IV., 275; *Am. Hist. Review*, IV., 445; letter of Jefferson (1803), in *Writings* (Ford's ed.), VIII., 261–263; Henry Adams, *United States*, II., 6.

[2] Ficklin, "Was Texas Included in the Louisiana Purchase?" in Southern Hist. Assoc., *Publications*, V., 384–386.

[3] J. Q. Adams to Rush, in *Am. State Papers, Foreign Relations*, V., 791.

[4] Channing, *Jeffersonian System* (*Am. Nation*, XII.).

the leading settlement, and the depot of a considerable trade between the Mississippi Valley and France and the West Indies. Its French population in 1763 was possibly three thousand, and its chief exports indigo, deer-skins, lumber, and naval stores. Elsewhere in Lower Louisiana the most important fortified villages were Point Coupée (on the Mississippi River, below the Red), Natchez, Natchitoches, and Mobile; the chief dependencies of the last-named were Fort Toulouse, at the junction of the Coosa and Tallapoosa rivers, and Fort Tombechbé, on the Tombigbee, controlling the Creeks and Choctaws respectively.[1] In addition to these were several shifting Jesuit missions and temporary fortified posts of wilderness traders, extending even into the country of the Osage and the Kansa. In the Illinois, or Upper Louisiana, the chief defence was Fort Chartres, with perhaps eleven hundred white inhabitants; other forts and hamlets in that district being Cahokia, St. Philippe, Kaskaskia, Ste. Geneviève, and Prairie du Rocher, on the Mississippi, Peoria on the Illinois, Massac on the lower Ohio, and Vincennes on the Wabash.[2] All holdings lying east of the Mississippi, save New Orleans, of course fell into the hands of the British as a result of the treaty of 1763.

[1] Hamilton, *Colonial Mobile*, chap. xxi.
[2] Turner, in *Chautauquan*, December, 1896, pp. 295–300; *Canadian Archives*, 1890, p. 109, Hinsdale, *Old Northwest*, 48; Winsor, *Mississippi Basin*, 462, *Westward Movement*, 22–30; Wallace, *Illinois and Louisiana under French Rule*, 377.

We have seen[1] that Detroit and the posts on or near the Great Lakes and the upper Ohio had passed into possession of their new owners within a year of the fall of Montreal. East and West Florida were taken over by British troops in the autumn of 1763, as soon as possible after the signing of the treaty of Paris. It had been deemed essential to penetrate to the Illinois at the earliest opportunity, in order to give to the savages visual evidence of Great Britain's power; but owing to the Pontiac uprising British soldiers found their road thither blocked by the confederated tribesmen. Several expeditions were sent out, but they met with persistent opposition, and occupation was delayed for two years.

The settlement of Ste. Geneviève, on the western side of the Mississippi, about twenty miles below Fort Chartres, was planted certainly as early as 1741–1742, and tradition places the date at 1735.[2] It soon became of considerable importance in the fur trade. The hamlet was visited early in November, 1736, by Pierre Laclede Liguest, a successful trader, who had ventured up the river from New Orleans in a barge laden with goods for Indians and settlers. Finding no room there for his projected trading-post, he selected the site of the present St. Louis. While spending the winter at Fort Chartres, news arrived of the treaty of Paris, which much disheartened the Illinois French, for they had hoped

---

[1] See chap. xvi., above.   [2] Scharf, *Saint Louis*, I., 65.

that their country would not be ceded to England.
They now wished to retire to the west of the river,
within what was understood as remaining French
territory, for as yet they were unaware of the
cession of Louisiana to Spain. The palisaded
village of St. Louis was accordingly, in February,
1764, laid out around Laclede's post, and thither
and to Ste. Geneviève perhaps half of the French
population in the Illinois soon drifted.

At the time of the founding of St. Louis, the commandant of Fort Chartres, and lieutenant-governor
of Illinois, was Neyon de Villiers, brother of the
officer to whom Washington had surrendered at
Fort Necessity. In June, 1764, disgusted at the turn
affairs had taken, and unwilling to be the instrument
through which the unpopular transfer should be
made, De Villiers summoned thither from Vincennes
the veteran Captain Louis St. Ange de Bellerive, and
to the latter and his small company of forty-two
men handed over the control of the district. Thereupon, with sixty-nine officers and men, and eighty
residents, including women and children, De Villiers
descended the Mississippi to New Orleans, where he
arrived July 2. Many of those in his following
settled in Lower Louisiana, but a few eventually
returned to the Illinois.[1]

St. Ange waited for sixteen months before the
British arrived — so long that he and his people

[1] Scharf, *Saint Louis*, I., 69–73; Wallace, *Illinois and Louisiana
under French Rule*, 353–360, 363.

began to trust that France might continue in possession. But Captain Thomas Sterling reached Fort Chartres October 10, 1765, with a hundred veteran Highlanders. Presenting Gage's proclamation,[1] he received from the reluctant commandant full "possession of the country of the Illinois." After hauling down the last French flag to float on the American main-land east of the Mississippi, St. Ange retired to St. Louis with his little garrison, now numbering some twenty men. There, without further warrant than the common consent of the French inhabitants, he served as acting governor until 1770, when Captain Pedro Piernas arrived from New Orleans to assume charge of Upper Louisiana as Spain's lieutenant-governor.[2]

Early in 1765, at a time when it was still hoped in New Orleans that Spain might not, after all, assume control, the chief citizens of Lower Louisiana met in New Orleans, and draughted a petition to Louis XV. not to sever them from France; but the messenger despatched to Paris was informed that restitution was impossible.[3] The first Spanish governor-general, Don Antonio de Ulloa, arrived at the then shabby little capital of Louisiana, March 5, 1766, accompanied by ninety soldiers, and took command of public affairs, although there was no formal transfer. A man of some excellent parts, and

---

[1] Text in Wallace, *Illinois and Louisiana under French Rule*, 361.   [2] Billon, *Saint Louis*, 27–30, 128.

[3] Wallace, *Illinois and Louisiana under French Rule*, 368.

with a scholarly reputation, Ulloa appears to have been tactless and arbitrary, and aroused intense opposition to Spanish authority. The only contented groups were a colony of Germans imported by Law's company to the neighborhood of New Orleans in 1722, and the Acadian refugees, of whom eight hundred and sixty-six arrived during 1765 and 1766, and received lands on both sides of the river between Baton Rouge and Point Coupée, the "Acadian Coast" of our day.[1]

In the closing months of 1768 the French king was again passionately appealed to by the people of New Orleans to "take back the colony instantly . . . [and] to preserve to us our patriotic name, our laws, and our privileges."[2] But Louis ignored this second petition wrung from the hearts of his former subjects, whom he had arbitrarily abandoned to a foreign master with whom they and their customs were wholly out of sympathy. Thereupon the obnoxious governor was placed on board of a vessel, November 1, 1768, and sent out of the colony, a revolutionary proceeding in which were involved "some of the most influential men in the colony." This conspiracy aroused a desire for vengeance in the court at Madrid, particularly because in the memorial to Louis these rebellious subjects had frankly described "the Spanish policy, which, gentle and insinuating in the beginning, becomes tyrannical

---

[1] Wallace, *Illinois and Louisiana under French Rule*, 368, 378.
[2] Text in Fortier, *Louisiana*, I., 172, 177–204

only when the yoke has been imposed." The following summer there arrived at New Orleans Don
Alexandro O'Reilly, newly appointed governor-general and commander of the province, backed by a
frigate and twenty - three transports, with three
thousand soldiers. The chiefs of the revolution
were arrested, several of them shot, and others
confined in the castle at Havana.[1]

Under Ulloa, French political methods had been
retained; but O'Reilly introduced Spanish law and
governmental machinery, and instituted a cabildo.
Execrated by the colonists because of his unneces-
sarily harsh treatment of the revolutionists of 1768,
although otherwise a man of good judgment,
"Bloody O'Reilly" was succeeded in 1770 by the
mild and humane Unzaga, who soothed the creoles
into a fair measure of contentment with Spanish
rule. He was followed seven years later by the
conciliatory and consequently popular Galvez, who
materially aided the cause of the American revolutionists by dealing severely with English traders on
the Mississippi, while at the same time Americans
were permitted to purchase munitions of war in
New Orleans and ship them by river to Fort Pitt.

When Spain declared war against England, in
1779, Galvez assembled a military force of six
hundred and seventy men, mostly French, and in
a brief but brilliant campaign conquered the English settlements of Manchac, Baton Rouge, and

[1] Fortier, *Louisiana*, I., chap. x.

Natchez.[1] In March, following, at the head of two
thousand men, he compelled the surrender of Mobile.
A few months later, with reinforcements from Havana, he proceeded against Pensacola, which surrendered May 9, 1781. While formulating schemes
for the capture of the Bahamas and Jamaica, the
news of peace arrived, thus putting a stop to the
governor's ambitious enterprises.

Meanwhile, important events had been occurring
in the Illinois. The British forts at Vincennes and
Kaskaskia, dependencies of Detroit, had been used
as rallying-points for Indian war-parties which were
threatening the very existence of Kentucky. No
British soldiers were in the Illinois at the time,
the posts being commanded by Frenchmen in their
employ, aided by small garrisons of militia recruited from among the neighboring *habitants*. A
force of Virginia frontiersmen, under Colonel George
Rogers Clark, descended from the Monongahela
River settlements to the Falls of the Ohio (later
Louisville), and marched across the Illinois prairies
to Kaskaskia, which was won without bloodshed
on the night of July 4, 1778. The French settlers
promptly fraternized with the Americans, and the
Spanish at St. Louis, under Lieutenant-Governor
Francisco de Leyba, did " every thing in their power,"
Clark writes, "to convince me of their friendship."
Upon his famous and difficult overland expedition
to Vincennes the succeeding February, through the

[1] Fortier, *Louisiana*, II., 63-65.

swollen marshes of eastern Illinois, French volunteers were an important element in his command; and when that post was captured, February 24, 1779, the Vincennes *habitants* at once entered into full fellowship with the conquering " Big Knives." [1]

In May, 1780, the English commandant at Mackinac sent an expedition consisting of "Seven Hundred & fifty men including Traders, servants and Indians . . . in an attack on the Spanish & Illinois Country." After a mild demonstration against St. Louis, the principal feature of which was the burning of outlying cabins, the raiders returned by various routes through Illinois and Wisconsin. "They brought off Forty-three Scalps, thirty-four prisoners, Blacks and Whites & killed about 70 Persons. They destroyed several hundred cattle, but were beat off on their attacks both sides o. the River." [2]

This enterprise was soon replied to by the Spanish, who in January, 1781, despatched a force of sixty-five militiamen—over half of them French— under Don Eugenio Pourré, against Fort St. Joseph, near the present Michigan town of Niles. After a weary midwinter march of four hundred miles across Illinois and northern Indiana, the small English garrison at St. Joseph was, together with a consider-

---

[1] Thwaites, *How George Rogers Clark Won the Northwest*, etc., 27–63; see also Van Tyne, *American Revolution* (*Am. Nation*, IX.), chap. xv.

[2] *Wisconsin Hist. Collections*, XI., 151–156.

able group of fur-traders, driven from the country, the Indian allies of the Spanish being rewarded with rich spoils. Large stores of goods and ammunition were also destroyed, whereupon Pourré retired to St. Louis. Because of this bold foray, the news of which only reached Paris a year later, Spain in the peace negotiations set up a claim to the Illinois country. Galvez's enterprise had led to similar demands upon the south; and it soon became evident that, as her price for the recognition of American independence, Spain aimed at obtaining a large slice of the country lying to the back of the Alleghanies and abutting on the east bank of the Mississippi. The firmness of the American commissioners, who persisted in maintaining the Mississippi as the western boundary of the United States, eventually warded off these pretensions.[1]

Galvez was, in 1785, followed by Don Estevan Miró, and he in turn (1791) by Baron de Carondelet. Both of these officials entertained hopes of alienating the people of Kentucky and Tennessee from the federal Union. Spain controlled the Mississippi, the commercial highway of the west, and on their part the westerners looked with hungry eyes upon the rich lands held by Spain. The federal authorities were slow to realize that the free navigation of the Mississippi was essential to western progress, and there was consequently much

---

[1] Mason, *Chapters in Illinois History*, 293–311; McLaughlin, *Confederation and Constitution (Am. Nation*, X.), chap. vi.

discontent in Kentucky, fomented by Spanish intrigues. All manner of schemes were advanced,
varying with men's temperaments and ambitions.
Filibustering expeditions against the Spanish were
first proposed. Then (1788), when this did not appear practicable, men like George Rogers Clark
were willing to join hands with Spain herself in
the development of the continental interior—and,
indeed, many Kentuckians, allured by promises of
large land grants, settled on Spanish territory to
the west of the great river, as did Daniel Boone
and his kindred in 1799. In 1793 and 1794 Clark
was ready to help France oust Spain from Louisiana.[1]
These several projects illustrate the unrest which
animated the trans-Alleghany region throughout
some twenty years of its formative period.[2] In
1795 the free navigation of the Mississippi was
granted to the Americans by treaty. But under the
governorship of Lemos (1797–1799) friction arose
with the United States over that official's arbitrary
regulations regarding American commerce through
the port of New Orleans; the trouble blew over,
however, and under Governor Salcedo amicable relations were resumed.

All this while life among the French, both in
Upper and Lower Louisiana—the number of Spanish was always small, and almost wholly confined

---

[1] Bassett, *Federalist System* (*Am. Nation*, XI.).
[2] Full treatment in Turner, "Correspondence of Clark and
Genet," in Am. Hist. Assoc., *Report*, 1896, pp. 930–1107.

to the official and military classes — ran on in a
placid stream. There was a small but steady
growth of population. The fur trade prospered,
with St. Louis as its chief entrepôt on the west
side of the great river and Kaskaskia on the east.
Itinerant merchants, usually French, pushed their
way to the upper waters of the Mississippi and its
northern tributaries, also into the southwest towards the Spanish commercial centre of Santa Fé.
By the close of the century French traders had
reached the Mandan villages at the great bend of
the Missouri, where they came in contact with the
agents of British fur - trade companies, who had
journeyed thither overland from their posts on the
Assiniboin and the Saskatchewan.

We are probably safe, judging from chance al-
lusions in the documents of the period, in estimat-
ing the population of New Orleans and its neighboring settlements, in 1803, at upward of eight
thousand, and of St. Louis and the Illinois at six
thousand—probably there were fifty thousand all
told, including West and East Florida, and counting
negro slaves, but eliminating Indians.[1] The aggregate value of the produce annually exported was
about $2,000,000, of which sugar contributed some
$32,000 and peltries and indigo $100,000 each. The
principal source of official revenue appears to have
been the $537,000 imported each year from Mexico
to pay the salaries of employés; for the province,

[1] Fortier, *Louisiana*, II., 301.

which was corruptly managed in every department of the service, remained a considerable expense to Spain as it had been to France.[1]

. Reflecting upon the tragic story of the ousting of France from North America, the great Napoleon deemed it possible to rehabilitate New France to the west of the Mississippi, thus not only reflecting glory upon the mother-land, but checking the United States in its westward growth. He therefore coerced Charles IV. of Spain to retrocede Louisiana to France by the secret treaty of St. Ildefonso, signed October 1, 1800—a cession supposed by Spain to be but nominal, but intended by Napoleon to be permanent.[2] There was, however, no formal transfer at the time. Three years later (April 30, 1803), Napoleon sold Louisiana to the United States for $15,000,000. His object was evident: the war-chest of France needed replenishment; during his projected war with Great Britain the latter's all-powerful navy might readily seize the capital of his far-off colony, and invasion from Canada was entirely practicable; moreover, by giving her great American rival the opportunity to expand its bounds westward, England's ambitions thither would be checkmated. Spain, whose dominion, despite the treaty of 1800, had not yet been disturbed, first formally transferred the province to France, November 30, and on

---

[1] Pontalba, "Memoir," cited in Fortier, *Louisiana*, II., 208–213.
[2] Becker, in *La España Moderna*, May, 1903; Channing, *Jeffersonian System* (*Am. Nation*, XII.).

December 20 the representatives of France with appropriate formalities handed it over to the United States. Similar ceremonials for Upper Louisiana occurred at St. Louis, March 9 and 10, 1804, and thus expired the last vestige of French power on the main-land of North America, almost exactly two centuries after the first successful settlement in Nova Scotia.

CHAPTER XIX

CRITICAL ESSAY ON AUTHORITIES

BIBLIOGRAPHICAL AIDS

WHILE not a formal bibliography of New France, a considerable list of books on the subject is given in Reuben Gold Thwaites, *Jesuit Relations and Allied Documents* (73 vols., 1896–1901), LXXI., 219–365. Justin Winsor, *Narrative and Critical History of America* (8 vols., 1888–1889), V., 420, 472, 560–611, is full, useful, and suggestive, but only includes material published to 1887. J. N. Larned, *Literature of American History, a Bibliographical Guide* (1902), 106–110, 391–405, 410–421, is a convenient introduction to the sources and literature. Channing and Hart, *Guide to the Study of American History* (1896), §§ 87–91, 131, 132, is brief but serviceable. The numerous and sometimes extended bibliographical notes in the twelve volumes of Francis Parkman, *France and England in North America* (complete ed., 1898), are of great value, but often lack definiteness in the matter of location of sources. The "Bibliography of Fellows of the Royal Society of Canada," in that society's *Proceedings*, XII., 1–79, is useful, for therein are listed many monographs on Canadian history, both in French and English. On the specific topic indicated by the title of the work, an elaborate bibliography will be found in Doughty and Parmelee, *The Siege of Quebec and the Battle of the Plains of Abraham* (6 vols., 1901), VI., 151–319.

Special bibliographies will be found in other volumes of the *American Nation* series, as follows: On early discoveries, III., Edward G. Bourne, *Spain in America*, chap. xxi.; on English colonial institutions and inter-colonial relations, IV., Lyon G. Tyler, *England in America*, chap. xx.; V., Charles McL. Andrews, *Colonial Self-Government*, chap. xx.; and VI., E. B. Greene, *Provincial America*, chap. xix.

GENERAL SECONDARY WORKS

The standard authority in English, on Canadian history in general, is William Kingsford, *History of Canada* (10 vols., 1887–1898)—fair and concise, but of course the English point of view. The best general works giving the French side, and dwelling particularly upon the history of that race in Canada, are M. E. Faillon, *Histoire de la Colonie Française en Canada* (3 vols., 1865); J. B. A. Ferland, *Cours d'histoire du Canada* (2 vols., 1861–1865); F. X. Garneau, *Histoire du Canada* (4 vols., 4th ed., 1882–1883)—an earlier edition has been unsatisfactorily Englished by A. Bell (2 vols., 1866); and B. Sulte, *Histoire des Canadiens-Français* (8 vols., 1882–1884).

Upon the topic of New France, of course the standard authority is Francis Parkman, *France and England in North America* (12 vols., 1851–1892). This series was not written in chronological order; the following is the proper sequence, with the years of first publication indicated: *Pioneers of France in the New World* (1865); *The Jesuits in North America* (1867); *La Salle and the Discovery of the Great West* (1869); *The Old Régime in Canada* (1874); *Count Frontenac and New France under Louis XIV.* (1877); *A Half-Century of Conflict* (2 vols., 1892); *Montcalm and Wolfe* (2 vols., 1884); *The Conspiracy of Pontiac, and the Indian War after the Conquest of Canada* (2 vols., 1851). Parkman is eminently readable, his style being picturesque and sympathetic, although sometimes too florid, and his development of the plot is dramatic. His treatment of the Jesuits is open to criticism, as frequently lacking in fairness to their point of view.

A brief, convenient, and impersonal manual of the subject is H. H. Miles, *History of Canada under French Régime* (1872). Justin Winsor, in his *Cartier to Frontenac* (1894) and *Mississippi Valley* (1895), studies New France largely from the side of exploration and cartography; very useful for reference, but rather unreadable. A. B. Hulbert, *Historic Highways of America* (15 vols., 1903–1905), especially II.–V., has much of importance on trails, trade-routes, and war-paths. Useful general suggestions of a like character are obtainable from Ellen C. Semple, *American History and its Geographic Conditions* (1903).

GENERAL COLLECTIONS OF SOURCES

There are several collections of prime importance. That edited by Pierre Margry, *Découvertes et Établissements des Français*, etc. (6 vols., 1879–1888), has chiefly to do with explorations, and is invaluable for La Salle's operations —but Margry is not above suspicion of having "doctored" some of his La Salle MSS. in order to prove his own historical contentions. O'Callaghan and Fernow, *Documents Relating to the Colonial History of New York* (15 vols., 1853–1883), cover the entire period of the French régime, with especial reference to intercolonial relations. The *Collection de documents relatif à l'histoire de la Nouvelle France* (4 vols., 1883) is general in character. Important series are those printed in Douglas Brymner, *Reports on Canadian Archives* (24 vols., 1874–1903): the Haldimand Collection was published in 1884–1885, Bouquet Collection in 1889, Murray Correspondence in 1890, Nova Scotia documents in 1894, Siege of Quebec material in 1895, and the Moreau-St. Méry Collection in 1899. Of general value, although specifically in the field of Jesuit missions and explorations, are R. G. Thwaites, *Jesuit Relations and Allied Documents*, cited above. P. G. Roy, *Bulletin de Recherches Historiques* (9 vols., 1895–1904), contains much of a general character; so also the Royal Society of Canada, *Proceedings and Transactions* (1st series, 12 vols., 1882–1893; 2d series, 9 vols., 1895), and the Société Historique de Montreal, *Mémoires à l'histoire du Canada* (9 vols., 1859–1880).

Taylor and Pringle, *Correspondence of William Pitt, Earl of Chatham* (4 vols., 1838–1840), is important. Lord John Russell, *Correspondence of John Russell, Fourth Duke of Bedford* (3 vols., 1842–1846), should be consulted for final peace negotiations. The *Gentleman's Magazine* (London, 1750–1763) and Robert Dodsley, *Annual Register* (London, 1758–1763), give contemporary reports and documents, often in full—the former, particularly vols. XXXII. and XXXIII., contains the treaty of Paris, Quebec Act, etc. For treaties, conventions, and other state papers, consult also George Chalmers, *Collection of Treaties between Great Britain and Other Powers* (2 vols., 1790); William Macdonald, *Select Charters Illustrative of American History* (1899); and William Houston, *Documents Illustrative of the Canadian Constitution* (1891).

Many contemporary or almost contemporary accounts have much the same value as documentary sources. Gabriel Sagard-Theodat, *Histoire du Canada* (Paris, 1836; new ed., 4 vols., 1865–1866), is from the Recollect standpoint; while the work of P. F. X. de Charlevoix, *Histoire et Description Générale de la Nouvelle France* (3 vols., 1744; trans. by J. G. Shea, 6 vols., 1866–1872), written nearly a century later, is a Jesuit publication. An English work is J. H. Wynne, *General History of the British Empire in America* (2 vols., London, 1770).

There are numerous other contemporaneous works of which we can but note a selection. The two standard contemporary English histories of the French and Indian War are John Entick, *History of the Late War* (5 vols., London, 1763–1764), and Thomas Mante, *History of the Late War* (London, 1772). A French account is by M. Pouchot, *Memoir upon the Late War in North America, 1755–1760* (English trans., 2 vols., 1866). John Knox, *Historical Journal of Campaigns in North America* (2 vols., London, 1769), is valuable. William Smith, *History of the Late Province of New York* (2 vols., 1830), is also a contemporary writer.

Topographical and social data are obtainable from Edmund Burke, *An Account of European Settlements in America* (2 vols., London, 1757); Jonathan Carver, *Travels through the Interior Parts of North America* (London, 1778) —although Professor E. G. Bourne, in a paper read at the Chicago meeting of the American Historical Association (December 29, 1904), casts doubt on the authenticity of this work; Thomas Hutchins, *Journals of 1760* (*Pennsylvania Magazine of History*, II., 149); Thomas Jefferys, *Natural and Civil History of the French Dominions in North America* (London, 1760); and Robert Rogers, *Concise Account of North America* (London, 1765).

SPECIAL COLLECTIONS OF SOURCES AND CONTEMPORARY ACCOUNTS

John Montressor's "Journal" of the Louisburg siege and "The Journal of an Officer at the Siege of Louisburg" are in New York Historical Society, *Collections* (1881), 151, 179. T. Pinchon, *Memorials on Cape Breton* (London, 1760), is also a valuable contemporary account.

The Nova Scotia Historical Society, *Collections* (11 vols., 1879–1900) contain much documentary material on Acadia. So also Gaston du Boscq de Beaumont, *Les derniers jours de l'Acadie* (1899), and T. B. Akins, *Selections from Public Documents of the Province of Nova Scotia* (1869).

Doughty and Parmelee, *The Siege of Quebec and the Battle of the Plains of Abraham*, already cited, is a comprehensive and invaluable collection of documentary material of every description, connected with this event. There are also several journals of the siege of Quebec in the Quebec Literary and Historical Society, *Historical Documents* (5th series, 1840–1877).

General operations in the St. Lawrence valley may be studied in *Siege of Quebec and Conquest of Canada in 1759, by a Nun of the General Hospital* (1855); H. R. Casgrain, *Lévis Documents* (8 vols., 1889–1895); *Official Documents Relative to Operations of the British Army in 1759–1760* (1813); C. J. de Johnstone, *Journal of Campaign of 1760* (Quebec Literary and Historical Society, *Historical Documents*, 2d series, No. 5, 1866); and *Canada Français*, a review published by professors of Laval University (1888–1891)—a supplementary volume contains *Documents inédits sur l'Acadie*.

Operations on our New England frontier are covered in Samuel Penhallow, *History of Wars of New England with the Eastern Indians* (Boston, 1726); Jeremy Belknap, *History of New Hampshire* (3 vols., Boston, 1792), II.; Nathaniel Bouton, *New Hampshire Provincial Papers* (7 vols., 1867–1873), VI.; William Livingston, *Review of Military Operations* (Massachusetts Historical Society, *Collections*, 1st series, V., 67), *Aspinwall Papers* (*ibid.*, 2d series, IX.), and *Pepperrell Papers* (*ibid.*, 6th series, X.); and documents (chiefly concerned with Rale and the Kennebec disturbances) in J. P. Baxter, *Pioneers of France in New England* (1894).

Hostilities on the New York frontier may be studied in J. M. le Moine, *Le Massacre au Fort George . . . documents historique* (1864); Daniel Shute, *Journal of Expedition to Canada in 1758* (Essex Institute, *Historical Collections*, 1859–1898, XII., 132); Caleb Rea, *Journal of Expedition against Ticonderoga* (*ibid.*, XVIII., 81–177); A. Tomlinson,*Military Journals of Two Private Soldiers* (1855); E. C. Dawes, *Journal of General Rufus Putnam . . . 1757–1760* (1886); and F. B. Hough, *Journals of Major Robert Rogers* (1883).

For data on the struggle for supremacy in the Ohio valley and along the western frontier generally, it will be essential to consult not only the *Documents Relating to the Colonial History of New York*, above cited, but the *Colonial Records of Pennsylvania* (16 vols., 1838–1853), particularly V.-VIII.; the *Calendar of Virginia State Papers* (9 vols., 1875–1890), particularly I.; and documents in N. B. Craig, *Olden Time* (2 vols., 1846–1848). Conrad Weiser, *Journal of a Tour to the Ohio, 1748*, and George Croghan, *Tours into the Western Country, 1750–1765*, volume I., of Thwaites, *Early Western Travels* (31 vols., 1904), may be studied for conditions on the extreme English-Indian frontier. William M. Darlington, *Gist's Journals* (1893), is invaluable. So also J. M. Toner, *Journal of Colonel George Washington, 1754* (1893); W. C. Ford, *Washington's Writings* (14 vols., 1889–1893), I., II.; A. T. Goodman, *Journal of Captain William Trent* (1871); *Dinwiddie Papers* (Virginia Historical Society, *Collections*, III., IV., 1883–1884); N. B. Craig, *Memoirs of Major Robert Stobo* (1854); and "Letters of Orme, on Braddock's Defeat," in *Historical Magazine*, VIII., 353. "Recollections of Augustin Grignon" (*Wisconsin Historical Collections*, III., 195) throw light on the operations of western Indians at Braddock's defeat. The *Captivity of Hugh Gibson, 1756–1759* (Massachusetts Historical Society, *Collections*, 3d series, V., 141) illustrates conditions in the Ohio valley.

On the French régime in the old northwest in general, but the upper lakes especially, consult Michigan Pioneer and Historical Society, *Historical Collections* (30 vols., 1877–1901), especially X., XIX.; and *Wisconsin Historical Collections* (17 vols., 1854–1905), especially V., XVI., XVII.

The Pontiac conspiracy may profitably be studied in James Bain, *Henry's Travels* (1901). Thomas Morris, *Journal, 1764*, in Thwaites, *Early Western Travels*, I., gives his thrilling experiences on the Maumee towards the close of Pontiac's war.

Southern documents of the period will be found in South Carolina Historical Society, *Collections* (5 vols., 1857–1897), and B. F. French, *Historical Collections of Louisiana and Florida* (1st series, 5 vols., 1846–1853; 2d series, 2 vols., 1869–1875).

Besides the New York, Pennsylvania, and Virginia colonial records and archives, above mentioned, the student of intercolonial politics should consult *Archives of the State of New Jersey* (22 vols., 1880–1900), particularly VIII.; *Records of the Colony of Rhode Island* (10 vols., 1856–1860), particularly V., VI.; G. S. Kimball, *Correspondence*

of *Colonial Governors of Rhode Island* (2 vols., 1902–1903);
Stephen Hopkins, *True Representation of Plan Formed
at Albany (Rhode Island Historical Tracts*, IX.); "Connecticut in Albany Conference," in *Massachusetts Historical Collections*, VII., 207; and Thomas Hutchinson,
History of Massachusetts Bay (3 vols., 1760–1828). Colonial
administration may be studied in Thomas Pownall, *Administration of Colonies* (2 vols., London, 1764–1774).

MODERN HISTORIES OF THE FRENCH AND INDIAN WAR

Contemporary accounts have been mentioned above;
so also Parkman, *Montcalm and Wolfe*, the chief single
modern authority. A. G. Bradley, *Fight with France for
North America* (1901), is highly commendable for breadth of
view and is recent. W. C. H. Wood, *The Fight for Canada*,
"a naval and military sketch of the great imperial war,"
has great merit, especially as showing that British sea
power was a leading element in the struggle. G. D.
Warburton, *Conquest of Canada* (2 vols., 1849) is old, but
still of much value. Careful French studies are Charles de
Bonnechose, *Montcalm et la Canada Français* (1877), a
good outline sketch; L. A. Bougainville, *Les Français au
Canada* (privately printed, 1896); H. R. Casgrain, *Montcalm et Lévis* (1891), important, as being based on the
Lévis MSS.; and Felix Martin, *Marquis de Montcalm et
les Dernières Années de la Colonie Français* (4th ed., 1898), a
standard work. Some interesting side-lights on details are
obtainable from F. W. Lucas, *Appendiculæ historicæ* (1891).

The New England phase of the war has been treated in
J. P. Baxter, *Pioneers of France in New England*, already
cited, and John Fiske, *New France and New England*
(1902), a series of more or less connected sketches.

MISCELLANEOUS

Many authorities have been cited in foot-notes to the
text, reference to each of which it seems unnecessary here

to repeat.   A few have, however, been selected, some of
which are not mentioned in the foot-notes of this volume,
with which the student will find it desirable to become
acquainted.

In *Revue Canadienne*, particularly I., IV., X., XVI., are
articles by E. Rameau de St.-Père on colonial administration in New France; also by the same authority is *France
aux Colonies* (1859).   Military history is well summarized
in J. W. Fortescue, *History of the British Army* (3 vols.,
1899), and naval in W. L. Clowes, *The Royal Navy* (7
vols., 1897–1903).   Canadian conditions are summarized
in P. A. de Gaspé, *Les Anciens Canadiens* (1863).

The standard history of Newfoundland is D. W. Prowse,
*History of Newfoundland from the English, Colonial, and
Foreign Records* (1895).   On Acadia, the latest authority
for the side of the *émigrés*, is Edouard Richard, *Acadia*
(2 vols., 1895), written in English.   An excellent account,
in French, is E. Rameau de St.-Père, *Une Colonie féodale
en l'Amérique* (2 vols., 1889).   James Hannay, *History of
Acadia* (1879 and several subsequent editions), is the
standard English authority outside of Parkman's works.
The chief authorities on Cape Breton and the siege of Louisburg are J. G. Bourinot, *Historical and Descriptive Account of Cape Breton* (1892), and R. Brown, *History of the
Island of Cape Breton* (1869).   On the siege of Quebec,
consult Doughty and Parmelee, above cited, and Ernest
Gagnon, *Le fort et le château de St. Louis* (1893)—less local
than the title indicates.   The Hudson Bay region may be
studied in Beckles Willson, *The Great Company* (1899), and
George Bryce, *Remarkable History of the Hudson's Bay
Company* (1900).

On the New York frontier, see *Pennsylvania Magazine
of History*, III., 11; J. R. Simms, *Frontiersmen of New
York* (2 vols., 1882); and F. W. Halsey, *The Old New
York Frontier* (1901).   On the Pennsylvania frontier, see
*Report of Commission to Locate the Sites of the Frontier
Forts of Pennsylvania* (2 vols., 1896).   The war and condi-
tions in the Ohio valley may be studied in T. J. Chapman,

French in Alleghany Valley (1897); J. A. McClung, *Sketches of Western Adventure, 1755–1794* (1832, 1872); and W. H. Lowdermilk, *History of Cumberland, Maryland* (1878). On the French in the west, consult Silas Farmer, *History of Detroit and Michigan* (2d ed., 1890); S. S. Hebberd, *Wisconsin under French Dominion* (1890); and Joseph Wallace, *Illinois and Louisiana under the French Rule.* For Louisiana and the southwest, leading authorities are J. F. H. Claiborne, *Mississippi* (1880); C. E. A. Gayarré, *Louisiana under French Dominion* (4 vols., new ed., 1903), II.; Alcée Fortier, *History of Louisiana* (6 vols., 1904), I., II.; and Marc de Villiers du Terrage, *Les Dernières Années de la Louisiane Française* (1903).

David Mills, *Boundaries of Ontario* (1873), should be consulted in connection with the boundaries and the peace of Paris.

The biographical material is considerable; lives of such English notables as William Pitt, Philip Schuyler, Benjamin Franklin, Robert Rogers, and others prominently connected with the intercolonial contest, diplomatic and military, are easily obtainable. The standard on Wolfe is Robert Wright, *Life of Wolfe* (1864). Eugène Guénin, in his *Montcalm* (1898), has given us a notable study. Camille la Jonquière, *Marquis de la Jonquière* (Paris, n.d.), is worthy of attention. Lives of Sir William Johnson are by Augustus C. Buell (1903), W. E. Griffis (1891), and W. A. Stone (2 vols., 1865). In tracing the careers of prominent French participants, an invaluable aid will be found in Cyprien Tanguay, *Dictionaire généalogique* (7 vols., 1871–1890).

INDEX